MC

The Power of Meaning

"The search for meaning just got a little easier, and a little more fun. To follow Emily Esfahani Smith in this great human quest is to undertake a rewarding journey with a sure-footed guide."

—DARRIN M. McMAHON
author of *Happiness: A History*; Mary Brinsmead Wheelock Professor of History, Dartmouth College

"All too often, we sleepwalk through life without examining it. *The Power of Meaning* shows us another path. How can we find purpose? What role does our work have in the search for meaning? This deeply researched—yet highly readable—book can help you answer those questions."

—CHRIS GUILLEBEAU
author of *Born for This* and *The $100 Startup*

"A powerful invitation to live a life that is not only happy but filled with purpose, belonging, and transcendence. By combining scientific research and philosophical insights with moving accounts of ordinary people who have deeply meaningful lives, Smith addresses the most urgent questions of our existence in a delightful, masterful, and inspiring way."

—EMMA SEPPÄLÄ
author of *The Happiness Track*; Science Director, Stanford University's Center for Compassion and Altruism Research and Education

The POWER of MEANING

Crafting a Life That Matters

EMILY ESFAHANI SMITH

CROWN
NEW YORK

Published in the United States by Crown, an imprint of the Crown Publishing Group, a division of Penguin Random House LLC, New York.
crownpublishing.com

CROWN is a registered trademark and the Crown colophon is a trademark of Penguin Random House LLC.

Library of Congress Cataloging-in-Publication Data
Names: Smith, Emily Esfahani, author.
Title: The power of meaning : crafting a life that matters / Emily Esfahani Smith.
Description: First Edition. | New York : Crown, 2017.
Identifiers: LCCN 2016010610 (print) | LCCN 2016043371 (ebook) | ISBN 9780553419993 (hardback) | ISBN 9780553446562 (paperback) | ISBN 9780553446555 (eISBN) | ISBN 9780553446555
Subjects: LCSH: Self-actualization (Psychology) | Meaning (Psychology) | Emotions. | BISAC: SELF-HELP / Personal Growth / General. | PHILOSOPHY / Ethics & Moral Philosophy. | PSYCHOLOGY / Emotions.
Classification: LCC BF637.S4 S6336 2017 (print) | LCC BF637.S4 (ebook) | DDC 128—dc23
LC record available at https://lccn.loc.gov/2016010610

Hardcover ISBN 978-0-553-41999-3
Ebook ISBN 978-0-553-44655-5
International Edition ISBN 978-0-451-49730-7

Printed in the United States of America

Book design by Lauren Dong

10 9 8 7 6 5 4 3 2 1

First Edition

To my parents, Tim and Fataneh, and
brother, Tristan, affectionately known as T-bear,
doostetoon daram

Contents

What is the meaning of life? That was all—a simple question; one that tended to close in on one with years. The great revelation had never come. The great revelation perhaps never did come. Instead there were little daily miracles, illuminations, matches struck unexpectedly in the dark; here was one.

—Virginia Woolf

The POWER of MEANING

Introduction

On Thursday and Sunday evenings, a group of seekers gathered in a large room of my family's home in downtown Montreal, where my parents ran a Sufi meetinghouse. Sufism is the school of mysticism associated with Islam, and my family belonged to the Nimatullahi Sufi Order, which originated in Iran in the fourteenth century and today has meetinghouses all over the world. Twice a week, darvishes—or members of the order—would sit on the floor and meditate for several hours. With their eyes closed and their chins to their chests, they silently repeated a name or attribute of God as traditional Iranian Sufi music played.

Living in the Sufi meetinghouse as a child was enchanting. The walls of our home were decorated with sculptures of Arabic script that my father carved from wood. Tea was brewing constantly, perfuming the air with the fragrance of bergamot. After meditating, the Sufis drank the tea, which my mother served along with dates or Iranian sweets made with rosewater, saffron, cardamom, and honey. Sometimes, I served the tea, carefully balancing a tray full of glasses, saucers, and sugar cubes as I knelt down before each darvish.

The darvishes loved dipping a sugar cube in their tea, putting it in their mouths, and drinking their tea through the sugar. They loved singing the poetry of medieval Sufi sages and saints. There was Rumi: "Ever since I was sliced away from my home of reeds, each note I whisper would make most any heart weep." And there was Attar: "Since love," he writes of the seeker, "has spoken in your soul, reject The Self, that whirlpool where our lives are wrecked." They loved, too, sitting in silence, being together, and remembering God through quiet contemplation.

Darvishes call Sufism "the path of love." Those on the path are on a journey toward God, the Beloved, which calls them to renounce the self and to constantly remember and love God at every turn. To Sufis, loving and adoring God means loving and adoring all of creation and every human being that is a part of it. *Mohabbat,* or loving-kindness, is central to their practice. When we first moved into our new home in Montreal, Sufis from all over North America came and stayed for days to help my parents convert the brownstone, formerly a legal office, into a space fit for *majlis,* the name of the bi-weekly gathering for meditation. When a homeless man knocked on our door one evening looking for a meal and a place to sleep, he was welcomed in. And when my father complimented a darvish on a scarf he was wearing, the darvish gave it with pleasure as a gift to my dad. (After that, my family had a general understanding that you only complimented another darvish's possessions with great caution.)

On special occasions, like the visit of a sheikh or the initiation of a new darvish into the order, Sufis from Canada and the United States would stay at the meetinghouse for a few days, sleeping on thin cushions in the meditation room and library—really, anywhere there was space. There was a lot of snoring at night and lines for the bathroom during the day, but that didn't seem to bother anyone. The darvishes were full of joy and warmth. Though they spent many hours meditating during these weekends, they also passed the time by playing classical Sufi music on Persian instruments, like a frame drum called a *daf* and the stringed *tar,* always singing Sufi poetry to the music. I sat on a tattered Persian carpet and listened, dipping my sugar cubes in my tea, just like they did—and trying to meditate, just like they did, too.

Formal rituals also governed Sufi life. When the darvishes greeted each other, they said *Ya Haqq,* "The Truth," and performed a special handshake by putting their hands together like a heart and kissing that heart. When they entered or left the meditation room, they "kissed" the ground by touching their fingers to the floor and then to their lips. When my mom and other Sufis prepared Iranian dinners, the darvishes sat around a tablecloth spread on the floor. I helped arrange the place settings and then waited with my parents for the other darvishes to sit down before finding a spot. The Sufis ate in silence. Generally, nobody spoke unless the sheikh spoke first—and it was understood that everybody should finish their food before the sheikh did so that he was not kept waiting. (Though, often, the sheikh ate slowly so that no straggler would feel uncomfortable.) These humbling rituals were important to the Sufis, helping them break down the self, which Sufi teaching considers a barrier to love.

Such a way of life appealed to the darvishes, many of whom had left Iran and other repressive societies to live in Canada and the United States. Some Muslims consider Sufis to be mystic heretics, and they are severely persecuted in the Middle East today. But even though many of the Sufis I knew had led difficult lives, they were always looking forward. Their demanding spiritual practice—with its emphasis on self-denial, service, and compassion over personal gain, comfort, and pleasure—elevated them. It made their lives feel more meaningful.

The Sufis who meditated in our home were part of a long tradition of spiritual seekers. For as long as human beings have existed, they have yearned to know what makes life worth living. The first great work of human literature, the four-thousand-year-old *The Epic of Gilgamesh,* is about a hero's quest to figure out how he should live knowing that he will die. And in the centuries since Gilgamesh's tale was first told, the urgency of that quest has not faded. The rise of philosophy, religion, natural science, literature, and even art can be at least partly explained as a response to two questions: "What is the meaning of existence?" And, "How can I lead a meaningful life?"

The first question addresses big issues. How did the universe come to be? What is the point and purpose of life? Is there anything transcendent—a divine being or holy spirit—that gives our lives significance?

The second question is about finding meaning within life. What values should I live by? What projects, relationships, and activities will bring me fulfillment? What path should I choose?

Historically, religious and spiritual systems laid out the answers to both questions. In most of these traditions, the meaning of life lies in God or some ultimate reality with which the seeker yearns to be united. Following a moral code and engaging in practices like meditation, fasting, and acts of charity help the seeker grow closer to God or to that reality, endowing day-to-day life with importance.

Billions of people, of course, still derive meaning from religion. But in the developed world, religion no longer commands the authority it once did. Though most people in the United

States continue to believe in God and many consider themselves spiritual, fewer people go to church, pray regularly, or have a religious affiliation, and the number of people who believe religion is an important component of their lives has declined. If religion was once the default path to meaning, today it is one path among many, a cultural transformation that has left many people adrift. For millions both with and without faith, the search for meaning here on earth has become incredibly urgent—yet ever more elusive.

My family eventually moved out of the Sufi meetinghouse. We came to the United States, where the busyness of everyday life trumped the rituals of meditation, singing, and tea. But I never stopped searching for meaning. When I was a teenager, that search led me to philosophy. The question of how to live a meaningful life was once a central driving force of that discipline, with thinkers from Aristotle to Nietzsche all offering their own visions of what a good life requires. But after arriving at college, I soon learned that academic philosophy had largely abandoned that quest. Instead, the issues it addressed were esoteric or technical, like the nature of consciousness or the philosophy of computers.

Meanwhile, I found myself immersed in a campus culture that had little patience for the questions that had drawn me to philosophy. Many of my peers were driven by a desire for career success. They had grown up in a world of intense competition for the merit badges that would get them to an impressive college, then to an elite graduate or professional school or a job on Wall Street. When they picked their classes and activities, they did so with those goals in mind. By the time they graduated, these razor-sharp minds had already acquired specialized knowledge in fields that were even more specific than their particular majors. I met people who could share their insights on how to improve public health in third-world countries, how to use statistical modeling to predict election outcomes, and how to "deconstruct" a literary text. But they had little to no sense of what makes life meaningful, or of what greater purpose they might have beyond making money or landing a prestigious job. Outside of an occasional conversation with friends, they had no forum in which to discuss or deeply engage with these questions.

They were not alone. As tuition skyrockets and a college degree is seen as the ticket to economic stability, many people today consider education to be instrumental—a step toward a job rather than an opportunity for moral and intellectual growth. The American Freshman survey has tracked the values of college students since the mid-1960s. In the late sixties, the top priority of college freshmen was "developing a meaningful life philosophy." Nearly all of them—86 percent—said this was an "essential" or "very important" life goal. By the 2000s, their top priority became "being very well off financially" while just 40 percent said meaning was their chief goal. Of course, most students still have a strong yearning for meaning. But that search no longer drives their educations.

Educating students about how to live was once central to the mission of colleges and universities in the United States. In the first part of our nation's history, college students received a rigorous education in classics and theology. They followed a prescribed curriculum that was designed to teach them what matters in life, and their shared beliefs in God and Christian principles served as a common foundation in that endeavor. But by the 1800s, the religious faith that grounded their studies was gradually eroding. The question naturally arose, writes

Yale law professor and social critic Anthony Kronman, of whether it "is possible to explore the meaning of life in a deliberate and organized way even after its religious foundations have been called into doubt."

Many professors not only thought it was possible but that they had an obligation to lead students forward in this quest. Religion, it was true, no longer offered all students definitive answers to life's ultimate question, but some educators believed the humanities could step in. Rather than leaving students to search for meaning on their own, these professors attempted to situate them in a large and enduring tradition of arts and letters. And so in the mid- to late nineteenth century, many undergraduates followed a college curriculum that stressed the masterpieces of literature and philosophy—like Homer's *Iliad*, Plato's dialogues, *The Divine Comedy,* and the works of Cervantes, Shakespeare, Montaigne, Goethe, and others.

By reading these texts, students listened and ultimately contributed to a "great conversation" that had been going on for thousands of years. As they encountered competing visions of the good life, students were able to come to their own conclusions about how to live. Is Homer's glory-driven Achilles a better model than the pilgrim in Dante's poem? What can we learn about the purpose of our lives from Aristotle's writings on ethics? What does Gustave Flaubert's *Madame Bovary* reveal about love and romance? How about Jane Austen's *Emma*? There was no one right answer. But by drawing on these shared cultural touchstones, students developed a common language with which they could discuss and debate life's meaning with peers, professors, and the members of their community.

By the early twentieth century, however, the situation had again shifted. After the Civil War, the first research universities appeared on the American educational landscape. These institutions, modeled after German universities, prioritized the production of scholarship. To facilitate such scholarship, separate fields of study arose, each with its own rigorous, systematic, and objective "methods." Professors pursued highly specialized areas of research within those fields, and students, too, chose an area of concentration—a major—to help prepare them for a career after college. Eventually, the humanities-oriented curriculum disintegrated, leaving students essentially free to pick and choose their classes from a menu of options—which, of course, continues to be the case today at most schools.

The research ideal dealt a blow to the idea that living meaningfully could be taught or learned in an academic setting. Its emphasis on specialization meant that most professors considered the question of meaning beyond their purview: they did not believe they had the authority or knowledge to lead students forward in this quest. Others found the topic illegitimate, naïve, or even embarrassing. The question of how to live, after all, requires a discussion of abstract, personal, and moral values. It does not belong, these professors argued, in colleges and universities devoted to the accumulation of objective knowledge. "An increasing consensus in the academy," as one professor wrote several years ago, "is that faculty members should not help students discern a meaningful philosophy of life or develop character, but should instead help them master the content and methodology of a given discipline and learn critical thinking."

But something interesting has happened in recent years. Meaning has regained a foothold in our universities, and especially in an unexpected place—the sciences. Over the past few decades, a group of social scientists has begun investigating the question of how to lead a good life.

Many of them are working in a field called positive psychology—a discipline that, like the social sciences generally, is a child of the research university and grounds its findings in empirical studies, but that also draws on the rich tradition of the humanities. Positive psychology was founded by the University of Pennsylvania's Martin Seligman, who, after decades of working as a research psychologist, had come to believe that his field was in crisis. He and his colleagues could cure depression, helplessness, and anxiety, but, he realized, helping people overcome their demons is not the same thing as helping them live well. Though psychologists were charged with caring for and studying the human psyche, they knew very little about human flourishing. And so, in 1998, Seligman called upon his colleagues to investigate what makes life fulfilling and worth living.

Social scientists heeded his call, but many of them zeroed in on a topic that was both obvious and seemed easy to measure: happiness. Some researchers studied the benefits of happiness. Others studied its causes. Still others investigated how we can increase it in our day-to-day lives. Though positive psychology was founded to study the good life more generally, it was the empirical research on happiness that blossomed and became the public face of the field. In the late eighties and early nineties, there were several hundred studies about happiness published each year; by 2014, there were over 10,000 per year.

It was an exciting shift for psychology, one that the public immediately responded to. Major media outlets clamored to cover the new research. Soon, entrepreneurs began monetizing it, founding start-ups and programming apps to help ordinary people implement the field's findings. They were followed by a deluge of celebrities, personal coaches, and motivational speakers, all eager to share the gospel of happiness. According to *Psychology Today,* in 2000, the number of books published about happiness was a modest fifty. In 2008, that number had skyrocketed to 4,000. Of course, people have always been interested in the pursuit of happiness, but all that attention has made an impact: since the mid-2000s, the interest in happiness, as measured by Google searches, has tripled. "The shortcut to anything you want in your life," writes author Rhonda Byrne in her bestselling 2006 book *The Secret,* "is to BE and FEEL happy now!"

And yet, there is a major problem with the happiness frenzy: it has failed to deliver on its promise. Though the happiness industry continues to grow, as a society, we're more miserable than ever. Indeed, social scientists have uncovered a sad irony—chasing happiness actually makes people unhappy.

That fact would come as no surprise to students of the humanistic tradition. Philosophers have long questioned the value of happiness alone. "It is better to be a human being dissatisfied than a pig satisfied; better to be Socrates dissatisfied than a fool satisfied," wrote the nineteenth-century philosopher John Stuart Mill. To that, the twentieth-century Harvard philosopher Robert Nozick added: "And although it might be best of all to be Socrates satisfied, having both happiness and depth, we would give up some happiness in order to gain the depth."

Nozick was a happiness skeptic. He devised a thought experiment to emphasize his point. Imagine, Nozick said, that you could live in a tank that would "give you any experience you desired." It sounds like something out of *The Matrix*: "Superduper neuropsychologists could stimulate your brain so that you would think and feel you were writing a great novel, or making a friend, or reading an interesting book. All the time you would be floating in a tank, with electrodes attached to your brain." He then asks, "Should you plug into this machine for life, preprogramming your life's experiences?"

If happiness is truly life's end goal, most people would choose to feel happy in the tank. It would be an easy life, where trauma, sadness, and loss are switched off—forever. You could always feel good, maybe even important. Every now and then, you could exit the tank and decide which new experiences you wanted programmed into your head. If you are torn or distressed over the decision to plug in, you shouldn't be. "What's a few moments of distress," Nozick asks, "compared to a lifetime of bliss (if that's what you choose), and why feel any distress at all if your decision *is* the best one?"

If you choose to live in the tank and feel happy moment to moment, for all the moments of your life, are you living a good life? Is that the life that you would choose for yourself—for your children? If we report that happiness is our main value in life, as a majority of us do, then wouldn't life in the tank satisfy all of our desires?

It should. Yet most people would say no to a life of feeling good in the tank. The question is, why? The reason we recoil from the idea of life in the tank, according to Nozick, is that the happiness we find there is empty and unearned. You may feel happy in the tank, but you have no real reason to be happy. You may feel good, but your life isn't actually good. A person "floating in the tank," as Nozick puts it, is "an indeterminate blob." He has no identity, no projects and goals to give his life value. "We care about more than just how things feel to us from the inside," Nozick concludes. "There is more to life than feeling happy."

BEFORE HIS DEATH in 2002, Nozick had worked with Martin Seligman and others to shape the goals and vision of positive psychology. Early on, they recognized that the happiness-focused research would be alluring and media-friendly, and they wanted to consciously avoid letting the field become what Seligman called "happiology." Instead, their mission was to shed the light of science on how people can lead deep and fulfilling lives. And over the last few years, that's precisely what more and more researchers have been doing. They have been looking beyond happiness in their search for what makes life worth living. One of their chief findings has been that there is a distinction between a happy life and a meaningful life.

This distinction has a long history in philosophy, which for thousands of years has recognized two paths to the good life. The first is *hedonia,* or what we today call happiness, following in the footsteps of Sigmund Freud. Human beings, he wrote, "strive after happiness; they want to become happy and to remain so"—and this "pleasure principle," as he called it, is what "decides the purpose of life" for most people. The ancient Greek philosopher Aristippus, a student of Socrates, considered the pursuit of *hedonia* the key to living well. "The art of life," Aristippus wrote, "lies in taking pleasures as they pass, and the keenest pleasures are not intellectual, nor are they always moral." Several decades later, Epicurus popularized a somewhat similar idea, arguing that the good life is found in pleasure, which he defined as the absence of bodily and mental pain, such as anxiety. This idea waned through the Middle Ages, but it saw a resurgence in popularity during the eighteenth century with Jeremy Bentham, the founder of utilitarianism. Bentham believed the pursuit of pleasure was our central driving force. "Nature has placed mankind under the governance of two sovereign masters, *pain* and *pleasure,*" he famously wrote: "It is for them alone to point out what we ought to do, as well as to determine what we shall do."

In line with this tradition, many psychologists today define happiness as a positive mental and emotional state. One tool commonly used in social science research to help assess happiness, for example, asks an individual to reflect on how often he feels positive emotions like pride, enthusiasm, and attentiveness versus how often he feels negative ones like fear, nervousness, and shame. The higher your ratio of positive to negative emotions, the happier you are.

But our feelings, of course, are fleeting. And as Nozick's thought experiment revealed, they're not everything. We may delight in reading the tabloids and feel stressed while taking care of a sick relative, but most of us would agree that the latter activity is more significant. It might not feel good in the moment, but if we skipped out on it, we'd later regret that decision. In other words, it's worth doing because it's meaningful.

Meaning is the other path to the good life, and it's best understood by turning to the Greek philosopher Aristotle and his concept of *eudaimonia,* the ancient Greek word for "human flourishing." *Eudaimonia* often gets translated as "happiness," and so Aristotle is often credited with saying that happiness is the highest good and chief goal of our lives. But Aristotle actually had pretty harsh words for those who pursued pleasure and "the life of enjoyment." He called them "slavish" and "vulgar," arguing that the feel-good route to the good life that he believed "most men" pursue is more "suitable to beasts" than to human beings.

To Aristotle, *eudaimonia* is not a fleeting positive emotion. Rather, it is something you do. Leading a *eudaimonic* life, Aristotle argued, requires cultivating the best qualities within you both morally and intellectually and living up to your potential. It is an active life, a life in which you do your job and contribute to society, a life in which you are involved in your community, a life, above all, in which you realize your potential, rather than squander your talents.

Psychologists have picked up on Aristotle's distinction. If *hedonia* is defined as "feeling good," they argue, then *eudaimonia* is defined as "being and doing good"—and as "seeking to use and develop the best in oneself" in a way that fits with "one's deeper principles." It is a life of good character. And it pays dividends. As three scholars put it, "The more directly one aims to maximize pleasure and avoid pain, the more likely one is to produce instead a life bereft of depth, meaning, and community." But those who choose to pursue meaning ultimately live fuller—and happier—lives.

It's difficult, of course, to measure a concept like meaning in the lab, but, according to psychologists, when people say that their lives have meaning, it's because three conditions have been satisfied: they evaluate their lives as significant and worthwhile—as part of something bigger; they believe their lives make sense; and they feel their lives are driven by a sense of purpose. Still, some social scientists are skeptical that happiness and meaning are distinct from each other at all. Yet research suggests that the meaningful life and the happy life can't be conflated so easily. The differences between the two were revealed in a study from 2013, in which a team of psychologists led by Florida State University's Roy Baumeister asked nearly 400 Americans aged 18 to 78 whether they were happy and whether they thought their lives were meaningful. The social scientists examined their responses alongside other variables, like their stress levels and spending patterns, and whether or not they had children. What they discovered is that while the meaningful life and the happy life overlap in certain ways and "feed off each other," they "have some substantially different roots."

Baumeister and his team found that the happy life is an easy life, one in which we feel good much of the time and experience little stress or worry. It was also associated with good physical health and the ability to buy the things that we need and want. So far, so expected. What was surprising, however, was that the pursuit of happiness was linked to selfish behavior—being a "taker" rather than a "giver."

"Happiness without meaning," the researchers wrote, "characterizes a relatively shallow, self-absorbed or even selfish life, in which things go well, needs and desires are easily satisfied, and difficult or taxing entanglements are avoided."

Leading a meaningful life, by contrast, corresponded with being a "giver," and its defining feature was connecting and contributing to something beyond the self. Having more meaning in life was correlated with activities like buying presents for others, taking care of children, and even arguing, which researchers said was an indication of having convictions and ideals you are willing to fight for. Because these activities require investing in something bigger, the meaningful life was linked to higher levels of worrying, stress, and anxiety than the happy life. Having children, for instance, was a hallmark of the meaningful life, but it has been famously associated with lower levels of happiness, a finding that held true for the parents in this study.

Meaning and happiness, in other words, can be at odds. Yet research has shown that meaningful endeavors can also give rise to a deeper form of well-being down the road. That was the conclusion of a 2010 study by Veronika Huta of the University of Ottawa and Richard Ryan of the University of Rochester. Huta and Ryan instructed a group of college students to pursue either meaning or happiness over a ten-day period by doing at least one thing each day to increase *eudaimonia* or *hedonia,* respectively. At the end of each day, the study participants reported back to the researchers about the activities they'd chosen to undertake. Some of the most popular ones reported by students in the meaning condition included forgiving a friend, studying, thinking about one's values, and helping or cheering up another person. Those in the happiness condition, by contrast, listed activities like sleeping in, playing games, going shopping, and eating sweets.

After the study's completion, the researchers checked in with the participants to see how it had affected their well-being. What they found was that students in the happiness condition experienced more positive feelings, and fewer negative ones, immediately after the study. But three months later, the mood boost had faded. The second group of students—those who focused on meaning—did not feel as happy right after the experiment, though they did rate their lives as more meaningful. Yet three months later, the picture was different. The students who had pursued meaning said they felt more "enriched," "inspired," and "part of something greater than myself." They also reported fewer negative moods. Over the long term, it seemed, pursuing meaning actually boosted psychological health.

The philosopher John Stuart Mill wouldn't have been surprised. "Those only are happy," he wrote, "who have their minds fixed on some object other than their own happiness; on the happiness of others, on the improvement of mankind, even on some art or pursuit, followed not as a means, but as itself an ideal end. Aiming thus at something else, they find happiness by the way."

PSYCHOLOGISTS LIKE Baumeister and Huta are part of a growing new movement, one that is fundamentally reshaping our understanding of the good life. Their work shows that the search for meaning is far more fulfilling than the pursuit of personal happiness, and it reveals how people can go about finding meaning in their lives. Through their studies, they're seeking to answer big questions: Does each person have to find meaning on his or her own, or are there certain universal sources of meaning that we can all lean on? Why are people in some cultures and communities more likely to consider their lives meaningful than those in others? How does living a meaningful life affect our health? How do we—and indeed can we—find meaning in the face of death?

Their research reflects a broader shift in our culture. Across the country—and across the world—educators, business leaders, doctors, politicians, and ordinary people are beginning to turn away from the gospel of happiness and focus on meaning. As I dug deeper into the psychological research, I began to seek these people out. In the pages ahead, I will introduce you to some of these remarkable individuals. We will meet a group of medieval enthusiasts who find fulfillment in their idiosyncratic community. We will hear from a zookeeper about what gives her life purpose. We will learn how a paraplegic used a traumatic experience to redefine his identity. We will even follow a former astronaut into space, where he found his true calling.

Some of their stories are ordinary. Others are extraordinary. But as I followed these seekers on their journeys, I found that their lives all had some important qualities in common, offering an insight that the research is now confirming: there are sources of meaning all around us, and by tapping into them, we can all lead richer and more satisfying lives—and help others do the same. This book will reveal what those sources of meaning are and how we can harness them to give our lives depth. Along the way, we'll learn about the benefits of living meaningfully—for ourselves, and for our schools, workplaces, and society at large.

As I interviewed researchers and chased stories of people searching for and finding meaning, I was reminded at every turn of the Sufis who first set me on this journey. More often than not, these paragons of meaning were living humble lives. Many of them had struggled in their pursuit of meaning. Yet their primary goal was making the world better for others. A great Sufi once said that if a darvish takes only the first step on the path of loving-kindness and goes no farther, then he has contributed to humanity by devoting himself to others—and it's the same with those focused on living meaningful lives. They transform the world, in big and small ways, through their pursuit of noble goals and ideals.

Indeed, just as new scientific findings have brought us back to the wisdom of the humanities, writing this book has affirmed the lessons I learned as a child living in the Sufi meetinghouse. Though the darvishes led seemingly normal lives as lawyers, construction workers, engineers, and parents, they adopted a meaning mindset that imbued everything they did with significance—whether it was helping to clean up a dinner spread or singing the poetry of Rumi and Attar and living by its wisdom. For the darvishes, the pursuit of personal happiness was completely beside the point. Rather, they focused constantly on how they could make themselves useful to others, how they could help other people feel happier and more whole, and how they could connect to something larger. They crafted lives that mattered—which leaves just one question for the rest of us: How can we do the same?

I

The Meaning Crisis

ON A FALL DAY IN 1930, THE HISTORIAN AND PHILOSOPHER Will Durant was raking leaves in the yard of his home in Lake Hill, New York, when a well-dressed man walked up to him. The man told Durant that he was planning to commit suicide unless the popular philosopher could give him "one good reason" to live.

Shocked, Durant attempted to respond in a way that would bring the man comfort—but his response was uninspired: "I bade him get a job—but he had one; to eat a good meal—but he was not hungry; he left visibly unmoved by my arguments."

Durant, a writer and intellectual who died in 1981 at the age of 96, is best known for his books that brought philosophy and history to the public. *The Story of Philosophy,* published in 1926, became a bestseller, and his multivolume work *The Story of Civilization,* cowritten with his wife, Ariel Durant, over the course of forty years, was awarded the Pulitzer Prize for its tenth volume, *Rousseau and Revolution.* During his life, Durant was a thinker with far-ranging interests. He wrote fluently about literature, religion, and politics, and in 1977, he received one of the highest honors bestowed by the U.S. government on a civilian, the Presidential Medal of Freedom.

Durant was raised Catholic, attended a Jesuit academy, and planned to join the priesthood. But in college, he became an atheist after he read the works of Charles Darwin and Herbert Spencer, whose ideas "melted" his "inherited theology." For many years following his loss of religious faith, he "brooded" over the question of meaning, but never found a satisfactory answer to it. An agnostic and empirically minded philosopher, Durant later came to see that he was unsure of what gives people a reason to go on living even when they despair. This wise man of his time could not offer a compelling answer to the suicidal man who came to him in 1930—the year after the stock market crash that inaugurated the Great Depression.

So Durant decided to write to the great literary, philosophical, and scientific luminaries of his day, from Mohandas Gandhi and Mary E. Woolley to H. L. Mencken and Edwin Arlington Robinson, to ask them how they found significance and fulfillment in their own lives during that tumultuous period of history. "Will you interrupt your work for a moment," Durant begins his letter, "and play the game of philosophy with me? I am attempting to face a question which our generation, perhaps more than any, seems always ready to ask and never able to answer—What is the meaning or worth of human life?" He compiled their answers into a book, *On the Meaning of Life,* which was published in 1932.

Durant's letter explores why many people of his time felt like they were living in an existential vacuum. For thousands of years, after all, human beings have believed in the existence of a transcendent and supernatural realm, populated by gods and spirits, that lies beyond the sensory world of everyday experiences. They regularly felt the presence of this spiritual realm, which infused the ordinary world with meaning. But, Durant argued, modern philosophy and science have shown that the belief in such a world—a world that cannot be seen or touched—is naïve at best and superstitious at worst. In doing so, they have led to widespread disenchantment.

In his letter, he explains why the loss of those traditional sources of meaning is so tragic. "Astronomers have told us that human affairs constitute but a moment in the trajectory of a star," Durant writes; "geologists have told us that civilization is but a precarious interlude between ice ages; biologists have told us that all life is war, a struggle for existence among individuals, groups, nations, alliances, and species; historians have told us that 'progress' is delusion, whose glory ends in inevitable decay; psychologists have told us that the will and the self are the helpless instruments of heredity and environment, and that the once incorruptible soul is but a transient incandescence of the brain." Philosophers, meanwhile, with their emphasis on reasoning their way to the truth, have reasoned their way to the truth that life is meaningless: "Life has become, in that total perspective which is philosophy, a fitful pullulation of human insects on the earth, a planetary eczema that may soon be cured."

In his book, Durant relates the old story of a police officer who attempted to stop a suicidal man from jumping off a bridge. The two talked. Then they both jumped off the ledge. "This is the pass to which science and philosophy have brought us," Durant says. Writing to these great minds, he sought a response to the nihilism of his time—a response to the despondent stranger who had left him speechless. Durant begged them for an answer to what makes life worth living—what drives them forward, what gives them inspiration and energy, hope and consolation.

* * *

DURANT'S QUESTIONS MATTER today more than ever. Hopelessness and misery are not simply on the rise; they have become epidemic. In the United States, the rate of people suffering from depression has risen dramatically since 1960, and between 1988 and 2008 the use of antidepressants rose 400 percent. These figures can't just be attributed to the increasing availability of mental health care. According to the World Health Organization, global suicide rates have spiked 60 percent since World War II. Some populations have been particularly vulnerable. In the United States, the incidence of suicide among 15- to 24-year-olds tripled in the last half of the twentieth century. In 2016, the suicide rate reached its highest point in nearly thirty years in the general population, and for middle-aged adults, it has increased by over 40 percent since 1999. Each year, forty thousand Americans take their lives, and worldwide that number is closer to a million.

What is going on?

A 2014 study by Shigehiro Oishi of the University of Virginia and Ed Diener of Gallup offers an answer to this question. Though the study was enormous, involving nearly 140,000 people across 132 countries, it was also straightforward. A few years earlier, researchers from Gallup had asked respondents whether they were satisfied with their lives, and whether they felt their lives had an important purpose or meaning. Oishi and Diener analyzed that data by country, correlating the levels of happiness and meaning with variables like wealth, rates of suicides, and other social factors.

Their findings were surprising. People in wealthier regions, like Scandinavia, reported being happier than those in poorer ones, like sub-Saharan Africa. But when it came to meaning, it was a different story. Wealthy places like France and Hong Kong had some of the lowest levels of meaning, while the poor nations of Togo and Niger had among the highest, even though people living there were some of the unhappiest in the study. One of the most disturbing findings involved suicide rates. Wealthier nations, it turns out, had significantly higher suicide rates than poorer ones. For example, the suicide rate of Japan, where per-capita GDP was $34,000, was more than twice as high as that of Sierra Leone, where per-capita GDP was $400. This trend, on its face, didn't seem to make sense. People in wealthier countries tend to be happier, and their living conditions are practically heavenly compared with places like Sierra Leone, which is racked by endemic disease, dire poverty, and the legacy of a devastating civil war. So what reason would they have to kill themselves?

The strange relationship between happiness and suicide has been confirmed in other research, too. Happy countries like Denmark and Finland also have some high rates of suicide. Some social scientists believe that this is because it is particularly distressing to be unhappy in a country where so many others are happy—while others suggest that the happiness levels of these countries are being inflated because the unhappiest people are taking themselves out of the population.

But Oishi and Diener's study suggests another explanation. When they crunched the numbers, they discovered a striking trend: happiness and unhappiness did not predict suicide. The variable that did, they found, was meaning—or, more precisely, the lack of it. The countries with the lowest rates of meaning, like Japan, also had some of the highest suicide rates.

The problem many of these people face is the same one the suicidal man struggled with over eighty years ago when he asked Durant for a reason to go on. Though the conditions of his life were generally good, he nonetheless believed life was not worth living. Today, there are millions of people who join him in that belief. Four in ten Americans have not discovered a satisfying life purpose. And nearly a quarter of Americans—about one hundred million people—do not have a strong sense of what makes their lives meaningful.

The solution to this problem, obviously, is not for the United States to become more like Sierra Leone. Modernity, though it can sap life of meaning, has its benefits. But how can people living in modern societies find fulfillment? If we do not bridge the chasm between living a meaningful life and living a modern life, our drift will continue to come at a major cost. "Everyone at times," wrote the religious scholar Huston Smith, "finds himself or herself asking whether life is worthwhile, which amounts to asking whether, when the going gets rough, it makes sense to continue to live. Those who conclude that it does not make sense give up, if not once and for all by suicide, then piecemeal, by surrendering daily to the encroaching desolation of the years"—by surrendering, in other words, to depression, weariness, and despair.

SUCH WAS THE case with the famous Russian novelist Leo Tolstoy. In the 1870s, around the time he turned fifty, Tolstoy fell into an existential depression so severe and debilitating that he was seized by the constant desire to kill himself. His life, he had concluded, was utterly meaningless, and this thought filled him with horror.

To an outsider, the novelist's depression might have seemed peculiar. Tolstoy, an aristocrat, had everything: he was wealthy; he was famous; he was married with several children; and his two masterpieces, *War and Peace* and *Anna Karenina*, had been published to great acclaim in 1869 and 1878, respectively. Internationally recognized as one of the greatest novelists of his time, Tolstoy had little doubt that his works would be canonized as classics of world literature.

Most people would settle for far less. But at the height of his fame, Tolstoy concluded that these accomplishments were merely the trappings of a meaningless life—which is to say that they were nothing at all to him.

In 1879, a despairing Tolstoy started writing *A Confession*, an autobiographical account of his spiritual crisis. He begins *A Confession* by chronicling how, as a university student and later a soldier, he had lived a debauched life. "Lying, stealing, promiscuity of every kind, drunkenness, violence, murder—there was not a crime I did not commit," he writes, perhaps with some exaggeration, "yet in spite of it all I was praised, and my colleagues considered me and still do consider me a relatively moral man." It was during this period of his life that Tolstoy began writing, motivated, he claims, by "vanity, self-interest, and pride"—the desire to acquire fame and money.

He soon fell in with the literary and intellectual circles of Russia and Europe, which had built a secular church around the idea of progress. Tolstoy became one of its adherents. But then two dramatic experiences revealed to him the hollowness of believing in the perfectibility of man and society. The first was witnessing the execution by guillotine of a man in Paris in 1857. "When I saw how the head was severed from the body and heard the thud of each part as it fell into the box," he writes, "I understood, not with my intellect but with my whole being, that no theories of rationality of existence or of progress could justify such an act." The second was the senseless death of his brother, Nikolai, from tuberculosis. "He suffered for over a year," Tolstoy writes, "and died an agonizing death without ever understanding why he lived and understanding even less why he was dying."

These events shook Tolstoy, but they did not shatter him. In 1862, he got married, and family life distracted him from his doubts. So did writing *War and Peace,* which he started working on soon after his wedding.

Tolstoy had always been interested in the question of what gives life meaning, a theme that runs through his writings. Levin, who is widely considered an autobiographical representation of Tolstoy, famously wrestles with the problem in *Anna Karenina*. He eventually concludes that his life is not pointless: "my life, my whole life, independently of anything that may happen to me, is every moment of it no longer meaningless as it was before, but has an unquestionable meaning of goodness with which I have the power to invest it."

But soon after he completed *Anna Karenina*, Tolstoy took a bleaker view. The question of meaning cast a shadow over everything he did. A voice inside his head started asking—Why? Why am I here? What is the purpose of all that I do? Why do I exist? And, as the years went on, that voice grew louder and more insistent: "Before I could be occupied with my Samara estate, with the education of my son, or with the writing of books," he writes in *A Confession,* "I had to know why I was doing these things." Elsewhere in *A Confession* he puts the question in other ways: "What will come of what I do today and tomorrow? What will come of my entire life . . . Why should I live? Why should I wish for anything or do anything? Or to put it still differently: Is there any meaning in my life that will not be destroyed by my inevitably approaching death?" Because he could not answer the "why" of his existence, he concluded that his life was meaningless.

"Very well," he writes, "you will be more famous than Gogol, Pushkin, Shakespeare, Molière, more famous than all the writers in the world—so what?" Tolstoy felt like the prophet of Ecclesiastes, who wrote, "Vanity of vanities; all is vanity! What profit hath a man of all his labour which he taketh under the sun? One generation passeth away, and another generation cometh: but the earth abideth for ever." The only truth we can absolutely know, Tolstoy believed, is that life ends with death and is punctuated by suffering and sorrow. We and all that we hold dear—our loved ones, our accomplishments, our identities—will eventually perish.

Tolstoy eventually found his way out of nihilism. He began by searching for people who were at peace with their lives to see where they found meaning. Most people in his own milieu—aristocrats and the literary elite—were leading superficial lives and knew nothing about life's meaning, Tolstoy argued. So he looked beyond his own social set and was struck to realize that millions of ordinary people around him had found, it seemed, a solution to the problem that had consumed him. These "simple people," as Tolstoy called them, the uneducated peasants, derived meaning from faith—faith in God and the teachings of Christianity.

Though Tolstoy had fallen away from religion by the time he was in university, his midlife search for meaning led him back to it. Curious about the faith that was so indispensable to the peasants, he studied various religious and spiritual traditions, including Islam and Buddhism. During that spiritual voyage, he became a practicing Christian. He first found a home in his native Russian Orthodox church, but he eventually broke away and started living according to his own stripped-down version of Christianity, which focused on adhering to Christ's teachings in the Sermon on the Mount.

Tolstoy's definition of "faith" is vague: he sees it as a fundamentally irrational "knowledge of the meaning of human life." What's clear, though, is his belief that faith ties an individual to something larger or even "infinite" that lies beyond the self. "No matter what answers a given faith might provide for us," he writes, "every answer of faith gives infinite meaning to the finite existence of man, meaning that is not destroyed by suffering, deprivation, and death." Though Tolstoy did not believe in the miracles or sacraments of the church, he found meaning in living "a life as it was meant by God to be led," as one of his biographers puts it—which, to Tolstoy, meant a Christ-like devotion to others, especially the poor.

Completing *A Confession* did not mark the end of Tolstoy's search for meaning. He continued his quest in the final decades of his life. He adopted a simple lifestyle, giving up alcohol and meat, rejecting his aristocratic titles of "Sir" and "Count," and learning the craft of shoemaking, believing that manual labor was virtuous. He devoted much of his time to improving the plight of the peasants in his community, and even tried to give all of his property to the poor (a plan his wife bitterly rejected). He also advocated progressive ideas like the abolition of private property, pacifism, and the doctrine of nonresistance to evil. With these beliefs, Tolstoy attracted a group of disciples who followed his teachings as they would a guru's.

At the same time, his final years were not easy. His attempt to live meaningfully upended his life. The Russian government denounced him as a radical; the Russian Orthodox church excommunicated him; and his marriage was left in ruins. Weary of constantly fighting with his wife, and yearning for an even more spiritual life, he fled their estate in October 1910, journeying by train to the Caucasus. He hoped to live the remaining years of his life in religious solitude. It was not to be: he died of pneumonia during the journey. His ideas, though, continued to make their mark on the world—and not just through his novels. His doctrine of nonresistance to evil inspired Gandhi's political campaign in India—which, in turn, helped spark Martin Luther King Jr.'s civil rights movement.

For Tolstoy, the meaning of life was found in faith. But many people do not believe in God or are unmoved by religious teachings. Others have faith, but are still searching for answers about how to live meaningfully here on earth. These people may not be satisfied by religion alone. Is it possible to find meaning in life without relying on faith in something infinite that gives our finite existence meaning, to paraphrase Tolstoy? For many people today, this is the question.

Tolstoy, it seems, would have answered no. But maybe there are other routes to meaning that either complement those offered by faith or, for nonbelievers, help to replace them. Maybe we can live meaningful lives even if everything for which we labor, everything and everyone we love, and everything we are and hope to be—our legacy—will one day perish and be forgotten. This is what the French novelist and intellectual Albert Camus set out to prove in his essay "The Myth of Sisyphus."

It is not surprising that Camus, who wrote that essay in his late twenties, would have been drawn to the problem of meaning. Unlike Tolstoy, Camus was not born into a wealthy family. His father, Lucien Camus, was a farmworker. His mother, a partially deaf and illiterate woman named Catherine, worked in a factory during World War I and later as a house cleaner. They married in 1910, the same year Tolstoy died. Three years later, Catherine gave birth to Albert in a small coastal town in Algeria called Mondovi (today Dréan). After World War I broke out, Lucien was drafted into the French army. He did not fight for long: one month later, he was wounded in the carnage of the Battle of the Marne, and soon succumbed to his injuries. Albert Camus had been alive for less than a year when his father was killed in the war.

Some sixteen years later, Camus's life was once again interrupted. In 1930, he was diagnosed with tuberculosis, which in his poor Algiers neighborhood often meant death. Still a teenager, Camus was forced to grapple with his mortality and with the fragile, arbitrary hold each of us has on life. From bed, he read the Stoic philosopher Epictetus, who meditated frequently on the subject—"For it is not death or pain that is to be feared," Epictetus wrote, "but the fear of pain or death"—and, as he recovered, tried to find some significance in what he was enduring. The upside of his illness, he concluded, was that it was preparing him for the inevitable end that awaited him, that awaits us all.

By the time he returned to school, Camus had decided that life had no meaning, a position he expressed in an autobiographical story published in a literary journal called *Sud*: "I haven't got anything anymore, I don't believe in anything, and it's impossible to live like this, having killed morality inside me. I have no more purpose, no more reason to live, and I will die." After he enrolled at the University of Algiers, his writing improved, and he continued exploring the question of meaning by studying philosophy. He graduated in 1936. That spring, he wrote a note in his journal expressing interest in writing a "philosophical work" on "absurdity."

Camus began writing "The Myth of Sisyphus" as another world war was overtaking Europe. He was living in Paris when Nazi planes showered down bombs on the city at the beginning of June in 1940. By the middle of the month, German forces marched into the capital, casting the shadow of totalitarian occupation over France for four years. Camus fled just a few days before they arrived. He worked on the essay during the bitterly cold winter of 1940 from a heatless apartment in Lyon—handwriting parts of it with "blistered and stiffened fingers," as one biographer has put it—and completed it in 1941.

Though Camus's interest in meaning is part of a long tradition of philosophy and literature, the times in which he lived made his search for it particularly urgent. In the chaos of France's collapse, in the cowardice of the Vichy government, and in the early triumphs of fascism across Europe, the world appeared meaningless and absurd. "The Myth of Sisyphus" is about how to live in such a world. "There is but one truly serious philosophical problem," Camus famously begins the essay, "and that is suicide. Judging whether life is or is not worth living amounts to answering the fundamental question of philosophy." No one, he quips, has ever died for the ontological argument, a proof of the existence of God. But many people die for meaning: some kill themselves because they judge their lives to be worthless, while others sacrifice their lives for their ideals. Whether life has meaning is the only life-or-death question that philosophy has ever asked and attempted to answer. It is, therefore, the most important question of all.

As Camus writes, we long for rational explanations of the world and seek order and unity, but the world is chaotic, disordered, and senseless—it has no "rational and reasonable principle." We wonder why we exist, how we came into being and for what purpose, but the world responds with silence. We can try to satisfy our yearning by making a leap to God, religion, or some other transcendent source of meaning that we take on faith. But if we accept as true only what we absolutely know, then there are "truths," as Camus puts it, but no single Truth.

To Camus, the fact that humans search ceaselessly for meaning but do not find it anywhere in the world renders life absurd; everything—from grand historical events to the great effort we all put into living our lives—seems pointless. The realization that there is no external source of meaning, no greater point or purpose to anything we do, inundates us with "nausea," to use the word of Camus's onetime friend, the existentialist philosopher Jean-Paul Sartre.

Of course, you don't have to be a French existentialist—or, for that matter, a Russian novelist—to feel the weight of the absurd descend on you. On the Conan O'Brien show in 2013, the comedian Louis C.K. described coming into contact with something like Sartre's nausea, Camus's absurd, and Tolstoy's horror. Like all great comedians, C.K. is a philosopher masquerading as a funny man: "Underneath everything in your life," he told O'Brien, "there is that thing, that empty—forever empty. That knowledge that it's all for nothing and that you're alone. It's down there. And sometimes when things clear away, you're not watching anything, you're in your car, and you start going, 'Oh no, here it comes. That I'm alone.' It starts to visit on you. Just this sadness. Life is tremendously sad, just by being in it."

When an inconsolable Tolstoy arrived at this point in his reasoning, he concluded that suicide was the only reasonable escape from the absurdity of life. Tolstoy, of course, eventually took another path. He found meaning in faith. But Camus rejects both faith and suicide as solutions to the problem of life's meaninglessness. For Camus, it's impossible to know whether God exists or whether any of the beliefs we take on faith are true. Given that, we must learn to live significant lives "without appeal" to God or faith. Yet to commit suicide would be to yield to the blind forces of a meaningless world. It would be to give in to the absurd and, in doing so, to compound it.

This might sound pretty grim, but the absurdity of life,

Camus argues, does not inevitably lead to despair. Rather, it opens up new opportunities. "Even within the limits of nihilism," Camus writes, "it is possible to find the means to proceed beyond nihilism." With meaning no longer imposed on us from an outside source, we have the freedom to create it for ourselves. As Sartre wrote, "Life has no meaning a priori. . . . [I]t's up to you to give it a meaning, and value is nothing but the meaning that you choose."

Camus illustrates this point by ending his essay with an ode to the ancient Greek hero Sisyphus, who was condemned by the gods to carry a boulder up to the peak of a mountain only to have it come tumbling down right before he reaches the summit. He performs this futile task for all of eternity. It's difficult to imagine a more meaningless existence than the one that Sisyphus ekes out. But Camus wants us to see that Sisyphus's life is extremely valuable. In fact, it serves as a model for us all.

To Camus, living a meaningful life requires adopting an attitude of defiance toward the absurd, which is precisely what Sisyphus does. Sisyphus, who is being punished for deceiving the gods and attempting to escape death, does not lament his fate or hope for a better life. Rather, in contempt of the gods who want to torment him, he embodies the three qualities that define a worthwhile life: revolt, passion, and freedom.

Each time he returns to the base of the mountain, he faces a choice: to give up or to labor on. Sisyphus chooses the struggle. He accepts his task and throws himself into the grueling work of carrying the boulder up the mountain. Having scorned the gods, he becomes the master of his own fate. "His rock is his thing," as Camus puts it—it's what gives his life meaning and purpose. Though his labors may seem pointless, they are endowed with meaning through the triumphant attitude with which he approaches his task. "The struggle itself toward the heights," Camus writes, "is enough to fill a man's heart. One must imagine Sisyphus happy."

The struggle *itself.* When Camus tells us to imagine Sisyphus happy, he does not mean a feel-good kind of happiness. He is talking about the sense of accomplishment and contentment that results from devoting yourself to a difficult but worthwhile task. Camus wants us to see that like Sisyphus, we can live our lives to the fullest by embracing the struggle with dignity—by embracing, as he puts it in his notebooks, the "misery and greatness of the world."

Camus obeyed this imperative in his own life. As he was working on "The Myth of Sisyphus" in Paris in 1940, he wrote a letter to a friend expressing his state of mind: "Happy? Let's not talk about it. . . . But even if my life is complicated, I haven't stopped loving. At this time there is no distance between my life and my work. I'm doing both at the same time, and with the same passion." If Tolstoy found meaning in the infinite, Camus finds it in the finite, in the daily task of living. The epigraph to "The Myth of Sisyphus" is a verse from Pindar, the ancient Greek poet: "Oh my soul, do not aspire to immortal life, but exhaust the limits of the possible."

Rather than give up on the world, we can confront it directly and with passion, and create for ourselves a meaning out of the pain, loss, and struggles that we endure. "To the question of how to live without God," Camus's biographer Olivier Todd writes, "Camus had three answers: live, act, and write."

Just as Sisyphus's rock was the "thing" that gave his life meaning, Camus's "thing" was his writing. Everyone, Camus believed, needs some "thing," some project or goal, to which he chooses to dedicate his life, whether it's a large boulder—or a small rose. Consider the beloved children's story *The Little Prince,* which is a wonderful expression of this wisdom. The prince lives on a tiny planet where he spends his time tending the plants and flowers in his garden. "It's very tedious work," he says, "but very easy." One day, he notices a rose that is growing on its surface—a flower unlike any he's seen on his planet before. The prince falls in love with the mysterious rose, whom he devotedly waters and shields from the wind. But she is a vain and needy flower, and the prince eventually grows weary of her, deciding to leave his planet and explore the broader universe.

He is on a quest for knowledge and understanding, and sees many strange sights during his travels. After visiting a few other planets, the prince finds his way to Earth, where he comes across a rose garden. Though the prince left his rose behind, he still cares for her, and seeing these other roses makes him disconsolate; he thought that *his* rose was the only flower of its kind in the universe, but now he sees that there are hundreds of others like her.

Just as he has reached the bottom of his despair, a wise fox calls out to him. The fox teaches the prince many lessons, but the most important one concerns the rose the prince left behind. The rose is not just another rose out of many, he tells the prince; it is special because of what the prince gave to the flower: "It's the time you spent on your rose that makes your rose so important . . . You become responsible forever for what you've tamed. You're responsible for your rose."

When the prince returns to the field of roses, he takes the fox's wisdom with him and addresses them: "You're lovely, but you're empty," he tells them. "One couldn't die for you. Of course, an ordinary passerby would think my rose looked just like you. But my rose, all on her own, is more important than all of you together, since she's the one I've watered. Since she's the one I put under glass. Since she's the one I sheltered behind a screen. Since she's the one for whom I killed the caterpillars (except the two or three for butterflies). Since she's the one I listened to when she complained, or when she boasted, or even sometimes when she said nothing at all. Since she's *my* rose."

In other words, it was the prince's investment of time, energy, and care into the rose that made her special—and that made their relationship meaningful.

This is not just literary or philosophical fancy. Social scientists, too, have found that when we put effort into building something, we tend to value it more—a phenomenon psychologists call the "IKEA effect." Putting together IKEA furniture makes people like it more, and what holds true for cheap Swedish furniture can also be applied to our lives more broadly. When we devote ourselves to difficult but worthwhile tasks—whether that means tending a rose or pursuing a noble purpose—our lives feel more significant.

The converse, of course, is also true. The most important parts of life require hard work and sacrifice. This is a lesson that many of us learn as children as we're first trying out sports, struggling through a hard class, learning how to play an instrument, or discovering how to nurture and maintain close friendships. Unfortunately, as we grow up, we tend to forget that lesson. The busyness of adult life makes quick and easy solutions to difficult life problems alluring. But to live well, we should take to heart the wisdom we learned in our younger years. Only by facing challenges head-on can we truly find meaning in our lives.

* * *

THOUGH THE MEANING of life may remain obscure, we all can and must find our own sources of meaning within life. This was the great insight of existentialist thinkers like Camus—and, a decade before "The Myth of Sisyphus" was published, Will Durant came to the same conclusion. After reading through the responses to the letter he sent to his friends and colleagues, he discovered that each of them found meaning in their own way. Gandhi wrote that he found meaning in the "service of all that lives." The French priest Ernest Dimnet found it in looking beyond his personal interest. "You ask what life has done for me?—It has given me a few chances to break away from my natural selfishness and for this I am deeply grateful." The filmmaker Carl Laemmle, one of the founders of Universal Studios, mentioned his children: "You ask 'where in the last resort my treasure lies?'—I think it lies in an almost frenzied desire to see my children and my children's children well cared for and happy." Owen C. Middleton, who was serving a life term in prison, found meaning in simply being part of the world: "I do not know to what great end Destiny leads us, nor do I care very much. Long before that end, I shall have played my part, spoken my lines, and passed on. How I play that part is all that concerns me. In the knowledge that I am an inalienable part of this great, wonderful, upward movement called life, and that nothing, neither pestilence, nor physical affliction, nor depression—nor prison—can take away from me my part, lies my consolation, my inspiration, and my treasure."

In 1930, the year that the suicidal man approached Durant in his yard, several others wrote to the philosopher expressing their desire to kill themselves. Durant wrote back, explaining, as best he could, why he believed life was worth living. Later, he synthesized his responses into a single statement that concludes *On the Meaning of Life.*

To Durant, meaning arises from transcending the self. "If, as we said at the outset," he writes, "a thing has significance only through its relation as part to a larger whole, then, though we cannot give a metaphysical and universal meaning to all life in general, we can say of any life in particular that its meaning lies in relation to something larger than itself." The more you connect with and contribute to that something, Durant believed, the more meaningful your life is. For Durant specifically, that "something" was work and family.

Some of the people who wrote to Durant were almost certainly out of work as a result of the Great Depression. They were not the only ones down on their luck. Joblessness rates skyrocketed during the Great Depression and peaked at 25 percent in 1933. At the same time, the suicide rate in the United States reached an all-time high. Researchers have found that across history, suicide rates tend to rise with unemployment—and it's easy to understand why: Work is a major source of identity, value, and purpose for people. It gives them something to do with their time, a sense of worth, and an opportunity to contribute to society and to support their families. When people lose their jobs, they are losing not only their livelihood, but a powerful source of meaning.

Durant counseled those who did not believe their lives were meaningful to find some sort of work, even if it was helping out on a farm in exchange for food and a bed until something better came along. To be productive and in the service of another person was a first step toward reengaging with life. "Voltaire once remarked," he writes, "that he might occasionally have killed himself, had he not had so much work on his hands."

In 1988, some fifty years after Durant published his book, *Life* magazine undertook a similar venture. The editors there wrote to over one hundred influential individuals of the time—from the Dalai Lama, Rosa Parks, and Dr. Ruth to John Updike, Betty Friedan, and Richard Nixon—asking them about the meaning of life. The magazine's editors did not learn of Durant's project until they were already well into collecting and editing the responses, but like Durant, they found that their respondents drew meaning from a wide variety of sources.

The psychologist and cell biologist Joan Borysenko, for example, told the story of one of her patients, who discovered the meaning of her life during a near-death experience, when she saw the key moments of her past play out in her mind like a movie. "She was amazed," Borysenko explains, "that her achievements as a lawyer meant little; the highlight of this 'replay' was a chance meeting she'd had years ago with a teenager who had checked out her groceries in the supermarket one day. Sensing sorrow in the boy's eyes, she'd patted his hand and whispered a few words of reassurance. Eyes locked in empathy, they had momentarily forgotten the illusion that they were strangers and shared a moment of deep connection." For the lawyer, meaning was kindled by sparks of love, compassion, and understanding in the checkout line.

Jason Gaes, a twelve-year-old boy with cancer, offered a touching explanation of what makes life meaningful for him. "I used to wonder," he wrote to *Life,* "why did God pick on me and give me cansur. Maybe it was becausc he wanted me to be a dr. who takes care of kids with cansur so when they say 'Dr Jason, Sometimes I get so scared I'm going to die' or 'you don't know how weird it is to be the only bald kid in your whole school,' I can say, 'Oh yes I do. When I was a little boy

I had cansur too. And look at all my hair now. Someday your hair will grow back too.' " For Gaes, confronting death helped him discover the purpose of his life.

For the novelist Madeleine L'Engle, meaning came from being a storyteller, taking the strands of human experience and weaving them into a coherent narrative. Echoing Camus, she wrote: "The only certainty is that we are here, in this moment, in this *now*. It's up to us: to live fully, experiencing each moment, aware, alert and attentive. We are here, each one of us, to write our own story—and what fascinating stories we make!"

Rabbi Wolfe Kelman wrote about the historic civil rights march from Selma to Montgomery in 1965. Martin Luther King Jr. was walking ahead of him, and as the large group crossed the Edmund Pettus Bridge in Selma, they sang together. "We felt connected, in song, to the transcendental, the ineffable," Kelman wrote to *Life*. "We felt triumph and celebration. We felt that things change for the good and nothing is congealed forever. That was a warming, transcendental, spiritual experience. Meaning and purpose and mission were beyond exact words: meaning *was* the feeling, the song, the moment of overwhelming spiritual fulfillment. We were experiencing what [Rabbi Abraham Joshua] Heschel called the meaning beyond mystery."

Each of the responses to Durant's letter and *Life*'s survey was distinct, reflecting the unique values, experiences, and personalities of the respondents. Yet there were some themes that emerged again and again. When people explain what makes their lives meaningful, they describe connecting to and bonding with other people in positive ways. They discuss finding something worthwhile to do with their time. They mention creating narratives that help them understand themselves and the world. They talk about mystical experiences of self-loss.

As I conducted my research for this book, those four themes came up again and again in my conversations with people living meaningful lives and those still searching for meaning. Those categories were also present in the definitions of a meaningful life offered by both Aristotle and the psychologists mentioned in the introduction—who argued, in different ways, that meaning arises from our relationships to others, having a mission tied to contributing to society, making sense of our experiences and who we are through narrative, and connecting to something bigger than the self. I found them, too, in the emerging social science research on a meaningful life and how people can achieve it. And I found them in works of philosophy, literature, religion, and popular culture—in Buddhist teachings, in American Transcendentalism, in novels, and in film.

They are the four pillars of meaning: belonging, purpose, storytelling, and transcendence.

For Laemmle and Borysenko's patient, for instance, meaning came from loving others and connecting to them with compassion and empathy. For Gandhi, as for young Jason, living a meaningful life involved doing some kind of good in the world so that others could live better lives. Then there was L'Engle, who found meaning in understanding life as a story. Rabbi Kelman and Middleton, meanwhile, found meaning by losing themselves in something bigger, whether a spiritual reality or the mystery of the tangible world itself.

These pillars are central to religious and spiritual systems, and they are the reason why those traditions historically conferred (and continue to confer) meaning in people's lives. They situated individuals within a community. They gave them a purpose to work toward, like getting into heaven, growing closer to God, or serving others. They offered them explanations for why the world is the way it is, and why they are the way they are. And they provided them with opportunities for transcendence during rituals and ceremonies. Each of these pillars was present in the lives of the Sufis I knew, which is why their lives were so meaningful.

But the beauty of the pillars is that they are accessible to everyone. Both with and without religion, individuals can build up each of these pillars in their lives. They are sources of meaning that cut through every aspect of our existence. We can find belonging at work and within our families, or experience transcendence while taking a walk through the park or visiting an art museum. We can choose a career that helps us serve others, or draft our life story to understand how we got to be the way we are. We may move from one city to another, change jobs, and lose touch with friends as the years go by, but we can continue to find meaning by harnessing the pillars in new ways in our new circumstances. And when we keep the pillars in mind, we find meaning in even the most unexpected of places, whether we're on our commute, inside of a prison, at the top of a mountain in West Texas—or on an island in the middle of the Chesapeake Bay.

2

Belonging

EVERYWHERE YOU GO ON TANGIER ISLAND, VIRginia, there are graves. There are graves in the front and back yards of the island's small houses, where people bury their dead family members. There are cemeteries near the beach, alongside the church, in the shadow of the powder blue water tower, and creeping into the narrow roads, their headstones crowded right next to each other. And there is the old island graveyard, now fifty feet under water. During severe storms, its skeletons and casket debris wash up in the surf.

Unlike modern urban and suburban communities, where cemeteries are marginalized, the cemeteries of Tangier are, by necessity, part of daily life. They serve as a constant reminder of the past. To the nearly five hundred residents of this tiny island, this is as it should be. Their community, they say, includes not just the living, but also the dead. Many of today's islanders can trace their line of descent to the original settlers who came to Tangier in the eighteenth century. Many of them still carry their ancestors' last names: Crockett, Pruitt, Park, Thomas.

Tangier sits in the middle of the Chesapeake Bay and is an hour away by ferry from both the Virginia and Maryland coasts. Only 1.2 square miles in size, it emerges from the water as little more than a sandbar, its harbor surrounded by a maze of docks, where the island's watermen keep their fishing boats. On the docks sit ramshackle shanties, with wire crab traps, or "pots," as the watermen call them, haphazardly stacked outside. Considered the soft-shell crab capital of the world, Tangier is also one of the last communities of its kind.

Swain Memorial Methodist Church is the physical, communal, and spiritual center of Tangier. On Sunday mornings, rows of golf carts, the island's principal mode of transit, line up outside the white clapboard building. The congregation, diminished over the years but still vibrant, fills up half of the church's pews. I attended a service hoping to catch a glimpse of the community in action, and on the morning I was there, worship began with a memorial for the recently departed: the preacher commemorated one former parishioner's "first birthday in heaven," and invited congregants to recall those they had lost. Everyone referred to each other, and to their dead, by their first names.

The service was intimate, more like a family reunion than a religious gathering. As an outsider, I felt self-conscious and out of place. At the end, I tried to slip out of the church without drawing attention to myself. But before I could, half a dozen people came up to me and formed a line. Each of them extended a hand to shake mine. "You must be staying at the Bay View," one woman said. "Well, we are so glad to have you in Tangier with us." Outsiders do not go unnoticed on Tangier. Nor do they go unwelcome.

"It's like one big family here," said Peggy Gordy, a lifetime resident of Tangier. "When someone is grieving, we grieve with them. When someone is celebrating, we celebrate with them. When there's a fundraiser, everyone goes. When there's a bridal shower, everyone chips in. Even if it's twenty dollars, everyone helps." It's inconceivable to the residents here that people on the mainland have neighbors whose names they do not know. "There are 480 people on this island," said Gordy, "and we all know each other."

The congregants spoke with a lyrical brogue that is unique to the people of Tangier. Though travelers over the years have attributed the accent to the remaining vestiges of Elizabethan England, its likely explanation is simpler: physically isolated from the world, Tangier's idiosyncratic folkways have managed to survive the homogenizing tides of language and culture.

But isolated though Tangier may be, cultural and economic forces have been crashing down on its shores in recent years. The distance between the island and the mainland is far more easily bridged today than it was in the past, thanks, in large part, to the recent adoption of wireless Internet and the growth of satellite television. The influx of media is not just exposing islanders to new ideas, but also giving them another vision of living well. Younger generations see people on television who are going to the mall and driving around in their cars, and—though they love Tangier—decide that that is the kind of life they want for themselves. For better and for worse, Tangier is entering the modern era.

The economics don't add up in Tangier's favor, either. The island's main industry is fishing and crabbing. But the state of Virginia has put a cap on fishing licenses and enacted catch limits to preserve the limited stock of fish and crab, making it nearly impossible for aspiring watermen to get into the business. "The younger guys," Tangier's mayor, James "Ooker" Eskridge, told me, "can't get a crabbing license unless somebody older drops out."

So they leave. Young men graduating from high school

today typically find work operating tugboats out of cities like Baltimore, while many of the women go on to college. Few return home. It used to be that people who grew up in Tangier would stay in Tangier their whole lives. But with every passing year, that has become less and less true. Fifty years ago, there were about 900 residents on the island and over 100 students at the island's only K–12 school. Today, there are fewer than 500 islanders and only 60 grade-school students.

Tangier has been called "the vanishing island" due to the erosion that has washed away twenty-five feet of its shore in the last few years. But it is vanishing in another way, too. The community of Tangier—its people and their way of life—is slowly disappearing.

EDWARD PRUITT is one of those who left. But in 2013, he returned for Memorial Day. Memorial Day is a big deal on Tangier, as residents come together to remember and celebrate those islanders who served—and died—for their country. That morning, American flags fluttered along the narrow streets. Someone was giving out paper cups of lemonade to the passersby. A handful of children wearing red, white, and blue ran through the small openings in the crowd that had gathered outside Swain Memorial Methodist Church. Pruitt, a thirty-two-year-old senior chief petty officer in the navy who had recently returned from a tour in the Middle East, stood on the porch of the church in his white uniform and sailor's hat, looking out at the faces of several hundred of his neighbors and friends. All of the islanders, it seemed, had turned up to hear him speak.

Edward's speech was about the importance of community. When he was getting ready to set off for college, he said, his school librarian—who is now the principal—gave him some advice. She told him not to be afraid to tell other people that he was from an island and not to be afraid to tell people that he was from Tangier. They would know from his accent that he was from somewhere unusual anyway, she had said, and when they asked him what it was like, he should proudly tell them that Tangier Island was a special place.

"Don't shy away from where you're from," Edward recalled her saying, "because it's a unique place and worth talking about."

It took Edward some time to fully heed her wisdom. Edward left Tangier in 1998 to attend Christopher Newport University in Newport News, Virginia, three hours away from the island. It was the first time he had been away from home—and it was an uneasy transition for him. Newport News was enormous compared to Tangier, and he wasn't used to having so many options and so much freedom. "In Tangier," he said, "there's just one grocery store. Off Tangier, there's a million."

But the hardest adjustment was learning how to make friends. Growing up, Edward knew all of the kids on the island; they were like his brothers and sisters. School was a comfortable and nurturing environment. There were seven people in his class year and, because all of the children of Tangier attend the same schoolhouse, the teachers he had in kindergarten were still around when he was in high school. "It's like growing up with an extended family," he said.

As wonderful as that tight-knit community was, it had one major drawback: when Edward got to college, he didn't have a whole lot of experience meeting new people. "I was shy," he said, "and I was self-conscious about my accent because most people start teasing you about it." Edward met a few people through his freshman year roommate—another young man from Tangier, who was a couple of years ahead of him in school—but he didn't really connect with any of them. So from time to time Edward got, in his words, "the college blues"—he felt lonely. He missed his friends and family. He missed Tangier.

In Tangier, Edward explained, you could always find someone to hang out with. In the evenings, young people would congregate at a seafood shack called Lorraine's or at Spanky's, an ice cream shop. Once together, they wouldn't do a whole lot. They'd grab some food, catch up, and maybe, later at night, wander around the island. In college, though, there was no equivalent of Lorraine's or Spanky's, no preexisting community in which he felt comfortable. "You don't realize how important those daily interactions are until they're gone," he said. "It's those conversations that are trivial and don't mean much that you miss—the daily stuff, not the big stuff. It was the same thing with the conversations you'd have every morning at school with the same people. In college, that was gone, and I didn't know how to fill that gap."

Edward didn't get good at making friends until he joined the navy after graduation. "The navy forces you to get to know people," Edward said. "You are being moved every couple of years or so, so you have to build new relationships all the time." As Edward got older and more self-assured, he no longer felt as self-conscious as he did when he first left home.

"A lot of people who leave Tangier Island," Edward said, "they'll drop the accent, and they'll try not to draw attention to themselves. But, after school, I realized that it could be a conversation starter, an easy way to break the ice with someone. They'll hear you talk and ask you where you're from. Some people think it's southern or Australian or English. So you have to explain you're from an island, and you start talking about your hometown—and then conversation just goes. They'll talk about their hometown, and a friendship can be made from there."

Edward's closest friends are still from Tangier, but he has found community in places beyond his little island. He has been in the navy for over a decade and has formed many close bonds there. "The connections you form on a ship when you're deployed are unlike anything else," he said. "You understand what each other has left behind and the difficulty of being gone, but you come together to complete the mission." When he sees shipmates from a previous deployment, he feels close to them, even if they were not good friends on the ship, because of that shared experience.

And, in 2010, Edward fell in love with a woman from Iowa. Their relationship has been through some trying times—several weeks after they were engaged in 2009, Edward was deployed to Iraq for a year. But though they were half a world apart, he and Katie talked almost every day. Those conversations, Edward said, sustained him. They married in 2011. Today, they live in Norfolk, Virginia, where they met, and have a three-year-old daughter named Laura.

Edward visits Tangier every five or six weeks, though he doubts he'll ever move back. Still, he said, "it's always good to be home."

WE ALL NEED to feel understood, recognized, and affirmed by our friends, family members, and romantic partners. We all need to give and receive affection. We all need to find our tribe. In other words, we all need to feel that we belong.

Research has shown that among the benefits that come with being in a relationship or group, a sense of belonging clocks in as the most important driver of meaning. When people feel like they belong, according to psychologists, it's because two conditions have been satisfied. First, they are in relationships with others based on mutual care: each person feels loved and valued by the other, just as Edward did when Katie called him regularly during his deployment. When other people think you matter and treat you like you matter, you believe you matter, too. Second, they have frequent pleasant interactions with other people. Those moments can be joyful and fun, like when a parent and child play, or more emotionally neutral, like when a content couple watches television together. But the key is that they happen on a regular basis and are not negative. When Edward was living on Tangier, he saw and spoke to his friends every day at school and around the island. In college, he had fewer of those daily interactions, which is why he felt lonely.

Though we all share a need to belong, in the first decades of the twentieth century many influential psychologists and physicians—those guardians of the mind and body—did not acknowledge this fundamental aspect of human nature. The idea that children needed parental love and care to live a full and meaningful life was not only considered medically dangerous; it was dismissed as immoral and mawkish. But the fruits of their labor reveal how fundamental it is for us to find belonging from our very first moments on earth.

Doctors' mistrust of parental care was a natural response to the horrific fact that children were dying all around them. Over a quarter of all children born in the United States from 1850 to 1900 died before they turned five. Yet thanks to the groundbreaking work of scientists like Louis Pasteur, doctors were beginning to understand that tiny pathogens caused certain diseases, an idea known as "germ theory." Medical professionals "still didn't fully understand how those invisible infections spread," explains the science writer Deborah Blum, but their "logical response was to make it harder for germs to move from one person to the next." Doctors established antiseptic environments in children's hospital wards where, as a pediatrician in New York wrote in 1942, "masked, hooded, and scrubbed nurses and physicians move about cautiously so as not to stir up bacteria. Visiting parents are strictly excluded, and the infants receive a minimum of handling by the staff." They also advised parents to minimize the amount of affection they gave to their children at home. Kissing, touching, hugging—all were ways to spread disease and therefore were discouraged for the sake of the child's health.

Meanwhile, behavioral psychology was coming into vogue, and academic psychologists began turning their attention to child-rearing. In 1928, John B. Watson, a former president of the American Psychological Association and founder of behaviorism, published an important new book called *Psychological Care of Infant and Child*. In it, Watson warned against the "dangers of too much mother love." Showering a child with affection, he said, will spoil his character by breeding "weaknesses, reserves, fears, cautions and inferiorities." Activities that we today take for granted—hugging a child, kissing her, letting her sit on her parent's lap—were roundly criticized by Watson as "sentimental." So destructive was parental love that Watson "dreamed of a baby farm where hundreds of infants could be taken away from their parents and raised according to scientific principles," writes Blum.

People took Watson's ideas seriously. His book became a bestseller and was widely praised in the press. But what Watson's book didn't discuss is that places much like those baby farms already existed. They were called foundling homes, or orphanages. In the early twentieth century, the mortality rate for children in orphanages could approach 100 percent—that is, almost every single child in the orphanage died before they were one or two years old. To spare the children from the pathogens that were surely the cause of their untimely deaths, scientifically minded caregivers established conditions of complete sterility and cleanliness, the same sort of conditions that doctors were implementing in hospital wards and that the medical community was advocating parents implement in their homes. The attendants in the foundling homes isolated the children from most human contact. They separated the children's beds from one another, covered their cribs with mosquito netting, and touched them only when absolutely necessary, which is to say hardly ever.

Children living in such environments did fare better. But even after orphanages and hospitals took these drastic measures, many infants were still inexplicably getting sick and dying. They had good food, good shelter, and as much protection from communicable diseases as possible, but they were continuing to develop infections and fevers that would not go away. What was going on?

That's when René Spitz entered the picture. In 1945, Spitz published the results of a seminal study on the critical role that love plays in the healthy development of a child. Spitz, who had come to the United States after fleeing from Europe to escape the Nazis, was not just a pioneer in this area of research; he was a renegade. In the study that he conducted, he compared two groups of disadvantaged children—infants who lived in an unnamed orphanage, and infants who attended a nursery at a prison in upstate New York, where their mothers were incarcerated.

The children in the orphanage, all younger than three years old, were kept in a state of what Spitz called "solitary confinement." Every measure was taken to prevent the spread of germs. Hanging sheets separated the cribs from one another. The attendants wore gloves and masks. They rarely handled the infants.

The prison nursery was a very different environment. Children were free to play with each other and to climb into each other's cribs. Toys were everywhere. And, most important, mothers were permitted to spend time in the nursery with their children, and would often play with and comfort them.

Unlike the foundling home, the nursery was a chaotic place, the perfect breeding ground for disease. But when Spitz looked at the mortality rates of the children in each group, he was stunned. Of the 88 children in the orphanage, where human contact was avoided, 23 had died by the end of his study. None of the children in the nursery had died.

The finding exploded the idea that the children in the orphanages were dying simply because of exposure to germs. Rather, Spitz argued, they were dying from a lack of love, which compromised their health. There were probably other factors at work, too, like the lack of a stimulating environment, but it was undeniable that the children Spitz studied did not have a core person in their lives with whom they could forge a lasting, intimate bond—in whose company they felt comfortable, safe, accepted, welcomed, and wholly cared for. They were prevented from feeling any sort of belonging. As a result, they languished and suffered.

In 1947, during a meeting at the New York Academy of Medicine, Spitz showed his colleagues video footage of the psychologically impoverished children at the unnamed orphanage he studied. The black-and-white film, crude and grainy, was called *Grief: A Peril in Infancy*. In one of the first title cards, the audience read, "During early infancy the sum total of the baby's human relations is represented by its mother or her substitutes." Then Spitz's colleagues saw a little girl named Jane, who had just been dropped off at the foundling home by her mother. At first, Jane was happy and full of life. When Spitz leaned over her in the crib smiling and playing, she smiled back and laughed joyously.

Then the film cut to footage of her taken a week later. She had become an altogether different child, with a depressed and searching look on her face. When a female attendant came over to her crib to play, as Spitz had done the week before, Jane looked at her and then started to cry. When Spitz came over and tried to comfort her, she was inconsolable. During the three-month period she was observed, Jane appeared to be in a state of grief, moaning with tears in her eyes.

The other children also suffered. Upon entering the orphanage, they smiled, played, and explored the world around them—they were normal infants. But after having spent time in the orphanage, their personalities transformed. Their eyes went blank. They looked scared and worried. One baby trembled in her crib as if she were having a psychotic episode. Another avoided making eye contact with an attendant trying to play with her, burying her head into her crib. Instead of crying, the infants let out "a thin wailing" sound.

These babies were, Spitz said, in despair. It was like they were giving up on life. Those whose lives prematurely ended died from what almost seemed to be a broken heart. Modern research helps explain why: chronic loneliness, scientists have found, compromises the immune system and leads to early death. Those infants who lived suffered physically and psychologically. They were smaller, less confident, and more socially maladapted than the prison nursery children.

As the film went on, a title card appeared that read: "The

cure—give mother back to baby." Jane was on the screen again, this time after being reunited with her mother. The infant was her old happy self. Rather than rejecting a researcher's affection by crying, she welcomed it, bouncing and smiling in an attendant's arms. But the psychologists and doctors watching the video knew that Jane was the exception, not the rule. Most of the children in an orphanage would never receive anything approximating parental care.

The video was heartbreaking and shocking. It drove at least one of Spitz's hard-nosed colleagues to tears. It also helped spark a shift in how psychologists understood human nature. In time, as a result of studies like Spitz's, psychologists began examining and affirming the vital importance of attachment early in life. They discovered that people, young and old alike, need more than food and shelter to live full and healthy lives. They need love and care. They need to belong to someone.

THE WAY WE satisfy our need to belong transforms over the course of our lives. In our early years, the love of a caregiver is essential; as we grow older, we find belonging in our relationships with friends, family members, and romantic partners. What remains the same, though, is the vital importance of these bonds.

But sadly, many of us lack close ties. At a time when we are more connected digitally than ever before, rates of social isolation are rising. About 20 percent of people consider loneliness a "major source of unhappiness in their lives" and one third of Americans 45 and older say they are lonely. In 1985, when the General Social Survey asked Americans how many people they'd discussed important matters with over the last six months, the most common response was three. When the survey was given again in 2004, the most common response was zero.

These figures reveal more than a rise in loneliness—they reveal a lack of meaning in people's lives. In surveys, we list our close relationships as our most important sources of meaning. And research shows that people who are lonely and isolated feel like their lives are less meaningful.

Émile Durkheim, the father of sociology, died a hundred years ago, but his insights about social isolation and meaning are more relevant now than ever. In his groundbreaking empirical study *Suicide* (1897), Durkheim explored the question of why people killed themselves. Why do some European societies, he wondered, have higher suicide rates than others? To answer that question, Durkheim investigated the relationship between suicide and variables like marriage, education levels, and religious orientation. What he found is that suicide is not just an individual phenomenon arising from people's personal troubles. It is also a social problem.

Here in the West, we take individualism and freedom to be foundational to the good life. But Durkheim's empirical research revealed a more complicated picture. He found that people are more likely to kill themselves when they are alienated from their communities and free from the social constraints those communities impose on them. Places where individualism is highly valued; places where people are excessively self-sufficient; places that look a lot like twenty-first-century America, Canada, and Europe—people don't flourish in these environments, but suicide does.

Durkheim combed through statistics from a number of European nations—including France, Sweden, Austria, and Italy—to examine how "integrated" people were into their various social networks. When he looked at the family, he saw suicide rates were generally higher among unmarried people than married people, and among people who didn't have children versus those who did. Turning to religion, he found that more Protestants killed themselves than Catholics and Jews, who lived in more tightly knit communities and had more religious obligations. Education, too, was associated with suicide. Educated people, like the Protestants he examined, tended to leave home for school and work—and, thanks to their education, they were also more likely to challenge traditional values. Going against the grain can be lonely. But being integrated into a community offset these effects. The Jewish people Durkheim studied, for example, were highly educated, but their strong bonds and traditional beliefs buffered them against suicide.

Meanwhile, factors that united people and imposed more duties on them, like living in a nation at war or having a large family, were associated with lower suicide rates. Without the constraints and traditions of the community, Durkheim argued, society devolves into a purposeless and normless state that he called *anomie,* where people feel directionless and despairing.

Recent empirical research confirms Durkheim's points. In the first chapter, I described a study by Shigehiro Oishi and Ed Diener, which showed that wealthy countries have higher suicide rates than poor ones, and that their inhabitants are less likely to consider their lives meaningful—but I didn't explain why. Beyond asking respondents about meaning, the researchers also gathered demographic and social information from each country on religiosity, education, fertility, and individualism. When they looked at the data, they saw that Durkheim was right. In wealthier countries, people are more educated and individualistic, have fewer children, and are less religious.

Poorer countries showed the opposite pattern: people overall were less educated and individualistic, more religious, and had more children. Oishi and Diener found that these factors, with religiosity leading the pack, made individual residents rate their lives as more meaningful.

In a similar vein, a study from 2010 probed into what was driving the increase in mental illness among high school and college students. The researchers discovered that the young people they studied were significantly more likely to suffer from poor mental health than older generations did as students—and that this was associated with a decreased concern for meaning among the students and an increase in social detachment across society. And when Australian researchers Richard Eckersley and Keith Dear looked at societal factors predicting the incidence of youth suicide, they found that it was associated with several measures of individualism, like personal freedom and control, just as Durkheim had suggested.

In our age of isolation, it's more critical than ever to actively seek out social groups and work hard to build close relationships, especially because many traditional forms of community are dissolving. People like Edward are leaving their small towns—and sometimes their countries—to go to school or find work, or because they want to see and experience the bigger world. Across society, people are spending less time with friends and neighbors and more time in front of television, phone, and computer screens—we are "privatizing our leisure time," as the sociologist Robert Putnam puts it. Meanwhile our busy, increasingly mobile lives make it hard to integrate into local groups. The average American moves eleven times in his life; many will change jobs at least that many times, if not more. We are growing apart from one another in many important ways. The challenge we face, then, is figuring out how to build relationships in spite of these trends. Fortunately, there are still ways to cultivate meaning-building friendships.

IN THE FALL of 2015, I traveled to Cleveland, Ohio, to see how people come together to deliberately create community. As I approached the grand Gothic church of St. Stanislaus, located on the south side of the city, I saw several hundred people of all ages gathered in small groups laughing, talking, and joyously greeting one another.

"It's been—what—twenty-five years?" one man called out, pulling his old friend in for a hug. "It's marvelous to see you."

It could have been a college reunion—except that people were dressed in brocade and breeches, and some of the men were carrying shields. They were members of the Society for Creative Anachronism, an international organization of medieval enthusiasts and re-creationists. During the week, SCA members lead ordinary lives as accountants, students, construction workers, parents, and scientists. But on many weekends, they get dressed up in elaborate costumes, adopt medieval personae, and step into a make-believe world of armored combat, crown tournaments, and royal court. That day in Cleveland, some three hundred of them had traveled from all over the Midwest to attend the coronation of Nikolai and his wife Serena as Czar and Czarina of the Middle Kingdom.

Inside the church, women in billowing dresses fanned themselves in the pews as they waited for the coronation to begin. Knights with swords hanging from their leather belts took their seats next to ladies wearing white veils and dainty crowns. A count in breeches spoke to a duke in a wide-brimmed feathered hat about the celebratory feast that would take place that night. And a small troupe of musicians in matching linen garb played fourteenth-century court music on their recorders. Nearby stood the two wooden thrones of the soon-to-be king and queen. Later that morning, Nikolai would kneel at a sword there and solemnly take his oath of kingship.

The SCA was founded in May of 1966 when Diana Paxson, a graduate student at UC Berkeley, threw a medieval-themed party, complete with a tournament and feast, in her backyard. About fifty people came, all dressed in period attire or something close to it. After a tournament victor emerged and crowned his lady the fairest of them all, the group thought it would be appropriate to hold a demonstration—this was, after all, the Berkeley of the 1960s. So they marched down Telegraph Avenue "to protest the twentieth century."

That original group of fifty has, six decades later, blossomed into an organization with sixty thousand members worldwide. As the society grew, the members divided themselves into geographical regions or "kingdoms," like the Middle Kingdom, which includes Ohio, Michigan, Indiana, Illinois, and parts of Iowa, Kentucky, and Ontario. Twenty kingdoms make up the "Known World," each of them ruled over by a king and queen who host events like the one I attended in Cleveland. Every summer, members from all of the kingdoms in the Known World gather at a lakeside retreat in Pennsylvania for two weeks to camp, duel, teach and take classes, shoot archery, dance, display their artistry, and reunite with old friends. Over ten thousand society members come to the "Pennsic War" each year. When they arrive, they are met at the gate by a greeter who tells them, "Welcome home."

The SCA is an unusual organization with an unusually strong pull over its members. There are a few reasons why the community is so vibrant—and knowing what they are sheds light on how we all can build new relationships and strengthen old ones.

First, the SCA's structure encourages people to invest time and effort into the community. Many SCA members have been involved with the organization for decades; many raise their children in the organization; and many attend twenty to fifty events each year. The frequency of SCA events is particularly important, because research has found that people naturally grow to like others whom they see regularly. SCA members are together a great deal, which contributes to their feelings of closeness. Our culture makes it easy to dismiss potential friends or partners based on a single interaction: if two people on a first date don't click immediately, they usually won't invest the time in getting to know each other better afterward. SCA members don't have that supposed luxury, which gives them a leg up in forming close relationships.

Second, people are more likely to befriend those with whom they share common experiences and values. Beyond a fascination with medieval history, the members of the SCA also share a set of principles centered around the chivalric virtues of courtesy, service, loyalty, and honor. Those who are models of these knightly virtues receive awards, or "peerages." The Order of Chivalry is awarded to those who are outstanding in armored combat. The Order of the Laurel recognizes those who have mastered an area of medieval arts and sciences, like thirteenth-century stained glass. And the Order of the Pelican is for those who exemplify the virtue of service. These virtues inspire SCA members to treat others, both inside and outside the group, with dignity and respect, even when their worst instincts impel them to do otherwise. This is a major reason why SCA members have such a strong sense of belonging in their community: they know that their peers will aim to treat them with dignity and respect no matter what. "I have to remember," one baroness told me, "that my job is to love others even when they are bringing me down or being annoying."

Howard—who goes by Sir Laurelen—is an optical physicist living in Cleveland. He's been an active member of the SCA for more than forty years. "I was an outcast, a nerd, a geek all through elementary school and high school. When I got to college," he told me over the clanking of heavy-armored combat happening nearby, "I had the chance to ask myself, 'Who am I going to be?' I had a choice." Howard chose to be himself—a geek long before it was cool. One day during his sophomore year of college, Howard was on his way home from practice for the varsity fencing team when a man on the bus noticed the two swords sticking out of his backpack and struck up a conversation. The man was in the SCA, and after the two talked about fencing and medieval fighting, he immediately recruited Howard to join the society.

"When I was a kid," Howard said, "I told people I wanted to be a scientist and a knight when I grow up. Today, I'm both."

Kat, a federal bank regulator from Chicago, met her spouse through the SCA. She joined the society over thirty years ago when she was fifteen years old, met her husband-to-be there three years later, and married him when she was twenty-four. "Without our mutual interests in the SCA period of history," she said, "we never would have met." The great thing about the SCA, Kat said, is that it values people who have interests that are outside the norm. "I have one friend," Kat said, "who is passionate about woodworking from the fourteenth century. I have another who is passionate about how they did their laundry back then. Another is into Japanese tea ceremonies. Whatever your thing is, we value you because you are learning and sharing that knowledge with others."

The SCA also builds belonging by giving people a strong network of friends. At the coronation, I met a member named James from St. Louis, Missouri. James, who said he was "socially inept and awkward" before joining the SCA, struggles with depression. He often feels inadequate and like a failure. It took him nearly twenty years, he said, to complete college, and today he is an adjunct professor at a community college, "which is not where I want to be." But in the SCA, he is the event organizer, a role that makes him feel capable and appreciated by his peers. The SCA, he said, gave him the confidence that he could not only socialize gracefully with a group of people, but also have something to contribute to them.

Several years ago, during one of his depressive phases, James checked into a psychiatric ward and was placed on suicide watch. When he was released, one of the first things he did was get together with his SCA friends for dinner. One of them said to him, "You know, James, if you ever left this earth, that would make all of us here very unhappy." It was a simple statement—a small gesture of support. But James carries it with him. When he starts to doubt whether his life is worth living, he brings that memory to the front of his mind, and it brings him comfort, reminding him that he is cared for.

Like all tight-knit communities, the SCA helps its members develop close relationships to a small group of people. But it also creates a network of trust and support among all of its members. Whether they're best friends or mere acquaintances, members take their relationships to one another seriously and lean on each other in times of need. Several years ago, one of the members of the Middle Kingdom was diagnosed with a serious illness. He had health insurance, but because he was too sick to work, he was having a hard time paying his bills. When the members of his kingdom found out, they decided to raise money for him by holding a silent auction of medieval crafts they had made. They ultimately raised over $10,000. When Hurricane Katrina hit New Orleans, SCA members from all over the country raised money and sent food and supplies to their unknown friends in Louisiana. Some members even paid their own way to New Orleans to help the stricken rebuild their homes and their lives.

The duty members feel to serve and support one another doesn't just spring from the community—it's also what sustains it. And it's those bonds, as much as the medieval regalia, that keep people like James coming back. "This," he said, "is my tribe." He looked over at the rapier combat happening in the sweaty social hall of the church and smiled.

WHILE CLOSE RELATIONSHIPS are critical for living a meaningful life, they are not the only important social bonds we need to cultivate. Psychologists have also discovered the value of small moments of intimacy. "High quality connections," as one researcher calls them, are positive, short-term interactions between two people, like when a couple holds hands on a walk or when two strangers have an empathetic conversation on a plane. We can sometimes be distracted or aloof when we're with another person, but during a high quality connection, each person is tuned in to the other and both reciprocate positive regard and care. As a result, both people feel valued. High quality connections play a role, of course, in making our close relationships with friends or romantic partners meaningful—but they also have the potential to unlock meaning in our interactions with acquaintances, colleagues, and strangers.

Jonathan Shapiro, an entrepreneur in New York, has a regular morning routine. Every day on his way to work, he buys a newspaper from the same street vendor, whose newsstand is by a busy subway station on the Upper West Side. Though both Jonathan and the vendor have every incentive to rush through the exchange of goods for money and get on with their days, they always take a moment to have a brief conversation.

Buying a newspaper, a cup of coffee, or groceries can feel businesslike and impersonal. Many of us are so caught up in our own lives, so rushed and preoccupied, that we acknowledge the people we are interacting with only instrumentally—as a means to an end. We fail to see them as individuals. But Jonathan and the vendor—even with hundreds of people streaming by them at the busiest time of the day in one of the largest cities in the world—take a moment to slow down. They break outside of their cocoons and form a brief bond with one another. Each of them lets the other one know that he is heard, seen, and appreciated—that he matters. Each of them helps the other one feel a little less alone in a vast and impersonal city.

One day, when Jonathan went to buy the paper, he realized he had only big bills. The vendor could not make change for Jonathan's $20 bill, so he smiled widely and said, "Don't worry, you'll pay tomorrow." But Jonathan tensed up and shook his head. He insisted on paying for the paper, so he went into a store and bought something he did not need so he could make change. He handed the vendor a dollar and said, "Here you go, to be sure I don't forget."

In that instant, the dynamic of their relationship changed. The vendor reluctantly took Jonathan's money and drew back in sadness.

"I did the wrong thing," Jonathan later said. "I didn't accept his kindness. He wanted to do something meaningful, but I treated it as a transaction."

The vendor isn't the only person, of course, who has felt

cut down by rejection. Psychologists have shown that social exclusion—even in the context of an interaction with a stranger during a research study—is a threat to meaning. In one experiment, undergraduates were brought into the lab, broken into small groups, and instructed to socialize with one another for fifteen minutes. Then each student was led into a separate room where he was told to nominate two of those people to interact with again. Those nominations were not used. Rather, half of the students were told, by random assignment, that everyone wanted to see them again. The other half were told that not even a single person did. You can imagine how those responses made the students feel. Those who were made to feel rejected and left out—made to believe they did not belong—were significantly more likely to say that life in general was meaningless. Other research shows that rejected participants also rate their own lives as less meaningful.

Perhaps surprisingly, psychologists have also found that social rejection can make both the rejected *and* the rejecter feel alienated and insignificant. As Jonathan learned on a crowded street corner of the Upper West Side, the smallest moment of rejection can knock the meaning out of a connection as easily as the smallest moment of belonging can build it up. After Jonathan dismissed the vendor's bid for mutual trust, both of them left each other that morning feeling diminished.

Fortunately, the two men were able to restore their relationship. The next time Jonathan saw the vendor, he brought him a cup of tea. And the next time the vendor offered Jonathan a newspaper, Jonathan thanked him and humbly accepted his gesture of kindness. They continue to share a quick conversation each day.

Jane Dutton, an organizational psychologist at the University of Michigan, coined the phrase "high quality connections" along with her colleague Emily Heaphy. Dutton studies the ways we interact in the workplace, and she has found that our connections there have a significant effect not just on our experience at work, but also in our lives as a whole. Given that work is where many people spend most of their waking hours, that shouldn't be too surprising. But it means that if we don't feel a sense of belonging on the job, both our jobs and our lives will feel less meaningful.

In one study, Dutton and her colleagues interviewed the cleaning and janitorial staff at a large hospital in the Midwest. They chose to focus on cleaners because they are vital to the operation of a hospital but are often ignored and disrespected. Their so-called dirty work is not generally valued by society. People talk about how meaningful it is to be a nurse who cares for the sick or a doctor who saves a person's life; they rarely talk about how meaningful it is to clean toilets.

Dutton and her colleagues randomly selected twenty-eight cleaners and interviewed them about their job responsibilities, how significant they believed their work to be, and their relationships with other people on the job, including doctors, nurses, patients, and visitors. The researchers were particularly interested in whether the cleaners felt respected and valued by their peers—whether their belonging needs were being met.

The cleaners told some two hundred stories about their time at work. When the researchers analyzed those stories, they discovered the powerful role that belonging plays in how people experience their jobs. Brief interactions, they found, could be deeply hurtful. When cleaners felt devalued by their colleagues, their work felt less meaningful.

The most common way the cleaners felt devalued was by being ignored. Doctors were particularly egregious offenders. One cleaner named Harry said, "The doctors have a tendency to look at us like we're not even there, like, you know, we'll be working in the hallways, and you know, no recognition of what you are doing whatsoever." A cleaner might be sweeping the hallway, but a group of doctors is standing in the way, which means, as Harry said, that "you have to ask them to move, every day, the same doctors every day." Several other cleaners told a similar story. The doctors, the cleaners felt, had "no regard" for them or what they were doing. It was like they were telling the cleaners that the cleaners do not exist and that their work does not matter. As a cleaner named Sheena told the researchers, "Sometimes you get the impression like, you know, they think they are more important than you are. And I mean their job is very important, but you know, cleaning the hospital is very important, too."

The cleaners spoke often about how doctors and nurses, whom they would see and work with every day, would walk right past them in the hallway without saying hello. One cleaner said that being ignored made her feel like "an invisible person that sort of floats around on the outside looking in." Another spoke of how the patients and their visitors disregarded them, too. Visitors, he said, often walked right through an area of floor he was mopping. "I think that this indicates they don't care about the cleaning people," he said.

Thankfully, those were not the only types of interactions the cleaners had. A "Good morning" from a patient could be packed with meaning. "They look at you like a person, you know?" said Kevin about patients who would acknowledge him as he cleaned their rooms. Another talked about how meaningful it was when the patients expressed gratitude. "They are not required to say thank you," he said. It's his job to clean their rooms, after all. "I guess," he said, "I feel appreciated by these things."

Positive experiences with colleagues, too, helped the cleaners feel a sense of belonging. One cleaner named Ben told a story about coming to work with a terrible stomachache. He was trying to sweep the floor, but the pain was so overwhelming that he bent over his broom in distress. A doctor came up to him and asked what was wrong, and Ben told him. The doctor told Ben he might have an ulcer (and, as it turned out, he did). It was kind of the doctor to stop and talk to Ben, but Ben's story focused on how the doctor treated him after that encounter. Every time the doctor saw Ben in the hospital, he would say, "Hey, Ben, how are you doing? Is everything better?" The doctor showed concern for Ben, and that made Ben feel valued.

Another cleaner named Corey talked about how the nurses he worked with made him feel like part of the team. When they would move patients from bed to bed or room to room, he would help them—and they, in turn, included him not just in professional tasks, but also in social gatherings: "When they have potluck or a dinner, or doughnuts, or rolls or whatever, or coffee, they invite me. . . . It lets me know that they appreciate me and that I'm likable."

When the hospital cleaners experienced these high quality connections, their relationship to their work changed. They saw themselves as caregivers rather than merely janitors, and they felt more closely tied to the mission of the hospital, which is to heal patients. Small inconsiderate acts, on the other hand, made them reevaluate the significance of their work, their ability to perform their tasks competently, and, even more gravely, their own worth as people.

The beauty of a high quality connection approach is that you don't have to overhaul the culture at your workplace to create meaning. Anyone, in any position, can change how they feel, and how their coworkers feel, simply by fostering small moments of connection. The results would be transformative. Dutton has found that high quality connections can revitalize employees emotionally and physically, and help organizations function better. They lead employees to feel more energized and engaged at work, make them more resilient when they encounter setbacks or frustration, and help teams work together more cohesively. Feeling like part of the group can make even the most mundane tasks seem valuable and worth doing well. Yes, brief interactions can be demeaning—but they can also be dignifying.

We can't control whether someone will make a high quality connection with us, but we can all choose to initiate or reciprocate one. We can decide to respond kindly, rather than antagonistically, to an annoying colleague. We can say hello to a stranger on the street rather than avert our eyes. We can choose to value people rather than devalue them. We can invite people to belong.

CLOSE RELATIONSHIPS and high quality connections have an important feature in common: both require us to focus on others. Think of René Spitz and how he tried to comfort baby Jane, or the SCA members who supported their acquaintances in New Orleans, or the doctor in Dutton's study who checked on Ben. They all put the needs of others before their own and helped them during a difficult period or moment in their lives; they all felt moved by what another person was going through, and they did something to make that person's life a little bit better. The recipients of their kindness were, in turn, elevated.

Compassion lies at the center of the pillar of belonging. When we open our hearts to others and approach them with love and kindness, we ennoble both those around us and ourselves—and the ripples of our compassionate acts persist, even long after we're gone. A story from the life of the Buddha offers an instructive parable. After the Buddha had his awakening beneath the Bodhi tree, he devoted his life to traveling through India teaching people of all classes the dharma, the basic principles of Buddhism—that life is full of suffering, which is caused by our endless cravings, and that we can be liberated from suffering by cultivating wisdom, living morally, and disciplining our minds through meditation.

When he was eighty years old, the Buddha was still traversing the countryside in his robes and bare feet, but he no longer had the energy of his younger years. "I am old and worn out," he said, "like a dilapidated cart held together with thin straps."

Approaching a tiny village, the Buddha grew frail and weak. When he arrived, a local blacksmith named Cunda, in a gesture of devotion and hospitality, offered him a meal that, the story goes, the Buddha knew was spoiled. The Buddha, however, did not want to hurt Cunda by rejecting the kind and generous offer of food. So he ate the food, even though he knew he would fall ill. "And soon after the Blessed One had eaten the meal provided by Cunda the metalworker," we learn, "a dire sickness fell upon him, even dysentery, and he suffered sharp and deadly pains."

When it became clear he was going to die, the Buddha once more exhibited a heroic compassion for Cunda. "It may come to pass," Buddha told his attendant, "that someone will cause remorse to Cunda the metalworker, saying: 'It is no gain to you, friend Cunda, but a loss, that it was from you the Buddha took his last alms meal, and then came to his end.' "

The Buddha instructed his attendant to dispel Cunda's

remorse by telling him that he played an indispensable role in the Buddha's life. Cunda, after all, gave the Buddha his final meal: "There are two offerings of food," the Buddha explained to his attendant, "which are of equal fruition, of equal outcome, exceeding in grandeur the fruition and result of any other offerings of food. Which two? The one partaken of by the Buddha before becoming fully enlightened in unsurpassed, supreme Enlightenment; and the one partaken of by the Buddha before passing into the state of Nirvana in which no element of clinging remains." In other words, the meal Cunda had prepared was one of the most important ones the Buddha ever ate.

The Buddha didn't have to extend his compassion to Cunda in those final moments of his life. He was deathly ill and in a great deal of pain. Instead of worrying about the blacksmith who had inadvertently poisoned him, the Buddha could have devoted his precious time to preparing for death or meditating or contemplating the legacy of Buddhism. But he didn't. Instead, he turned his attention to Cunda and assured him that the bond the two of them formed was meaningful.

The Buddha's story contains a lesson for all of us. The search for meaning is not a solitary philosophical quest, as it's often depicted, and as I thought it was in college—and meaning is not something that we create within ourselves and for ourselves. Rather, meaning largely lies in others. Only through focusing on others do we build the pillar of belonging for both ourselves and for them. If we want to find meaning in our own lives, we have to begin by reaching out.

3

Purpose

Ashley Richmond spends the majority of her time at work cleaning poop out of stalls. Her hours are rough, and she rarely gets holidays off. She earns significantly less money than most college graduates her age. And her body often aches at the end of the day. And yet, she says, this is her dream job: "I can't imagine doing anything else."

Ashley is a zookeeper at the Detroit Zoo, where she cares for giraffes, kangaroos, and wallabies. It's a role she knew she wanted to play from a young age. One of her earliest memories is of driving through a safari park in Canada when she was three years old. As her family's station wagon motored along through the park, a giraffe approached the vehicle and suddenly stuck its large head into the open window. "Everyone—all of my sisters—were screaming, but I was laughing and trying to stick my hand in his mouth," she said. "I've had a strong draw to animals since the beginning." When Ashley was six, a neighbor hatched a pet chick for a class project. Ashley was riveted. She wanted to grow up, she remembers thinking, so she could take biology and have the opportunity to care for an egg—to be "the reason why it hatched." Just a few years later, she took charge of caring for and training her family's pet dogs.

When Ashley was nine, a relative who had noticed her affinity for animals told her that she should consider becoming a zookeeper as an adult. It was the first time Ashley had heard of zookeeping as a career, but after she learned more about it, she knew that it was what she was meant to do. In the sixth grade, when she was assigned to write an essay on how she would like her life to unfold in five, ten, and fifteen years, Ashley wrote that she wanted to enroll at Michigan State University, get her degree in zoology, and work at the Detroit Zoo.

She graduated from Michigan State with a degree in zoology in 2006 and has been working at the Detroit Zoo ever since.

When I first met Ashley at the Giraffe Encounter, a feeding platform overlooking the giraffe habitat at the Detroit Zoo, her hands were covered in dirt, and she was carrying a bundle of branches in one arm. "Sorry I'm a mess," she said. She threw the branches on the ground, picked one up, and held it straight up in the air.

"Grab one from the pile," she said, "and hold on to it tightly with both hands."

A giraffe named Jabari galloped toward us. His geometric spots were chestnut brown, and they radiated in the October sun.

"Jabari is friendly. But," Ashley said as I lifted my hand toward his muzzle, "he doesn't like to be petted." On the other end of the habitat stood Jabari's mate Kivuli and their son Mpenzi, a one-year-old calf named after the Swahili word for "love." Jabari sniffed my stalk of leaves and snorted. Then he galloped away.

Ashley rustled her branch and called out Jabari's name to

coax him back. He returned and examined my branch again. He bit into the leaves at the top of the branch, nearly pulling the stalk out of my hand. In a matter of seconds, he had stripped it clean of leaves. I put the branch down and turned my attention to my notebook. Jabari bent his neck over the wooden fence of the feeding platform and dragged his nose along the edge of the page I was writing on. He lifted his head and looked directly at me, his long and muscular neck curved like a wave. The tip of his nose was an inch away from my face.

"He's such a curious guy," Ashley said.

This feeding exercise is an example of what's known in the zoo community as "enrichment." In a zoo environment, life is easy for wild animals like giraffes. They are fed regularly, protected from disease, and do not encounter predators. Though the animals lead longer lives as a result, those lives may not be as interesting as they would be in the wild. Ashley's role at the zoo, she told me, is to do everything in her power to make the lives of animals she oversees—none of whom chose to be in captivity, she pointed out—richer, happier, and more exciting. "I can't re-create the wild for them," she said, "but I can try to help them live somewhat normal lives."

Enrichment is one way for zookeepers and staff to try to achieve that goal. By moving rocks or tree branches around to create a different environment for the animals to explore, hiding food so that the animals have to search for it, or giving the animals objects to manipulate, they help make life in the zoo more unpredictable and, therefore, more stimulating. Enrichment also helps animals feel a sense of control over their environment, which is critical to their well-being. Jabari chose to participate in the feeding activity, for example, while Kivuli and Mpenzi chose not to.

"We try to give them opportunities to behave in natural ways," Ashley said. "Giraffes spend most of their time eating, so I try to find ways to feed them that are new and challenging for them." It's a challenge for Ashley, too: she has to constantly think of new methods to spice up their environment so that the animals do not get bored.

The keepers know their animals are doing well when they see them act naturally. Toward the end of our discussion, for example, one-year-old Mpenzi rammed the side of his body into Jabari, who rammed the young giraffe right back. Mpenzi's neck swayed to the left with the force of his father's hit. Then the two of them slapped their necks together. When I asked Ashley what they were doing, she said, "They're necking. Jabari is showing his son how to be a boy. This is what they'd be doing in the wild."

Ashley joined the Detroit Zoo at a watershed moment. Over the last four decades, zoos have undergone a major shift in purpose. It used to be that the primary mission of zoos was entertaining the public, and the animals were a means to that end. As late as the 1980s, the Detroit Zoo had an enormously popular chimpanzee show featuring the primates dressed up in clownish outfits doing silly stunts like riding tricycles and drinking from teacups. Today, top zoos like the one in Detroit define their purpose as ensuring animal welfare and contributing to the conservation of species and natural habitats around the world. A chimp show—or anything like it—would be considered an unacceptable violation of the animals' dignity and a distortion of nature.

That mission—to put the animals first—is always at the forefront of Ashley's mind. And she isn't alone. According to social scientists Stuart Bunderson and Jeffery Thompson, zookeepers have an unusually strong sense of purpose. They often describe their work as a calling—as something they were destined to do from a very young age because of a preternatural ability to connect with, understand, and care for animals. Zookeepers, the researchers found, are willing to sacrifice pay, time, comfort, and status because they believe they have a duty to use their gifts to help vulnerable creatures in captivity lead better lives. And they derive an enormous sense of meaning from living out that purpose.

Ashley shares this mindset. She spends only 20 percent of her time doing fun or intellectually challenging work, like training the animals or providing them with enrichment. The other 80 percent of her time is devoted to far less glamorous tasks, like cleaning the habitats. But even menial tasks are meaningful for Ashley, because they are tied to her broader purpose. "Keeping the yards and stalls clean is important," Ashley said, "because that helps the animals. It keeps them healthy. My goal every day is to make sure they are enjoying their environment—and a big part of that is giving them a clean place to live."

PURPOSE SOUNDS BIG—*ending world hunger* big or *eliminating nuclear weapons* big. But it doesn't have to be. You can also find purpose in being a good parent to your children, creating a more cheerful environment at your office, or making a giraffe's life more pleasant.

According to William Damon, a developmental psychologist at Stanford, purpose has two important dimensions. First, purpose is a "stable and far-reaching" goal. Most of our goals are mundane and immediate, like getting to work on time, going to the gym, or doing the dishes. Purpose, by contrast, is a goal toward which we are always working. It is the forward-pointing arrow that motivates our behavior and serves as the organizing principle of our lives.

Second, purpose involves a contribution to the world. It is, Damon writes with his colleagues, "a part of one's personal search for meaning, but it also has an external component, the desire to make a difference in the world, to contribute to matters larger than the self." That could mean advancing human rights or working to close the achievement gap in education, but it works on a smaller level, too. Teens who help their families with tasks like cleaning, cooking, and caring for siblings, for example, also feel a greater sense of purpose.

People who have such a purpose believe that their lives are more meaningful and more satisfying. They are more resilient and motivated, and they have the drive to muddle through the good and the bad of life in order to accomplish their goals. People who fail to find purpose in their daily activities, however, tend to drift through life aimlessly. When Damon looked closely at emerging adults 12 to 22 years old in a major study he conducted with his colleagues between 2003 and 2007, he found that only 20 percent of them had a fully developed, prosocial purpose that they were actively working toward. Purposeful youth are more motivated at school, get better grades, and are less likely to engage in risky behaviors like drug use. But 8 out of 10 of the young people Damon studied did not yet have a clear sense of where their lives were going. Many of them had made some progress toward setting long-term goals, but they did not know how they would pursue those goals or whether their aspirations were personally meaningful to them. A quarter of the emerging adults were "disengaged, expressing virtually no purpose."

Twenty years ago, Coss Marte was one of those purposeless children. Coss grew up on New York's Lower East Side in the 1980s and 1990s with his parents and three siblings—two older sisters and a younger brother. As a kid, he was mischievous and got into trouble. He attended four different high schools, having been kicked out of three for offenses like smoking and fighting. Even so, he graduated at the top of his class. "I did well in school without trying," he said. He was smart, ambitious, and—when he wanted to be—a hard worker.

Coss's father, a Dominican immigrant, ran a bodega, and Coss worked there as a cashier, cleaner, and stocker. He also collected cans and bottles to exchange for cash. Coss hated that he was poor and wanted desperately to change that fact. "I was always on the hustle," he said. "I saw the other kids have better stuff than me and I wanted that stuff. I was hungry to make money."

With his drive and smarts, he could have gone to college like his siblings, who ended up working at companies like Goldman Sachs and IBM. Instead, he started selling drugs.

In the eighties and nineties, the crime rate in New York was spiking, and the Lower East Side was one of the epicenters of the drug trade. Coss recalls that people would line up on street corners waiting to buy drugs. A dealer in the apartments above would lower a bucket on a rope filled with drugs to the buyer below, who would fill the bucket with money before the dealer would pull the bucket back up.

Coss soon joined their ranks. He had started smoking weed when he was eleven years old. By the time he was thirteen, he was selling it. A few years later, he began selling crack and powder cocaine, too. At sixteen, he inherited the lucrative street corner at Eldridge and Broome from a respected drug dealer and began managing the other dealers who came with the corner.

Coss was a natural entrepreneur—a savvy businessman—and he saw that the Lower East Side was gentrifying. By 2000, young professionals in law and finance were flocking into his neighborhood, and Coss realized that if he expanded his market to them, his business would soar. He printed ten thousand business cards that listed his phone number underneath the words "Festival Party Services: No Event Too Large or Too Small 24/7." Then he put on a nice suit and tie and headed to Happy Ending, a trendy new bar in the area, to hand them out to the yuppies. He created, as he put it, a "private, bougie delivery service" for cocaine and marijuana. Clients placed orders over the phone, and Coss's workers delivered the drugs to them in luxury cars.

At nineteen years old, Coss was making $2 million a year. He had nice clothes, wore expensive shoes, drove a fancy car, and split his time between multiple apartments in New York. A decade after he had decided not to be another poor kid from the hood, he was living his dream. But living your dream, as Coss would soon find out, is not necessarily the same thing as finding your purpose.

The dream ended one evening in April of 2009. Coss, then twenty-three, was trying to reach his workers, but no one was picking up their phones. "So I'm wondering what the hell is going on," Coss said. "I stepped out of my house with a package to deliver myself." The feds were outside his door, ready to raid the apartment. Coss tried to run, but the agents caught him and searched the apartment, where they found over two pounds of cocaine and $5,000 in cash. He and eight other members of his operation were arrested in one of that year's biggest drug busts in New York.

Coss was sentenced to seven years in prison. He wasn't too worried. He had been in and out of correctional institutions since he was thirteen and figured this would be "just another road trip." But when he got upstate to the penitentiary, the doctors there gave him some unsettling news: he would probably die before he was released. He had high cholesterol, high blood pressure, and would likely have a heart attack if he did not start eating more healthily. Coss, who was five foot eight, weighed 230 pounds.

The prognosis was a wake-up call. Coss had never exercised. Even in New York, he used to drive to the corner store twenty feet away and double-park. "I just paid the tickets," he said. "I was super arrogant." In prison, Coss started working out and eating better. At first, the other inmates laughed at him—he couldn't even do one pull-up. But he pressed on. He began by doing cardio for ten to fifteen minutes each day. Within a few months, he was working out for two hours straight. He ultimately lost 70 pounds.

With his healthier lifestyle came a new insight: he wanted a different life from the one he had been living. But wanting and doing are not the same thing. In prison, Coss continued to deal drugs and sold moonshine made from fermented fruit.

When he wasn't working the black market, he took on the role of the prison's personal trainer, teaching inmates exercises they could do in their cells. "Helping other people," Coss said, "it was empowering: just to have people come up to you and ask you for knowledge of how to do something and to share my knowledge of how to do it." He helped over twenty inmates climb out of obesity. One man, whose 320-pound girth inspired the nickname "Big Papi," lost over 80 pounds with Coss. "He actually cried," Coss said, "saying, 'Thank you, I have never been this fit. I was one of the fat boys.' "

These experiences were fulfilling, but Coss had to hit rock bottom before he recognized his true purpose in life. Just before his release date, Coss landed in solitary confinement for thirty days after an altercation with an officer. In solitary, he was given only a pen, paper, an envelope, and a Bible. He used the pen and paper to write a ten-page letter to his family explaining that he wasn't going to be coming home as planned and telling them that he had "really fucked up this time." When he finished the letter, though, he realized that he couldn't send it. He didn't have a stamp.

As the days wore on, Coss obsessed over how to get the letter to his family. Then he received a letter from his sister, a devout Catholic. In the letter, she suggested that Coss read Psalm 91, a beautiful poem about God watching over his flock during danger and turmoil. "I didn't believe in God or religion," Coss said, "and I said, 'Hell no, I'm not reading that. That's a waste of time.' " But then he reconsidered. "I realized all I had was time," he said, "so I decided to pick up the Bible." He flipped to Psalm 91. "When I opened to that page, a stamp fell out of the Bible. I got goose bumps. It was a supernatural moment for me."

That moment changed Coss's life. "I read the Bible from front to back," he said, "and understood I was fucking up. I was not doing anything to help society. Before, I didn't think selling drugs was a problem. I thought it was another job. All I thought about was getting paid. But I realized that I was affecting my family and these people I was selling drugs to. I thought, 'I fucked up so many lives and I don't know how to pay it back.' "

But then he realized that he *was* beginning to pay it back—by encouraging other people to get in shape and lead better lives. Helping other people improve themselves through fitness, he decided, was the unique contribution he could make to society. That thought motivated him. He wrote out a business plan for a fitness center. "I used the side of the Bible as a ruler and made a spreadsheet," he said. "I used the nutritional info from the milk carton they gave me to devise a nutritional plan for people." When he came out of solitary confinement, he made a vow to himself to never sell drugs again. He served an additional year in prison and then went home in March 2013.

Back in New York, he had nothing. He had run out of money in jail, and the government had seized most of his assets. He slept on his mom's couch as he rebuilt his life. "I went to a whole bunch of nonprofits to help me out, and I would never have gone to any before," he said. "But I was super humble and started asking for help." He got a day job at Goodwill doing clerical work and in his spare time thought about how to launch his business.

One of the nonprofits he encountered was Defy Ventures, whose mission is to help entrepreneurs from the street turn into legal entrepreneurs—to "transform the hustle." They offered a business education program, which Coss completed. They also hosted a business competition. Just two months after he was released, Coss won first place in that competition for the business plan he initiated in solitary confinement.

With his award money, he opened Coss Athletics in 2014, a fitness studio on the Lower East Side that specializes in a prison-style workout. The workout he created relies exclusively on body weight and is designed for small spaces, like a prison cell—or an urban apartment. When I first spoke with Coss in 2014, he had 350 clients and was working full-time at Goodwill to support himself. When I followed up one month later, he had doubled his client list and was hoping to raise money from private investors. By 2016, he had attracted over 5,000 clients and raised $125,000. He rebranded the company ConBody, and he left his job at Goodwill to run it full-time.

"I always wanted to have my own business and step away from drugs, but I was stuck on making so much money," he told me. These days, he is focused on using his talent to create a product that contributes positively to his community. Coss's clients are mostly young professionals—"the same people I sold drugs to," he said. But now, he is touching their lives in a very different way.

COSS'S STORY CONTAINS an important insight: living purposefully requires self-reflection and self-knowledge. Each of us has different strengths, talents, insights, and experiences that shape who we are. And so each of us will have a different purpose, one that fits with who we are and what we value—one that fits our identity.

The famed twentieth-century psychologist Erik Erikson described identity as complex and multifaceted; it involves not only who a person is but also where he comes from, where he is going, and how he fits into society and the broader world. Someone who has a solid grasp of his identity knows his core beliefs, his values and life goals, and how his groups and communities have shaped him. He is able to answer the central question that emerges during young adulthood, which is: *What kind of person am I and what kind of person do I want to be?* And yet identity isn't static. At every stage of life, he must actively revisit these questions. Toward the end of life, that means asking not *What kind of person do I want to be?* but *What kind of person have I been, and am I okay with that?* A person who has lived according to his values and accomplished his life goals will feel "ego integrity," as Erikson put it, instead of "despair."

Researchers at Texas A&M University have examined the tight relationship between identity and purpose, and they've found that knowing oneself is one of the most important predictors of meaning in life. In one study, a group of psychologists led by Rebecca Schlegel had undergraduates list ten traits that best represented who they were deep down, their "true self," as opposed to the inauthentic self they sometimes presented to others.

About a month later, the students returned to the lab to complete the second part of the study. As the students performed random tasks on a computer, the researchers flashed the words that the students had used to define their true selves on the screen for 40 milliseconds—too fast to visually register and consciously process. The students who were subconsciously reminded of their true selves subsequently rated their lives as more meaningful than they had before the study. Being reminded of your authentic self, even subconsciously, makes life feel more meaningful.

There's a reason for that. "Our culturally shared sources of meaning are dwindling," Schlegel said, "so people have to turn inward to figure out how to best lead their lives. Knowing your true self is the first step of that journey." People who know themselves can choose to pursue paths that align with their values and skills. Someone whose strengths are love and zest, for example, may make a great educator. But you don't have to change careers to put your talents to use. That same person could also use those gifts to connect with and serve his clients as a lawyer. Research shows that when people use their strengths at work, they find more meaning in their jobs and ultimately perform better. And when they pursue goals that align with their core values and interests, they feel more satisfied and competent. They're also likelier to persevere through challenges to actually accomplish those goals—that is, they are more purposeful.

The story of Manjari Sharma, a Brooklyn-based photographer, reveals the central role identity plays in helping us discover our purpose. Manjari's purpose as an artist is tightly tied to who she is and where she came from, and her journey offers some clues about how people come to know themselves.

Manjari was born in Mumbai, India. She grew up in a Hindu household where the divine was a constant presence. Her childhood home was filled with representations of deities—as were the shows she watched on television, like *Mahabharat* and *Ramayan,* both based on ancient Hindu epics whose myths captivated her growing up. When Manjari went on family vacations across India with her parents, her mother always took her to visit the nearby Hindu temples, some of them over five thousand years old, where she stood in awe before paintings and sculptures of deities like Vishnu, the majestic protector of the universe, and Shiva, its ferocious destroyer and transformer, who is often depicted dancing on the back of a demon.

Viewing these figures as a child inspired a *darshan* in Manjari. *Darshan* is the Sanskrit word for "glimpse" or "apparition"; it means seeing the essence of something. In Hinduism, a *darshan* refers to having a momentary connection to the divine in worship. Manjari only had such experiences from time to time in the temples, but they left their mark on her imagination.

Though Manjari has devoted her adult life to art, she had no intention of becoming an artist when she was younger; she wanted to be a dietitian. But when she got to college in Mumbai and saw the thick textbooks that she would be required to read, with their unending lists of caloric counts, her eyes glazed over. She decided to study visual communications instead, though she had no clear idea of what she wanted to do with the degree.

But then serendipity struck. With the help of a mentor, Manjari began to discover where her calling lay. A freshman photography class required her to snap some pictures every now and then. At the end of the year, her professor gave her the equivalent of the "best student of the year" award in photography.

She was shocked. "Really? Was I really that good?" she wondered. "I was completely caught off guard. I was just taking pictures without paying much attention," she said. "What if I started to pay more attention?"

To this day, Manjari, who has had her work exhibited internationally, considers her professor's award the most meaningful piece of recognition she has received as an artist. He not only awakened Manjari's calling in art, but also encouraged her to travel to the United States to study photography, which she did in 2001 at the Columbus College of Art and Design in Ohio.

There, she was "culture shocked," she said. For one thing, her ideas about America came to her via Hollywood. When she got to Columbus, she looked around and wondered, "Where are all the people?" She was lonely and missed home, but eventually she adjusted—and she soon realized that those feelings of estrangement could be transformed into something artistically productive. "When you are pushed out of your comfort zone—when you experience alienation—amazing things happen," she said. For Manjari, coming to America pushed her into developing an artistic vision tied to her childhood experiences.

Once Manjari left home, she did not continue to practice Hinduism regularly. Though religious ritual was central to her daily life in India, in America her focus shifted to immersing herself in art, from the art history classes that she took, to the art projects she was working on, to the museums that she visited with classmates. "I went from being in a country where art was worshipped in temples to a country where art was venerated and placed on a pedestal in museums," she said. The art museums recalled the Hindu temples she visited as a child on road trips with her family. As in a temple, there was a ritualistic component to going to the museum: the standing in line, the anticipation, the connection with a piece of art. "It had all the ingredients of a *darshan,*" Manjari said.

That insight sparked Manjari's most ambitious project to date. *Darshan,* as it's called, is a series of nine large photographic representations of Hindu gods and goddesses. These images, Manjari told me, are meant to stir the viewer in the same way that being in a temple, surrounded by the presence of the divine, electrifies the pilgrim.

Creating *Darshan* involved more than just taking pictures of nine models in fancy clothes. It was itself a ritual. For each portrait, Manjari worked with a crew of over thirty craftsmen to create an elaborate diorama that she then photographed. All of the objects that appear in the final portrait—from the jewelry and costumes to the props and sets—were handcrafted, painted, sewn, and assembled in a workshop in India into a traditional representation of the deity. The craftsmen, painters, workers, and models were not just hired help—what was most important to Manjari was that each person working on the project shared her vision. "I wanted everyone to have a special relationship to the set we were building together. That way, each crewmember would be personally invested in the project. Many people can come together to create something bigger than themselves," Manjari said.

The series is full of rich, bright colors and psychedelic imagery, and each portrait, like each deity, is utterly unique. The first portrait that Manjari completed with her crew is a radiant image of the goddess Lakshmi seated on a pink lotus flower with white bejeweled elephants behind her. Lakshmi is the goddess of material and spiritual fortune and, in the image, gold coins drop from the palm of her hand. In another portrait, Maa Saraswati, the goddess of art, music, and education, sits on a clay-colored boulder in a jungle and plays a stringed instrument with a peacock at her foot. And in yet another, Lord Hanuman, the monkey god, holds up a mountain with one hand as his tail floats in the air behind him.

Hanuman was the deity that made the greatest impression on Manjari when she was young. The story goes that Hanuman was very mischievous as a child, using his special powers of flight and transformation to sneak up on meditating sages and disturb them with pranks. One day, the sages punished him with a curse: Hanuman would forget his special gifts and powers, and would only remember them when he was truly in need of them to do good. That myth taught Manjari a valuable lesson about purpose. "We are capable of something unique, each one of us, but it takes time to find out what that is," she said. "There are all these layers that cover up our true potential, and it's not until the time is right that we might discover who we are truly meant to become or transform into. Just like Lord Hanuman."

Manjari's journey of self-discovery took nearly a decade, and it involved lots of twists and turns. With the help of a mentor, she devoted herself to pursuing art. Then, moving to an unfamiliar place, the United States, expanded her boundaries and gave her the opportunity to gain greater clarity about who she was—which, in turn, helped her develop a series of topics to address in her art. She was, she realized, someone who has a deep connection to myth, religion, and spirituality, and her works bear this imprint of her identity. "I learned that my artistic sense comes from the fact that I love myths and people's stories," she said. "I love telling them, hearing them, learning from them, and re-creating them in pictures."

Manjari looked over at the prints tacked across the white walls of her studio—pictures of her mother in a sari on an Indian beach, of the god Vishnu rising from the clouds like Venus from the sea, and of a father holding his newborn child to his chest in the shower. "That's my purpose," she said, "to tell a meaningful story that moves people the way I was moved by these stories."

Of course, self-knowledge is not enough on its own. Coss knew his strengths from a very young age and used them to achieve his goals as a drug dealer. Manjari took longer to discover her unique gifts and didn't find her purpose as an artist until she discovered that her work had the capacity to inspire others. For both of them, finding purpose required a critical step beyond self-knowledge: using that knowledge to figure out how they could best contribute to society. Today, they employ their skills to help others live better lives—Coss by helping people stay healthy and Manjari by creating an elevating experience for her audience.

THOUGH LIVING WITH purpose may make us happier and more determined, a purpose-driven person is ultimately concerned not with these personal benefits but with making the world a better place. Indeed, many great thinkers have argued that in order for individuals to live meaningful lives, they must cultivate the strengths, talents, and capacities that lie within them and use them for the benefit of others.

That idea was expressed forcefully by the eighteenth-century German thinker Immanuel Kant. Kant asks us to consider a man—one like so many of us today—who "finds in himself a talent that by means of some cultivation could make him a useful human being in all sorts of respects. However, he sees himself in comfortable circumstances and prefers to give himself up to gratification rather than to make the effort to expand and improve his fortunate natural predispositions." What should this man do? Should he abandon the cultivation of his natural talents for a life of enjoyment and ease? Or should he pursue his purpose?

These questions are the driving force behind the 1997 movie *Good Will Hunting*. The story begins with Will, a psychologically troubled twenty-year-old from South Boston. Will drifts purposelessly through life, working as a janitor at MIT and spending most of his free time drinking with his friends, even though he is a genius who can solve math problems that the graduate students at MIT cannot. When he gets in trouble for assaulting a police officer, Will gets a lucky break: an MIT professor, Gerald Lambeau, intervenes on his behalf. The judge agrees to release Will to Lambeau's supervision under the condition that he meet with Lambeau regularly to work on math.

Lambeau wants Will to put his talent to good use, so he does his best to mentor him and arranges job interviews for him with prestigious employers. But Will is defiant. He is not interested in developing his mathematical genius. He mocks his interviewers during their meetings and insults Lambeau, calling his research a joke. Later, when Will's best friend,

Chuckie, asks him how his interviews are going, Will implies he's not interested in being a "lab rat." He'd rather stay in South Boston and work in construction.

But Chuckie, like Lambeau, doesn't want Will to waste his potential—and he tells his friend that his attitude is selfish. "You don't owe it to yourself. You owe it to me. 'Cause tomorrow," Chuckie says, "I'm gonna wake up and I'll be 50, and I'll still be doin' this shit. And that's all right, that's fine." Will, however, has the chance to live a better life by putting his skills to work—skills that his friends, Chuckie explains, would do anything to have. But he's too afraid. It would be an "insult to us if you're still here in 20 years," Chuckie says, and a waste of Will's time.

Should Will throw away his gifts because he does not want to cultivate them, or should he doggedly work to perfect his skills and master his craft, as Lambeau and Chuckie want him to do?

For Kant—as for Chuckie and Lambeau—the answer is clear: a rational person, Kant explains, "necessarily wills that all capacities in him be developed, because they serve him and are given to him for all sorts of possible purposes." That is, his talents can benefit others and society, and so he has a moral obligation to cultivate them. Kant's ideas, as the contemporary philosopher Gordon Marino points out, fly in the face of the current cultural imperative, often heard during graduation season, to "do what you love." To Kant, the question is not what makes you happy. The question is how to do your duty, how to best contribute—or, as the theologian Frederick Buechner put it, your vocation lies "where your deep gladness and the world's deep hunger meet."

* * *

NOT EVERYONE HAS a calling as obvious as Will Hunting's, of course. In the real world, the majority of people have to choose jobs that they are qualified to get, and that hopefully pay enough to support them and their families. The four most common occupations in America are retail salesperson, cashier, food preparer and server, and office clerk, low-paying and often rote jobs that don't scream "meaningful work"—at least not on their face.

Even those with more options often find themselves at sea when it comes time to find a fulfilling career. Amy Wrzesniewski, a professor at the Yale School of Management and a leading scholar on meaning at work, told me that she senses a great deal of anxiety among her students and clients. "They think their calling is under a rock," she said, "and that if they turn over enough rocks, they will find it." If they do not find their one true calling, she went on to say, they feel like something is missing from their lives and that they will never find a job that will satisfy them. And yet only about one third to one half of people whom researchers have surveyed see their work as a calling. Does that mean the rest will not find meaning and purpose in their careers?

Adam Grant, a Wharton School of Business professor who studies how people find meaning at work, would argue that it does not. Grant points out that those who consistently rank their jobs as meaningful have something in common: they see their jobs as a way to help others. In a survey of over 2 million individuals across over 500 different jobs, those who reported finding the most meaning in their careers were clergy, English teachers, surgeons, directors of activities and education at religious organizations, elementary and secondary school administrators, radiation therapists, chiropractors, and psychiatrists. These jobs, Grant writes, "are all service jobs. Surgeons and chiropractors promote physical health. Clergy and religious directors promote spiritual health. Educators promote social and mental health. If these jobs didn't exist, other people would be worse off."

Grant's research offers a clue about how people working in any sector can find purpose at work—by adopting a service mindset. In one study, Grant and his colleagues tracked a group of university-call-center fundraisers who each met a student whose scholarship was being funded by their work. These callers took on a different attitude toward their jobs: seeing how their work affected another person's life made the fundraisers become much more purposeful—and more effective—compared with a control group. They spent 142 percent more time on the phone with potential donors and raised 171 percent more money.

In a study led by Jochen Menges, Grant and his colleagues discovered a similar phenomenon among women working at a coupon-processing factory in Mexico. Typically, workers who do not find their jobs interesting are less motivated and purposeful, and so are less productive on the job. Processing coupons can be dull and repetitive, so you might expect the women at the factory who found the job boring to be less productive than those who found it rewarding. That, indeed, is what Grant and Menges found. But that trend was reversed among a certain subset of women—those who adopted a service mindset. The women who found their work dull were just as productive and energized as those who found it rewarding, but only if they saw their work as a way to support their families. Even the most tedious tasks can be made purposeful when they benefit the people you love.

Parents perhaps know the value of a service mindset better than anyone. Raising children is one of the most stressful but crucial jobs a person can have—and though children can be a source of joy, an oft-cited finding from the psychological research on parenting is that raising kids makes parents unhappy. Parents sacrifice their personal time and space for their children, they lose sleep as a result of their kids, and they are constantly engaged in tiring tasks like changing diapers and enforcing discipline. At the same time, though, many studies show that raising children is a powerful source of meaning. As one mother told me, "It's blood and guts and makes me want to pull out my hair sometimes." But, she added, it is also "tremendously rewarding." Parenting gives people an opportunity to put aside their own interests for the sake of another. All of the difficult and tedious work of being a parent lies in the service of a larger purpose—helping a child grow into a responsible adult.

IN THE FINAL paragraph of *Middlemarch,* the novelist George Eliot pays a tribute to those individuals who keep the world moving forward in small yet indispensable ways: "The growing good of the world is partly dependent on unhistoric acts; and that things are not so ill with you and me as they might have been, is half owing to the number who lived faithfully a hidden life, and rest in unvisited tombs."

Those many millions of people, though they may not be remembered or known by you and me, made a difference for the people they encountered in their daily lives.

The ability to find purpose in the day-to-day tasks of living and working goes a long way toward building meaning. It was the mindset, for instance, adopted by the janitor John F. Kennedy ran into at NASA in 1962. When the president asked him what he was doing, the janitor apparently responded saying that he was "helping put a man on the moon." It was the mindset adopted by a roadworker who was directing the flow of traffic near a repair site on a stretch of Colorado highway several years ago. Standing in the sun, he periodically turned a sign that read "Stop" on one side and "Slow" on the other. "I keep people safe," he told a driver who asked him how he could stand such boring work. "I care about these guys behind me," he continued, "and I keep them safe. I also keep you safe, and everyone else in all those cars behind you." And it was a mindset adopted by a food cart owner a few years ago when my friend realized, after ordering, that he had forgotten his wallet. "My job isn't to take your money," he told my friend. "My job," he said, handing my friend his taco, "is to feed you."

Not all of us will find our calling. But that doesn't mean we can't find purpose. The world is full of retail clerks, coupon sorters, accountants, and students. It is full of highway flaggers, parents, government bureaucrats, and bartenders. And it is full of nurses, teachers, and clergy who get bogged down in paperwork and other day-to-day tasks, and sometimes lose sight of their broader mission. Yet no matter what occupies our days, when we reframe our tasks as opportunities to help others, our lives and our work feel more significant. Each of us has a circle of people—in our families, in our communities, and at work—whose lives we can improve. That's a legacy everyone can leave behind.

4

Storytelling

Erik Kolbell vividly remembers the summer in 2003 when his daughter Kate got her first job. Kate, who was then fourteen and living in New York with her family, had been hired to work as a mother's helper in the Hamptons. She was excited to move to Long Island and assume some of the responsibilities of adulthood. But her life, and Erik's, came to a screeching halt two weeks after she started working. On July 31, Erik received a call from his wife: "Kate's been hit by a car."

"The next thing I remember," Erik said, "was driving in the car out to Stony Brook Hospital and not knowing how serious it was, what condition she was in, where she was hit, or if she was alive." He eventually learned that she was in surgery with a pediatric neurosurgeon. That, Erik said, gave him three pieces of information: "Number one: she was alive. Number two: this was serious. Number three: neurosurgeon. She had a brain injury."

At the hospital, Erik was led to a private waiting area, where the neurosurgeon came in to see him and his wife. "She is in a medically induced coma," the doctor said. "Her vitals are stable. We had to remove a piece of her skull," he continued, "in order to relieve the pressure on her head, on her brain." The procedure had never been performed on a child before, Erik said, but it was the doctor's "Hail Mary. It was all he had." It was not enough. Late that night, her intracranial pressure spiked. She had to be taken into brain surgery once more.

Erik was telling this story into a microphone, on a velvet-curtained stage in a cozy wood-paneled room as part of an evening of storytelling organized by a group called The Moth. He looked out onto an audience of nearly three hundred people sitting in tightly packed rows and told them the thought that went running through his head when he found out that Kate was being wheeled into her second brain surgery of the night: "Where is the good in any of this?"

Just twenty minutes earlier, during a boozy intermission, the room had been filled with laughter and noise. Now the audience all leaned forward in rapt silence as Erik shared his story.

When Kate came out of her second brain surgery, Erik continued, it was 5 a.m. and she was stable. The doctors eventually transferred her to Mount Sinai Hospital in New York City, where she underwent intensive rounds of therapy. Because of the accident, she could no longer speak or do math, her depth perception was impaired, and she had lost nearly all of her memories. But by October, she was able to return to school part-time and continued to attend rehab. By November, she was well enough that she returned to Stony Brook so that the doctors could replace the part of her skull that they had removed in July. This would be her third brain surgery. "It was kind of a triumphal reentry," Erik said. "It's a way of sort of closing the door and saying, 'Yeah, she's going to make it.'"

Still, Erik continued searching for the meaning in everything that had happened: "I'm grateful she's alive," he thought on the eve of her third brain surgery. "I don't know how much more of her I am going to get back. Where is the good?"

He found it when Kate came out of the surgery. The two of them were in the recovery room. Kate was "still woozy" from the anesthesia when a series of visitors began arriving at her bedside.

The first person to come was a doctor. "Kate, you wouldn't remember me," he said. "I'm the admitting physician who was in the emergency room the day you came in."

Moments later, a nurse came by: "Kate, you would not remember me, but I was the nurse who was there when the original operating team came and started working on you."

"Kate, you wouldn't remember me," another guest said, "but I was the chaplain on duty when you came in and I spent time with your parents."

"Kate," said the next person, "you wouldn't remember me, but I was the social worker who oversaw your case."

"Kate," yet another said, "you wouldn't remember me, but I was the nurse on duty the second or third day."

It was, Erik recalled, "a parade of smiling faces." The last visitor was a nurse named Nancy Strong, who had overseen Kate's stay in the intensive care unit over the summer. "I pulled her aside and said, 'You know, I think it's great that you are all coming by to wish Kate luck. But there's something else going on here, isn't there?' "

"Yeah," Nancy said, "there is."

"What's going on?"

"Erik," she said, "for every ten kids we see with this injury, nine of them die. There is only one Kate. We need to come back and we need to see her, because she is what keeps us coming back to work in this place every day."

"This is the redemption," Erik realized. "This is the good."

* * *

AS A YOUNG MAN, George Dawes Green, the founder of The Moth, spent many evenings at his friend Wanda's home on St. Simon's Island in Georgia, where he grew up. He and his friends would sit around on Wanda's porch, drink bourbon, and tell each other stories from their lives—like the time one of them, Dayton, got drunk and let six thousand chickens escape from a barn he was responsible for tending, or the time that another, Kenny, forgot to take his lithium and swam a mile into the ocean stark naked before the coast guard caught him. Kenny, the story goes, told the coast guard to leave him alone: "Oh, I'm just fine," he insisted; "I'm a whale." As they took turns telling stories, Green recalls, "a troupe of moths staggered around the light, while the cicadas kept time in the live oaks."

Years later, Green was living in New York. He had published two novels, one of which, *The Juror,* became an international bestseller, adapted into a movie starring Demi Moore and Alec Baldwin. Green had made some money, was living in Manhattan, and attended fancy cocktail parties in the city. He was, from the outside, leading the sort of life that most writers dream about living.

But there was something missing. One evening, at a "particularly dull" poetry reading downtown, Green realized that he longed for those enchanting evenings on Wanda's porch. As literary as New York was, there was no place where ordinary people, like Green's neighbors in Georgia, could come onstage to simply deliver a well-crafted, well-told personal story. So Green decided to have some people over to his apartment, where he tried to re-create, in his New York loft, the experience he had on Wanda's porch.

By 1997, his idea had grown into a nonprofit organization named after the moths he remembered from those nights on St. Simon's Island. Twenty years later, The Moth has become a fixture of the New York cultural scene and an international phenomenon. Today, it puts on over five hundred shows a year in cities from London to Los Angeles to Louisville—there's even been one in Tajikistan. In addition to the live shows, which have brought over fifteen thousand stories like Erik's to the stage, The Moth hosts a weekly podcast and Peabody Award–winning radio show, and in 2013, it published its first story collection.

Under the leadership of artistic director Catherine Burns, The Moth carefully selects stories for meaning. They find these stories in a variety of ways: through The Moth's website; at StorySLAMs—open-mic competitions where anyone can sign up; and, of course, by word of mouth. No matter the source, Burns and her team look for stories that have conflict and resolution—stories that show how the storyteller developed into the person she is today—and they look for tales of change, stories that could end the way the Irish writer Frank O'Connor ended his short story "Guests of the Nation": "And anything that happened to me afterwards, I never felt the same about again."

The most moving stories, Burns has found, are rooted in vulnerability, but they are not too emotionally raw. The stories should come, as she put it, "from scars and not wounds." They should have settled in the storyteller's mind so that he or she can reflect back on the experience and pull out its meaning. "Sometimes," Burns said, "when you get on the phone with someone, they think they have a story worked out, but you'll see that it's not resolved."

Once they find a good story, Burns and her team take on

the role of directors. They work with the storytellers in rehearsal, helping them figure out the major narrative steppingstones to the climax and resolution, and might suggest some subtle feedback on delivery, like pausing here or slowing down there. Burns's intent is to make the stories resonate as strongly as possible with the audience members. But there's a secondary effect. After working with The Moth for more than fifteen years, Burns has seen that the process of crafting a story helps the storytellers connect the events of their life in new ways, gaining insight into their experiences and learning lessons that had previously eluded them.

At a 2005 Moth event in New York, Jeffery Rudell told a story about coming out to his parents when he was a freshman in college. He expected them to be accepting, so he was shocked when they responded by burning his possessions and cutting off all communication with him. For six years, he continued reaching out, regularly calling and writing letters, but they never responded. Eventually, he decided to make one last effort to reconnect with them. He flew home, unannounced, and showed up at his mother's office. Even then, she refused to see or talk to him. Two weeks later, he received a black funeral wreath at his office in New York with a note that said, "In memory of our son."

As Jeffery prepared this story for The Moth, he initially thought it would be about anger and pain. How could his parents, who had taught him the importance of love and kindness, treat him with such hatred and disgust? "I had the whole anger theme primed and ready to go," he said. "But there was a problem: I didn't particularly feel angry at my parents." After his family ostracized him, Jeffery had sought comfort from gay friends who assured him that their parents had also reacted poorly to their coming out—at least initially—but that they'd eventually grown more accepting and it was likely his parents would, too. All Jeffery needed was patience—and hope. He took their advice and for years held on to the hope that he and his parents would one day reconcile. As a result of that hope, though, his life "sort of came to a halt."

As he went through different drafts of the story for The Moth, Jeffery realized that he had been so focused on trying to earn back his family's love that he never thought about his future or his own needs. He declined job opportunities and broke up with a boyfriend who was moving to Los Angeles so that he could stay in Michigan, where his parents lived. He wanted to be nearby when they were ready to welcome him back into their lives. "For years," he said, "my relentless hoping did nothing more than keep me in a state of emotional stasis." Eventually, he came to understand that his hope had really been a form of denial. There was no chance of resurrecting his relationship with his parents, so he let go of that wish and moved on with his life. When he did so, he was finally able to find a sense of peace and resolution.

"The joke is," Burns said, "that telling a story on the main stage of The Moth is like ten years of therapy."

Few of us will reveal our personal histories in front of a crowd of strangers like Erik Kolbell did. But we are all storytellers—all engaged, writes the anthropologist Mary Catherine Bateson, in an "act of creation," which is the "composition of our lives." And yet unlike most stories we're used to hearing, our lives don't follow a predefined arc. Instead, she writes, "each of us has worked by improvisation, discovering the shape of our creation along the way." Our identities and experiences, in other words, are constantly shifting. Like a jazz musician in the middle of an improvisation, we may follow one path, then abandon it for another. Storytelling is how we make sense of that act. By taking the disparate pieces of our lives and placing them together into a narrative, we create a unified whole that allows us to understand our lives as coherent—and coherence, psychologists say, is a key source of meaning.

Our storytelling impulse emerges from a deep-seated need all humans share: the need to make sense of the world. We have a primal desire to impose order on disorder—to find the signal in the noise. We see faces in the clouds, hear footsteps in the rustling of leaves, and detect conspiracies in unrelated events. We are constantly taking pieces of information and adding a layer of meaning to them; we couldn't function otherwise. Stories help us make sense of the world and our place in it, and understand why things happen the way they do. "Storytelling is fundamental to the human search for meaning, whether we tell tales of the creation of the earth or of our own early choices," writes Bateson.

Stories are particularly essential when it comes to defining our identity—understanding who we are and how we got that way. Take the story of Emeka Nnaka. When he was twenty-one, Emeka was a defensive end with the semipro football team the Oklahoma Thunder. During one game in Arkansas, Emeka ran to make a tackle after the ball was snapped—a play he'd made many times before. When he hit the other player, his 250-pound body fell to the ground, as it usually did. But this time, something was different: he didn't actually feel himself fall. All he felt, lying there on the turf as the crowd fell silent, was the tingly feeling you get when you bump your funny bone. The trainers ran out. An ambulance wailed in the distance. Emeka was carried off the field on a stretcher. He tried to lift his hand to give the crowd a thumbs-up, but couldn't. At the hospital, he underwent a nine-hour neck surgery. When he woke up, he could not move his body below his chest.

Emeka had not grown up playing football. He threw the ball around a bit in high school, but it was not until he joined the Oklahoma Thunder during his sophomore year of college that he devoted himself seriously to the game. As a freshman, he explained, he was "a screwup." But "when football came to my doorstep," he said, "it was my chance to make everyone proud of me. I remember thinking, 'an opportunity has arisen for me to shine at what I'm good at, so let me use my gifts to pursue that.' It felt like I was moving to a bigger goal." He trained hard every day and, as he got stronger and faster, felt that his life was finally moving in a positive direction. After he played with the Thunder for two seasons, a coach at a college in Missouri called him, hoping to recruit him to play for the school's team.

Three weeks later, he injured his spinal cord.

In the days following his surgery, Emeka did not fully grasp the gravity of his situation. He thought he would spend two months in rehab before he could start playing football again. But by month three, when the hospital sent him home, Emeka still could not use his hands and arms, let alone move his legs—and that was when he realized that he was on a journey that would be much longer and more difficult than he had anticipated. "You are supposed to be in the hospital because you are sick," Emeka said. "When they tell you it's time to go home, it's because you're better. But when they told me it's time for me to go home, I didn't look or feel better." He thought, "What do you mean I'm ready to go?" The guy who had been able to lift 300 pounds couldn't even lift a 3-pound weight. His father had to move to Tulsa from Georgia to take care of him.

As Emeka adjusted to his new life, he spent a lot of time asking himself some big questions: "What is my life about? Am I going to get married? Will I have kids? Will someone love me? How will I support myself?" Before his injury, he had a clear sense of who he was: he was a football player; he was the life of the party; he was a college student with a future full of opportunities. Now he had to come to terms with the fact that the future he had always imagined for himself—the person he thought he would become—was gone.

To make matters worse, he came to see that the person he had been was seriously flawed. As Emeka evaluated who he had been before his injury, he realized that there were aspects of his identity that he did not like. "The truth is," he said, "I was really into who I was: I was a guy who partied a lot and didn't think a lot about others. I thought, 'You only live once, so do whatever you want to do right now.' I was living a purposeless life."

Emeka's identity was unraveling, but he started weaving a new one—a positive one. He told himself that he was better than the drifting and self-absorbed man he had been. In the spring of 2010, nearly a year after his injury, he began to volunteer at his church as an adviser to junior high school and high school students. Being a mentor helped him take his focus off himself and his circumstances and turn his attention to other people who needed his help and wanted to learn from his life experiences. "It wasn't until I started serving people that a light came on," he said, "and I realized who I really am—today, I'm someone who tries to put other people first." Two years after he began volunteering at his church, he went back to college. He graduated in 2015 and enrolled in a master's program for counseling. Emeka is still paralyzed and does not know whether he will ever walk again, but he is confident that the life he is leading now is far spiritually richer than the life he was leading before.

In the months after his surgery, Emeka spent a lot of time trying to make sense of his injury—of the moment when the story of his life took an abrupt turn. Before his injury, he said, "I was climbing up the wrong mountain." When he broke his neck, he fell down that mountain and "hit rock bottom." Then he discovered another mountain—the mountain he was supposed to be climbing all along, the mountain that contained his true path. He has been slowly climbing that mountain ever since.

THE STORY EMEKA tells about his injury is inspiring to the teenagers he mentors. But psychologist Dan McAdams would argue that it's even more important to Emeka himself. McAdams is a psychologist at Northwestern University and an expert on a concept he calls "narrative identity." McAdams describes narrative identity as an internalized story you create about yourself—a personal myth, as one writer puts it, "about who we are deep down—where we come from, how we got this way, and what it all means." Like fictional stories, it contains heroes and villains that help us or hold us back, major events that determine the plot, challenges that we overcome, and suffering that we have endured. When we want people to understand us, we share our story or parts of it with them; when we want to know who another person is, we ask them to share part of their story in turn.

It's important to understand that an individual's life story is not an exhaustive history of what happened to him. Rather, we make what McAdams calls "narrative choices." Our stories tend to focus on the most extraordinary events of our lives, good and bad, because those are the experiences that we need to make sense of, those are the experiences that shape us. But our interpretations of those events may differ wildly. For one person, for example, a pivotal childhood experience like learning how to swim by being thrown into the water by a parent might explain his sense of himself today as a hardy entrepreneur who learns best by taking risks. For another, that same experience might explain why he hates boats and does not trust authority figures. A third might leave the experience out of his story altogether, deeming it unimportant in the larger narrative of his life. For Erik Kolbell, an ordained minister and psychotherapist, his daughter's accident at first challenged and then affirmed an idea that is critical to his vocation, and therefore to his very self: that redemption is possible in a world where good people suffer unjustly.

McAdams has been studying life stories and meaning for over thirty years. In his interviews, he asks research subjects to divide their lives into chapters and to recount key scenes from their lives, such as a high point, a low point, a turning point, or an early memory. He encourages his participants to think about their personal beliefs, values, and philosophy of life. Finally, he asks them to reflect on the story's central theme.

After analyzing hundreds of these life stories, McAdams has discovered some very interesting patterns in how people living meaningful lives understand and interpret their experiences. People who are driven to contribute to society and to future generations, he found, all share a common pattern: they are more likely to tell redemptive stories about their lives, or stories that transition from bad to good. In these stories, the tellers move from suffering to salvation—they experience a negative event followed by a positive event that resulted from the negative event and therefore gives their suffering some meaning.

There was the man who grew up in dire poverty but told McAdams that his hard childhood circumstances brought him and his family closer together. There was the woman who told him that caring for a close friend as the friend was dying was a harrowing experience, but one that ultimately renewed her commitment to being a nurse, a career she had previously abandoned. And there was the father who shed his cynicism as he discovered the inherent kindness and generosity of the many people who helped his son when the child was diagnosed with a brain disorder: "As awful as the experience was," he said, "in retrospect we gained more from it, learned more about life and human nature and how many good people there are in the world." Erik, for his part, found redemption in how the hospital staff responded to Kate's survival. The redemption "doesn't make the crisis worthwhile," Erik said, "but it makes it worth *something*." These people, and others whom McAdams has studied, rate their lives as more meaningful than those who tell stories that have either no or fewer redemptive sequences.

It's important to note that telling a redemptive story doesn't necessarily mean that our lives have objectively improved. Erik, for example, could have easily crafted a narrative in which Kate's accident led to even more negative outcomes. Kate gets exhausted easily in social situations and continues to have problems with depth perception as a result of her brain injury. She also lost much of her memory of life before the accident. Erik could have dwelled on all of the ways that Kate's life has gotten harder—but he didn't. He told a story that in part redeemed what happened to her. Emeka was in a similar situation: he could have told a story about how being paralyzed spoiled his dreams, but instead he focused on how the injury changed him for the better.

The opposite of a redemptive story is what McAdams calls a "contamination story." In these stories, people interpret their lives or life events as going from good to bad. One woman he studied told the story of the birth of her child, a high point in her life. But then she made a striking narrative choice: she ended the story with the death of the baby's father, who was murdered three years later. In her telling, the joy that the birth of her child brought to her life was tainted by that tragedy. People who tell contamination stories, McAdams has found, are less "generative," as psychologists put it, or less driven to contribute to society and younger generations. They also tend to be more anxious and depressed, and to feel that their lives are less coherent compared to those who tell redemptive stories.

Redemption and contamination stories are just two kinds of tales we can spin about our lives. Some life stories, for example, are defined by inner transformation and personal growth, while others are defined by stagnation or regression; some by communion, love, and belonging and others by loneliness and isolation; some by agency—the belief that an individual is in control of his or her life—and others by helplessness; and some by a combination of these themes. McAdams has found that beyond stories of redemption, people who believe their lives are meaningful tend to tell stories defined by growth, communion, and agency. These stories allow individuals to craft a positive identity for themselves: they are in control of their lives, they are loved, they are progressing through life, and whatever obstacles they have encountered have been redeemed by good outcomes.

The stories we tell about our lives reveal how we understand ourselves and how we interpret the way our lives have unfolded. They can also reinforce different aspects of who we are. Someone who is depressed or pessimistic, for example, may be more likely to tell a contamination story about his life—and that harmful story could lead him to feel even worse about his circumstances. But there's a way to break out of this cycle. Just because some stories give rise to more meaning than others doesn't mean that people who tell negative stories about their lives are stuck in a meaningless rut. We are all the authors of our own stories and can choose to change the way we're telling them.

One of the great contributions of psychology and psychotherapy research is the idea that we can edit, revise, and interpret the stories we tell about our lives even as we are constrained by the facts. The psychologist Michele Crossley writes that mental illness is often the result of a person's inability to tell a good story about his or her life. Either the story is incoherent or inadequate, or it's a "life story gone awry." The psychotherapist's job is to work with patients to rewrite their stories in a more positive way. Through editing and reinterpreting his story with his therapist, the patient comes to realize, among other things, that he is in control of his life and that some meaning can be gleaned from whatever hardship he has endured. As a result, his mental health improves. A review of the scientific literature finds that this form of therapy is as effective as antidepressants or cognitive behavioral therapy.

Even making smaller story edits can have a big impact on how we live. So found Adam Grant and Jane Dutton in a study published in 2012. The researchers asked university-call-center fundraisers, a group Grant has studied before, to keep a journal for four consecutive days. In one condition, the beneficiary condition, the researchers asked the fundraisers to write about the last time a colleague did something for them that inspired gratitude. In the second condition, the benefactor condition, the participants wrote about a time they contributed to others at work.

The researchers wanted to know which type of story would lead the research subjects to be more generous—a story in which you define yourself as a recipient of someone's good graces or a story in which you define yourself as a giver of good graces. To find out, they monitored the fundraisers' call records. Since the fundraisers were paid a fixed hourly rate to call alumni and solicit donations for the school, the researchers reasoned, then the number of calls they made during their shift was a good indicator of prosocial, helping behavior. Someone who makes more calls in an hour is being more helpful to the university than someone who makes fewer calls.

After Grant and Dutton analyzed the stories, they found that fundraisers who told a story of themselves as benefactors—as givers—ultimately made 30 percent more calls to alumni after the experiment than they had before. Those who told stories about being recipients of generosity showed no changes in their behavior. It was an elegant demonstration that the kind of story we tell affects who we are. "When seeing themselves as benefactors," Dutton said, the fundraisers "now needed to act like givers, which called forth more pro-social behavior."

Grant and Dutton's study shows that the ability of a story to create meaning does not end with the crafting of the tale. The stories the benefactors told about themselves ultimately led to meaningful behaviors—giving their time in the service of a larger cause. Even though the fundraisers knew they were only telling their stories as part of a study, they ultimately "lived by" those stories, as McAdams would put it. By subtly reframing their narrative, they adopted a positive identity that led them, like Emeka, to live more purposefully.

In addition to story-editing, one of the best ways for people to make meaning through storytelling is to reflect on the pivotal moments of their lives—the central scene or scenes from their personal narratives—and consider how those moments shaped who they are and how their lives have unfolded. As Emeka told me his story, for example, there were a lot of "what ifs" peppered throughout his narrative. What if I could walk? What if I hadn't got involved in youth ministry? What if I could still play football? Of course, Emeka will never know the answers to these questions. But when he thinks about those critical moments in his life and the alternative paths his life could have taken had things turned out differently, Emeka is not just engaging in wishful thinking—he's making sense of his experiences and, in doing so, building meaning.

The exercise of imagining how life would have turned out if some event had or had not occurred is what academics call counterfactual thinking. In research published in 2010, psychologist Laura Kray of the University of California at Berkeley and her colleagues asked participants to come into their lab and reflect on significant experiences from their lives, and then consider how their lives could have developed differently had the experiences not occurred.

The researchers asked students at Northwestern, for example, to reflect on their decision to attend that school: "Think about how you decided where to go to college. How did you end up coming to Northwestern?" the students were asked. "Looking back, list the broad sequence of things that led to your decision." After responding to the essay prompt, half of the participants were asked to respond to one more statement: "Describe all the ways that things could have turned out differently."

This simple exercise, researchers found, made the participants rate an important life experience as more meaningful. They were more likely to endorse statements like "Coming to Northwestern has added meaning to my life" and "My decision to come to Northwestern was one of the most significant choices of my life," and to say that the event defined who they were. The researchers found similar results when they asked participants to reflect on a close friendship. Mentally subtracting meeting the friend, like mentally subtracting the decision to attend Northwestern, led participants to conclude that the friendship was more meaningful.

Why is counterfactual thinking so powerful? The answer, Kray suggests, is that this kind of exercise engages the sense-making process more rigorously than does simply thinking about the meaning of an event. First, it helps us appreciate the benefits of the path we ultimately took. As the study participants thought about what their lives would be like without the pivotal event, they mostly imagined alternative lives that were worse, not better. Without that event, they concluded, their lives would lack many relationships and experiences that were important to them. If I hadn't attended Northwestern, one perhaps realized, I would never have gotten that job at the company of my dreams. If I hadn't met Julie at the party, another may have reasoned, I would never have been introduced to the man I eventually married.

Second, counterfactual thinking leads us to tell more coherent stories about our lives. In another study, the researchers found that those who mentally subtracted a turning point from their lives, like meeting a future spouse, were more likely to believe that the event was "meant to be." Their life, they concluded, was not shaped by random chance; rather, it had followed a logical pattern that inevitably led them to meet their partner. Life doesn't just happen, they seemed to believe; it has an order and a design.

Of course, many of the subjects in Kray's studies were reflecting on positive moments in their lives—going to college and meeting a close friend. But some of the most important turning points in our lives are difficult or painful. When we subtract those experiences from our stories, we are forced to consider that life might have been better had they not occurred.

For Carlos Eire, that moment was the Cuban Revolution. He was eight years old when Fidel Castro marched into Havana in January 1959 and seized power from dictator Fulgencio Batista. Before the revolution, Carlos lived a privileged and idyllic life in Havana. His father was a respected judge and art collector who believed he had been Louis XVI in a former life and behaved accordingly. His mother was a beautiful woman and devout Catholic who adored her two sons. Carlos spent most of his time playing outside and trying not to get into trouble at his strict all-boys Catholic school.

Just days before Castro came to power, Carlos and his family spent Christmas Eve with his grandparents. It was a classic childhood scene. Roast pork for dinner, nougat for dessert; Carlos cracking nuts with his grandfather on a balcony; the women sharing stories together in the kitchen. "We didn't know it then," Carlos has written, "but it would be the last time my entire family would spend *Nochebuena* together at my grandparents' house." That night, Carlos's father drove the long way home so that they could see the Christmas lights and decorations adorning the city's houses and storefronts. It would soon "all be over," Carlos wrote—Castro's "guerrilla war and our future as a family."

Not long after that night, Castro's government began showing its teeth—torturing and executing political rivals, confiscating private property, and indoctrinating children at school. When Carlos's mother heard rumors that Castro planned to separate children from their parents, she panicked and decided to send Carlos and his brother Tony to the United States, where they would be safe. The boys were among the fourteen thousand Cuban children airlifted to Florida between 1960 and 1962 as part of Operation Peter Pan. Carlos's mother and thousands of other parents remained behind in Cuba awaiting their exit permits and the day that they would be reunited with their children.

For Carlos's mother, that day came three years later. In 1965, she left Cuba for Illinois, where Carlos and his brother were living with their uncle. Carlos's father was forced to stay behind in Cuba. By then, Carlos's life was very different. When they first came to America, Tony and Carlos had been living in a roach-infested orphanage in Florida, where they were served one meal a day and harassed by the other orphans. Life was slightly better in Illinois. But because their mother could not speak English and was disabled—she had a bad leg due to childhood polio—Tony and Carlos had to work to support both her and themselves. When he was fifteen, Carlos lied about his age and got a job washing dishes at the Conrad Hilton hotel in Chicago. From Wednesday through Sunday, he worked at the hotel from 4 p.m. to 2 a.m. He had only a few hours of sleep before getting up for school, where classmates called him a "spic." The pampered life he had lived in Havana seemed like a distant dream.

When Carlos was fifty years old, the news broke that a

young Cuban boy, Elián González, had washed up on a shore in Florida, precipitating an international crisis. A historian at Yale University by then, Carlos was living a happy and stable life in Connecticut with his wife and three children. He rarely thought about his early life in Cuba. But González's story opened a dam in Carlos's mind. Out of the dam came a flood of childhood memories. He felt compelled to write them down and assemble them together into a memoir to make sense of what had happened to him and his family.

During that process, Carlos thought a lot about the life he lost. In his memoir *Waiting for Snow in Havana,* he considers "what might have been" had the revolution not occurred, or had Castro been quickly overthrown. He imagines that the Bay of Pigs had been successful. He imagines Castro "lined up against a wall and shot with blanks for days on end," enduring the same psychological terror to which he subjected prisoners. He imagines staying in Havana rather than fleeing to the United States. He imagines himself as a young man applying cream to his hair and heading to the Havana clubs. He imagines attending the funeral of his father, whom Carlos never saw again after saying goodbye to him at the Havana airport in the spring of 1962.

"I don't know if it's possible to think of future nostalgia," he said. "But I do sometimes get nostalgic for the future I could have had. What would my life have been like? What kind of person would I have been? What would my relationship to my father have been like? I wouldn't have had this total break between my childhood and adulthood. I would have had a seamless life." His life without the revolution would have been much easier and more carefree, he believes—it would have been a life free of the worries and hardships he had to endure as a teenager, free of the bouts of depression he experienced as an adult, free of the anger he felt for the communists who destroyed his childhood, free of financial worry. "Yes," he said, "it would have been an easier life. But does that mean it would have been a better life? I don't think so. I'm old enough now that I understand that the break was a good thing. It made me who I am."

When Carlos left Cuba as a ten-year-old, he had just learned how to tie his own shoelaces, had never done any chores around his house, had never cut his own meat, and had never spent a night away from home. He had zero survival skills. In America, he had to learn how to take care of himself. Adversity also led to "moral growth," he said. "I got to experience what it's like to be at the bottom," he explained, "and that has shaped my perspective on everything. It's given me a certain kind of empathy for people who are at the bottom, and for understanding how unfair their situations can be."

Carlos lost a lot. But what he lost has been offset by what he has gained—which also includes a family, a meaningful career, and faith in God.

The University of Missouri's Laura King has spent much of her career trying to understand how narrative can help us make sense of our lost lives. In the late 1990s, she studied three groups of adults who had experienced challenges: parents of children with Down syndrome, gay men and lesbians who have come out of the closet, and women who got divorced after twenty years or more of marriage. Though she was studying people in specific circumstances, they all shared the universal human experience of loss.

King asked these three groups of research subjects to write two versions of the story of their future—the narrative of their current "best possible self," or how they hoped their lives would unfold, and the counterfactual narrative of their "lost possible self," the self that *could have been* had they not had to inhabit a difficult role. For example, gay men and lesbians wrote about their lives as if they were straight, while divorced women wrote about their lives as if they were still married. After they responded to the two prompts, they completed a questionnaire indicating how much they thought about each of these versions of themselves.

King found that the more people thought about their current future self, the happier they were. Visions of this future give hope because they are within reach. However, the more people thought about their lost possible self, the unhappier they were. At the time of King's research, discrimination against gays and lesbians was more pronounced than it is today. In no state could same-sex couples marry or enter into a civil union. And so coming out could represent a real loss. For gay men and lesbians, thinking frequently about the paths closed off to them led to distress and regret—they realized that a so-called normal life free of discrimination and other obstacles would have been so much easier than the life they were living. The same pattern held true for divorced women.

As both groups found, dwelling on "what might have been" can be an emotionally painful process. At the same time, though, this kind of counterfactual thinking led people to delve into their own humanity. Writing about the lost self in a detailed and complicated way, King found, was associated with more ego development among gays, lesbians, and divorced women two years after they responded to the prompt. Ego development measures how an individual sees and interprets reality—the extent to which they are able "to master, to integrate, and make sense of experience," to think about themselves and the world in complex ways. In other words, it's a measure of emotional depth, something that becomes clear in the stories King collected for her research. One gay man wrote this narrative about his lost possible self as a straight man:

> As I was growing up, I envisioned my life to be like the lives of those I admired. Those lives were something to aspire to. I grew up in a small town. . . . My parents and their friends were involved in volunteer work, owned businesses, and were active in community politics. My dream was to be a veterinarian. I imagined that I was married (as that is what is supposed to happen). I dreamed that my wife would be the manager of the pet store we both owned. . . . We would be active in the community. Small towns can be so much fun. . . . I would be well-known as someone who is a good person and down to earth. . . . The business would be successful and eventually passed down to our children.

People who wrote detailed, thoughtful narratives like this one—people who almost seemed nostalgic for the future, as Carlos would put it—had clearly thought a great deal about the path that was now closed off to them. Reconciling themselves to that loss was a difficult process, but a necessary one that left a positive mark on the lives they ended up living. "Avoiding thinking about loss may be one way to be happy," as King writes, "but it may also preclude the kind of examination necessary for growth."

THE STORIES we tell about ourselves help us understand who we are, how our lives developed, and how they could have unfolded differently. But we also find meaning in stories told by others. Whether in fiction or film, on the radio or on the stage, stories about others can help us reflect on our own values and experiences.

Consider the novel *Life of Pi*. It tells the story of a teenage boy named Pi, who, in the aftermath of a shipwreck that has killed his family, finds himself aboard a lifeboat with a Bengal tiger, a spotted hyena, an injured zebra, and a kind orangutan. Soon after being at sea, chaos breaks loose on the lifeboat: Pi watches in horror as the hyena decapitates and eats the helpless zebra, and then kills the orangutan. The butchery continues when the tiger kills and eats the hyena.

That leaves Pi and the tiger alone aboard the boat. Lost in the Pacific Ocean for 227 days, starved, desperate, and forced into a game of survival with the tiger, Pi pushes forward, even though he has lost everything. Pi's story of resilience is incredible once you realize what really happened on board the lifeboat. The animals, it turns out, were symbols for real people. Pi's mother was the orangutan; the zebra was an injured sailor; and the hyena was the ship's loathsome cook, who cannibalized the sailor and killed Pi's mother. Pi, we learn, was the tiger. He killed the cook and ate his liver and heart.

Pi's showdown with the tiger was really a confrontation he had with himself. After relating what happened to the zebra, hyena, and orangutan, Pi explains how he tamed the ferocious tiger that killed and ate the hyena. This parallels what truly happened: after ruthlessly killing the cook, Pi learned to control his own base impulses. Telling the story of the tiger allowed Pi to dissociate himself from the savagery he saw and committed. Only through doing so was he able to find meaning in the events that unfolded on the boat.

Research has shown that fiction can help people who have endured loss and trauma cope with their experiences. Reading tragic stories allows them to process what happened to them while maintaining distance from their painful memories and emotions. Alone on the lifeboat, Pi does something similar: he uses a fable to work through an experience that was too difficult to face in reality. For Pi, telling the story of the tiger's growth was a way to understand his own. Just as the tiger learned to control his violent nature with the discipline of a master, Pi developed a set of spiritual, emotional, and physical qualities that helped him survive the months he spent at sea before washing up on a beach in Mexico. "The world isn't just the way it is," as Pi says. "It is how we understand it, no?"

We don't need to have experienced a trauma like Pi's, of course, to gain wisdom from fiction. In a study published in 2002, David Miall and Don Kuiken of the University of Alberta asked participants to read the short story "The Trout" by Seán Ó Faoláin. The story is about a twelve-year-old girl named Julia who discovers a trout stuck inside a tiny pool of water near her family's summer home. The image of the trout thrashing around in "his tiny prison" haunts her. One night, she decides to set it free. She gets out of bed, ventures down to the pool in her pajamas, places the trout into a jug, and then runs to the river to release him into the water.

After the participants read the story, they were invited to think out loud about its most evocative parts. One reader saw her young self in Julia. She felt, she said, "a real kinship with her." As a young girl, she said, she would have wanted to save the trout, too. This reader was surprised, the researchers point out, by her admiration of Julia. "It recalled a sometimes submerged 'heroic' aspect of her younger self," they write. Another reader commented that Julia's decision to save the trout represented her "first step towards maturity." He added, as if from experience, that becoming mature does not happen overnight; it takes time. "You're not aware that you're becoming mature," he said, "until many years down the road when you look back and you can understand what was happening to you." These readers were most moved by the parts of Julia's story that related to their own narratives. As a result of reading "The Trout," they gained more insight into themselves.

Like the participants in "The Trout" study, the audience members at The Moth were deeply affected by the tales they heard the night Erik shared his story about Kate—and for the same reason. "You know, in the intermission I saw a friend who was really touched by a story from the first half," said David Crabb, the emcee. He was referring to a story that one of that night's storytellers told about the death of her mother. "And she was tearful," Crabb continued, "talking about someone she lost and how it made her connect more with that feeling and that memory."

The Moth has attracted all kinds of storytellers, including a former White House press secretary, an astronaut, Salman Rushdie, and Malcolm Gladwell. But no matter who is telling the story, the effect on the audience is always the same when the stories are told well. The stories that "levitate the room" have, as *The New Yorker* writer Adam Gopnik has put it, "some last rising touch, a note of pathos or self-recognition or poetic benediction, to lift the story, however briefly, into the realm of fable or symbol." By sharing their stories with the audience, storytellers aren't just creating meaning for themselves—they're helping others do so, too. "And that's why storytelling is so important," continued Crabb. "I think some people think it's all about talking about you, you, you. But what it really is is reaching out into the void and connecting with people and letting them know they're not alone."

5

Transcendence

I FLEW FROM NEW YORK TO SAN ANTONIO AND THEN drove another seven hours west through the land of rattlesnakes and armadillos, cowboys and cattle to make it to the McDonald Observatory in Fort Davis, Texas. The Chihuahuan Desert, which reaches from West Texas down to Mexico, is one of the largest in North America, and one of the least forgiving. Hundreds of miles separate cities of any size. You can drive along a major road for hours without seeing another car, or any other sign of life. At high noon, when I stopped for lunch, it was 96 degrees outside. By nighttime, the mercury had fallen to 34.

The final leg of the journey passed through the dramatic peaks and valleys of the Davis Mountains. El Paso, the nearest major city, was now about 200 miles away. As I wound my way up to the top of one of those mountains, the three great white domes of the McDonald Observatory appeared. Resting at an elevation of over 6,000 feet—the highest point that can be reached by car on the Texas highways—the telescopes form a desert acropolis. At night, they sit beneath some of the darkest skies in the continental United States—so black that after the sun and moon have set, you can't even see your hand when you hold it in front of your face.

This seemingly barren corner of the world was the last place I would expect to find hundreds of people coming together for a transcendent experience. But on the cool and clear night in July that I visited McDonald, five hundred others had journeyed to the observatory for its famed "star party" in order to reenact one of the oldest rituals known to man—stargazing.

At 9:45 p.m., the sky was dark. It was time to begin. A guide led us down a dimly lit path that zigzagged past a dozen telescopes toward an amphitheater. Huddled together with the other stargazers, I looked up to see the sky stretching uninterrupted from one horizon to the other like a great big dome over us. At first, there were just a handful of stars visible in the sky. A few minutes later, there were suddenly hundreds.

Most of the stars we saw were hundreds of millions of years old and dozens of light-years away—and some were much farther. Looking at them means looking back in time: because they are so distant from Earth, it takes many years for the light they emit to finally reach our eyes, which means that when we see stars in the sky, we are seeing them as they existed years ago. Even Alpha Centauri, the nearest star to our own solar system, is 26 trillion miles away from us; when it one day burns up and dies, observers on Earth (assuming there are any) will only find out four and a half years after the fact.

Our guide, Frank, started the "constellation tour" by pointing out the Big Dipper, which is part of Ursa Major, the Big Bear. The Big Dipper points to Polaris, the North Star, in the constellation Ursa Minor, the Little Bear. For years, Frank explained, "civilizations have seen this constellation as a bear." There's reason to believe, he went on, "that the Europeans and Native Americans, without knowing of the other, both saw the same animal in these random dots in the sky. From an anthropological perspective, that's very interesting."

Each civilization attached a story to these stars, too. In ancient Greece and Rome, the story of the two bears begins with the ever-lusty Zeus. The great god wanted to seduce the beautiful nymph Callisto, who as a follower of the virgin goddess Artemis had taken a vow of chastity. Zeus, not to be deterred, disguised himself as Artemis, approached Callisto, and forced himself upon her. Later, when Artemis saw that Callisto was pregnant, she furiously banished the nymph from her circle. Wandering in the woods, alone and vulnerable, Callisto gave birth to a son, Arcas. Soon after, Zeus's wife Hera, in a fit of jealousy, took revenge on Callisto by transforming her into a bear. Years later, when Callisto, as a bear, came upon her son Arcas in the woods, he nearly killed her. But Zeus then stepped in to (sort of) clean up the mess he had made. He transformed Arcas into a smaller bear and then threw both big bear and little bear up into the night sky.

To the ancient Greek and Roman people, this myth communicated some important lessons about being human. Our fate, as mortals, lies in the hands of capricious gods. Contact with a divine being can lead to immortality in the heavens above—unless, of course, it leads to savage death, like in the myth of Actaeon, who was torn to pieces by his hounds after Artemis transformed him into a stag. The cosmos is a chaotic, unpredictable place for us.

"One of the things you'll see in the telescopes tonight," Frank explained, "is the Ring Nebula, which we call the 'Cosmic Cheerio' around here." The nebula is the remains of a star whose center has released its gas into space so that it looks like a ring. "This is what's going to happen to our sun eventually," Frank said, "but not for a long time."

He then drew our attention to the southwest portion of the sky, where Mars and Saturn were visible as prominent red and yellow dots of light. As he was describing Saturn's rings, a meteor flew by. The crowd gasped in wonder. A little boy called out, "That was the first shooting star I ever saw!"

After the constellation tour, we were left to wander around to the telescopes, which were each focused on a particular point of interest, like Saturn, Mars, or the Swan Nebula, where, thousands of light-years from Earth, new stars are being born. Another telescope focused on Messier 51, two colliding galaxies 25 million light-years away. To look through that telescope was to look back to a moment when early horses and the first elephants with trunks were beginning to appear on Earth. Modern human beings were still another 24.9 million years away.

The line for Saturn wound all the way around the amphitheater, so I got in line to see the Cosmic Cheerio. When our sun reaches the same stage in its evolution as the Ring Nebula, it will have long before destroyed life on our blue planet. Standing in line next to me, a five-year-old boy asked his mom, "Mommy, is this what's going to happen to the sun?"

"Yes, baby," she said, taking a deep breath in, "but not for billions of years, long after you and me and Daddy are all gone."

The boy wrapped his arm around his mother's leg and looked up to the sky with wide eyes. "Wow."

ASTRONOMERS COME TO the McDonald Observatory from around the world. They stay in the Astronomers Lodge on the mountain, where they maintain a nocturnal schedule. During the day, they sleep in the lodge, where heavy curtains block the sun from entering their rooms; at night, when it is dark enough to observe the sky, they spend hour after hour in the telescope domes.

I arrived at the Astronomers Lodge in the afternoon, tiptoeing around the building so that I wouldn't disturb the researchers' slumber. Around three, I made my way to the cafeteria, where the astronomers were eating their first meal of the day. One of them—William Cochran, a professor at the University of Texas at Austin—invited me to join him up in the Harlan J. Smith Telescope. That night, using a small flashlight, I found my way through the observation dome to a cramped, quiet room full of old computers, in front of which Bill sat listening to music and patiently taking down data.

Bill researches exoplanets—planets orbiting stars other than our sun. Because planets don't produce their own light, they're very difficult to detect, and the search for exoplanets is still an emerging field of astronomy: the first confirmed discoveries of planets orbiting other stars came in the 1990s. Today, scientists believe that they've confirmed the existence of around 2,000 such bodies, a tiny fraction of the billions of planets that probably exist throughout the universe. Bill himself, in collaboration with other researchers, has been involved in the discovery of around 1,000 exoplanets.

Bill uses the Kepler spacecraft to track light emissions from distant stars over time and feeds his observations into a database shared with a group of other planet-searchers, who can then examine the data for patterns that might indicate the presence of an exoplanet. In the long run, Bill and others are looking for the kinds of planets—small, rocky, and with an appropriate distance from their star—that would, like Earth, sustain intelligent life. The odds that such a planet exists are "pretty good," Bill said. "There are one hundred billion other galaxies out there, each with hundreds of billions of stars. There are billions, if not trillions, of other solar systems. So I don't think we're the only ones here in this universe. But as of now, we don't know. There is so much that we just don't know."

A few hours later, Bill led me outside to a catwalk that circled the base of the dome. The moon had set and it was pitch black all around. The only noise in the air was the wind. I looked out straight ahead and saw a sky dotted with thousands of stars. One shooting star after another flared into and out of view. It was the most amazing thing I've ever seen.

When we went back inside, Bill pulled up a picture taken by the Hubble telescope. The image zooms in on a tiny portion of the universe—a pinprick in a sliver—known as the Hubble Ultra Deep Field. It shows 10,000 distant galaxies, some of them the oldest that are known to exist.

The universe began 13.8 billion years ago, and some of the galaxies in this image existed just 400 to 800 million years after that. If you compress the entire 13.8 billion years of the universe's existence into one hour, the galaxies we see in the Hubble Ultra Deep Field came into existence just a few minutes after the Big Bang. When we look at this picture, then, we are really looking back to the beginning of time—the beginning of the universe itself.

"This," Bill said, "this to me is awe."

SINCE THE DAWN of human consciousness, men and women have looked up to the night sky, marveling at the stars, wondering what they were and what they represented. Studying the celestial spheres, they sought answers to the biggest questions of human existence. How did the world begin? Will it end?

What else is out there? They sought omens, wisdom, and hints of ancestors past. But what they really sought was meaning.

The same is true today. When we look up at night, we do not see random balls of fire or scattered dots in the sky. We see bears and warriors. We see hunters and swans. We see the powder white band of the Milky Way, and, if we are religious, we think "heaven." We may know more about the stars than our ancestors did, but they still represent some of the most impenetrable mysteries of human existence. Though we invest so much into building our lives, the few decades we are on this earth amount to very little compared with the billions of years that the universe has existed before us and will continue to exist long after we are gone.

You might expect the insignificance we feel in the face of this knowledge to highlight the absurdity and meaninglessness of our lives. But it in fact does the opposite. The abject humility we experience when we realize that we are nothing but tiny flecks in a vast and incomprehensible universe paradoxically fills us with a deep and powerful sense of meaning. A brush with mystery—whether underneath the stars, before a gorgeous work of art, during a religious ritual, or in the hospital delivery room—can transform us.

This is the power of transcendence. The word "transcend" means "to go beyond" or "to climb." A transcendent, or mystical, experience is one in which we feel that we have risen above the everyday world to experience a higher reality. In Buddhism, transcendence is sometimes described through the metaphor of flight. The seeker begins on earth, but then flies upward, "breaking the roof." Then, writes the religious scholar Mircea Eliade, he "flies away through the air [and] shows figuratively that he has transcended the cosmos and attained a paradoxical and even inconceivable mode of being."

The metaphor of "breaking the roof" captures the key element of the mystical experience, whether religious or secular. You break out of the profane world of checking email and eating breakfast, and yield to the desire to commune, however briefly, with a higher and more sacred order. Many people have had transcendent experiences, and they consider them among the most meaningful and important events in their lives.

Such was the case with William James, the great American psychologist of the nineteenth century. James was so interested in transcendence that he inhaled nitrous oxide—laughing gas—on several occasions to "stimulate the mystical consciousness." Though a meticulous scientist and philosophical pragmatist, even James admitted feeling "the strongest emotion" he had ever had under the influence of the drug. Some time later, he described his experience to an audience in Edinburgh. "One conclusion," he said, "was forced upon my mind at that time, and my impression of its truth has ever since remained unshaken. It is that our normal waking consciousness, rational consciousness as we call it, is but one special type of consciousness, whilst all about it, parted from it by the filmiest of screens, there lie potential forms of consciousness entirely different. . . . No account of the universe in its totality can be final which leaves these other forms of consciousness quite disregarded."

In his masterpiece *The Varieties of Religious Experience*, James argues that mystical experiences share four qualities. First, they are *passive*. Though we can do certain activities to increase the likelihood that we will have a mystical experience—like meditating, fasting, or taking mind-altering drugs—the mystical feeling seems to descend as some sort of external force. The mystic, writes James, feels "as if he were grasped and held by a superior power." Second, they are *tran-*

sient. The mystical experience rarely lasts more than a few hours, and is often much shorter than that. The characteristic feeling of depth and importance—or of the divine, as the case may be—flows into and out of the person.

James suggests that the next two characteristics are particularly important. Mystical states, he points out, are *ineffable.* It is difficult if not impossible to capture the subjective feeling in words and fully do it justice. "It follows from this," James writes, "that its quality must be directly experienced; it cannot be imparted or transferred to others." Finally, they are *noetic*—that is, they impart knowledge and wisdom. "They are states of insight into depths of truth unplumbed by the discursive intellect," as James writes: "They are illuminations, revelations, full of significance and importance, all inarticulate though they remain; and as a rule they carry with them a curious sense of authority for after-time." The meaning we derive from the experience stays with us, often for our entire lives.

DURING TRANSCENDENT STATES, two remarkable things happen. According to psychologist David Yaden of the University of Pennsylvania, an expert on transcendence, first, our sense of self washes away along with all of its petty concerns and desires. We then feel deeply connected to other people and everything else that exists in the world. The result is that our anxieties about existence and death evaporate, and life finally seems, for a moment, to make sense—which leaves us with a sense of peace and well-being.

In recent years, scientists have begun to study the emotional response to mystery, which they refer to as awe. We feel awe when we perceive something so grand and vast that we cannot comprehend it, like a magnificent vista, an exquisite piece of music, an act of extraordinary generosity, or the divine. As the eighteenth-century philosopher Adam Smith wrote, awe occurs "when something quite new and singular is presented" and "memory cannot, from all its stores, cast up any image that nearly resembles this strange appearance." In other words, awe challenges the mental models that we use to make sense of the world. Our mind must then update those models to accommodate what we have just experienced. This helps explain why encounters with mystery and transcendence are so transformative—they change the way we understand the universe and our place in it.

In 2007, researcher Michelle Shiota and her colleagues Dacher Keltner and Amanda Mossman published some of the very first empirical studies to examine how awe affects our sense of self. They recruited 50 undergraduates for an experiment. When the students arrived, rather than attempting the nearly impossible feat of awaking wonderment in the fluorescent glow of their sterile psych lab, the researchers guided the participants to a different building on Berkeley's campus. An awe-inspiring sight awaited them there: in the main hall of the Valley Life Sciences Building was an enormous replica of a *Tyrannosaurus rex* skeleton. The replica was overwhelming. It was 25 feet long and 12 feet high, and it weighed about 5,000 pounds. In the presence of the massive skeleton, the students were instructed to respond to the question "Who am I?" by writing twenty sentences, each beginning with "I am."

When they analyzed the statements, the psychologists found that they fell into four broad categories. There were physical responses, like "I am tall" or "I am thin." There were character trait responses, like "I am funny" or "I am smart." There were relationship descriptions, like "I am dating John" or "I am a brother." And finally, there were responses that belonged to an "oceanic universal category." In these responses, people defined themselves in terms of something far larger than themselves. They wrote statements like "I am part of the universe" and "I am part of humanity."

It turns out that people in the awe condition saw themselves very differently from their peers in a control condition. In an earlier study, the researchers had found that awe-inspired subjects were far more likely to say that they felt "small or insignificant" and "unaware of my day-to-day concerns," and that they experienced "the presence of something greater than myself." In the dinosaur experiment, the participants' decreased self-focus translated into a feeling of connection with the broader world and all of those in it. This is the paradox of transcendence. It simultaneously makes individuals feel insignificant and yet connected to something massive and meaningful. How can this paradox be explained?

The experiences of practiced meditators, who describe similar phenomena, may offer a clue. At the peak mystical moment, they sense the boundaries of their selves dissolve and, as a result, feel no more separation between themselves and the world around them. They experience, as a meditator in one study put it, "a sense of timelessness and infinity. It feels like I am part of everyone and everything in existence." Angela of Foligno, a thirteenth-century Franciscan nun, described the feeling perfectly: "I possessed God so fully that I was no longer in my previous customary state but was led to find a peace in which I was united with God and was content with everything."

Cory Muscara has been there, too. Cory, originally from the South Shore of Long Island, entered college with the intention of going into finance. But by the time he graduated in

2012, he wanted to do something more with his life—and so he traveled to a monastery in Burma, where he was ordained as a Buddhist monk. During his six months there, Cory meditated for fourteen to twenty hours daily, slept on a thin mattress on a wooden plank, and ate two simple meals a day, one at 5:30 a.m. and one at 10:30 a.m. There was no talking, no music, and no reading—just an ascetic regimen meant to break down the walls of the self.

When Cory set off for the monastery, he was looking forward to an adventure. "I was wide-eyed and bushy-tailed," he said, "and excited about severing myself from everything that brought me comfort in my sheltered life." When he got to the monastery, situated on 100 acres of rolling hills, he found that his room, no bigger than a prison cell, was full of ants. "This is exactly what I want," he thought. Twelve hours later, he was not so sure: he was crying in his bed, questioning his reasons for coming to Burma.

The situation did not improve. Within days of practicing the strict meditation program, which began each morning at 3:30 a.m., Cory was in excruciating pain from sitting cross-legged on the floor of the meditation hall for most of the day. The "sheet of pain" started at his neck and went down his back and around to his abdomen, which would cramp up if he breathed too deeply. His pain interfered with his meditation: he couldn't distance himself from his thoughts. All he thought about was how much his body hurt. Five days after his arrival, Cory decided he couldn't live like this for six months; he was going to go home. But on the day he was scheduled to leave, Cory revisited the original reason for coming to the monastery—which was to understand suffering more deeply. He decided to stay and face suffering rather than to run away from the very thing he was seeking to know.

During those long and painful days, Cory was practicing, or supposed to be practicing, mindfulness meditation. Mindfulness meditation is meant to inspire a state of heightened awareness. Rather than repeating a mantra, as in other forms of meditation, the practitioner focuses on everything that is happening to him and around him, like the rising and falling of his breath or the subtle sensations of his body as he moves. "Mindfulness," as one of its most famous teachers, Jon Kabat-Zinn, has put it, "means paying attention in a particular way: on purpose, in the present moment, and nonjudgmentally."

Ultimately, the individual is supposed to realize that he can step away from his thoughts, feelings, sensations, and experiences and observe them neutrally, rather than allowing them to define him. In Buddhism, mindfulness meditation is a path toward enlightenment, or the realization that the self is an illusion. As the layers of the self are peeled away through meditation, all that is left is the individual's raw experience of the world as it really is—a reality defined by unity and interconnectedness rather than by the natterings of the ego.

Cory returned to the meditation hall hoping to gain some wisdom about suffering. Every time he focused on his pain, he noticed that his mind would race with thoughts: "Why are you doing this? You're not getting anything out of this experience. How can anyone meditate in this heat? There are way too many mosquitoes here. You should go to a different monastery. You should be out right now dating women, not sitting in silence all day long." Those thoughts, which triggered anger, compounded his physical pain. But, in time, Cory realized he had the power to break that negative cycle by distancing himself from his thoughts and emotions. He could "just be with the pain itself," as he put it—he could sit on the riverbank and watch the water flow by, to use a mindfulness metaphor, rather than be caught up in the current. Though his body still hurt, the "secondary pain" of emotional suffering no longer made it worse. Once he understood that he had control over his experience of pain, he knew that he could stay at the monastery for the full six months.

As the weeks passed, Cory had some days when his meditations were serene, and others when his mind was a turbulent mess. Every time a good feeling like tranquillity emerged, Cory would tell himself, "This is what you want, try to hold on to this." But the feeling would pass away. Every time he felt pain, he would tell himself, "This is bad, try to resist this." But then that feeling, too, would pass away.

"Eventually, I said, 'Screw it. Stop trying to hold on to the experiences you want and let go of experiences you don't want. In life there will be good things and bad things,' " he realized, " 'and you can try to pull in all of the good things and push away all of the bad things, but everything will change anyway, so just let go.' Once I did, there was no pushing or pulling anymore. I could just be with my experience, and that left me with a deep sense of equanimity."

Around this time, Cory intensified his meditation practice. When he first entered the monastery, he meditated the mandated fourteen hours a day and did so mostly in the meditation hall. Now he was meditating twenty to twenty-two hours a day, mostly in his small, dark room. He woke up at 2:30 a.m. and went to bed around midnight, leaving his room only for breakfast and lunch.

One day during his final few weeks at the monastery, Cory woke up feeling unusually focused. Before he opened his eyes, he could feel every sensation running through his body like an electric current. As he slowly got out of bed, he found that he was not just moving, but observing his body move. During the morning meditation, his mind did not wander at all.

Later, on his walk back to his room from breakfast, Cory stopped at a bridge and sat down at a spot overlooking a pond. On previous days, when Cory meditated at the bridge, he would feel peace and tranquillity, but nothing beyond that. But on that particular day, as Cory looked at the water, his concentration grew more and more intense, and then something remarkable happened: his sense of separation between himself and the pond vanished. Before, he always experienced himself as a distinct entity looking at the pond, another distinct entity. Now it was all "oneness, non-duality, communion," he said. He felt himself surrendering to all that was around him.

"I saw clearly that the idea of the self—of distinction, of me, of an inner and outer—is just an illusion," he said, "something created by the mind. It was like wisps of smoke from a pipe. The idea evaporates as soon as you cease to create it." When his mind stopped creating that illusion at the pond that morning, his heart burst open and a wave of compassion washed over him. "When you become nothing," he explained, "you realize that you are one with everything."

When Cory returned home to Long Island a month later, his approach to life had changed. Instead of searching for a lucrative career, Cory now wanted to help other people find relief from suffering. He began to work as a mindfulness teacher. The emotional high from the experience in Burma began to wear off, but what he learned there remained with him. Once he started teaching, for example, he found himself striving to make more money and become a great teacher. But as soon as he recognized that his ego was taking over, he surrendered his pride and focused on his students. "It's easier to let go of my self-focus now," he said, "because I've seen so clearly what an illusion the self is."

Scientists can actually see the mystical experiences of people like Cory unfold in the brain. Andrew Newberg, a neuroscientist at Thomas Jefferson University, investigates the brain activity of devoted meditators—including Buddhists, Catholic nuns, and Sufis—to determine what exactly happens during transcendent states. In one study, he and his colleagues studied eight experienced practitioners of Tibetan Buddhist meditation using a form of brain imaging called single photon emission computed tomography, or SPECT.

The scientists measured their subjects' baseline level of brain activity and then left them alone to meditate in a private room. When a meditator felt like he was approaching a moment of transcendence, he tugged on a long piece of string that Newberg and his colleague Eugene d'Aquili were monitoring in another room. The researchers then injected a radioactive substance into the meditator through a long intravenous line and, once the meditation was over, led him into a special high-tech camera that took a snapshot of his brain activity. The radioactive substance allowed researchers to see the amount of blood flowing into various regions of the brain: the more blood flow, the more activity there is in that part of the brain; the less blood flow, the less activity.

At the peak of the mystical moment, Newberg and d'Aquili found, the meditators had decreased activity in the posterior superior parietal lobe—an area of the brain that Newberg calls the "orientation association area," because its main functions are to locate the self in space, keep track of physical boundaries, and distinguish the self from the not-self. The orientation association area is usually highly active, taking in sensory information from the world and using that information to perform the crucial function of helping us navigate space. When neuronal inputs to the orientation association area from our senses decrease precipitously, as was the case with the meditators, the brain can no longer separate the self from the surrounding environment. Individuals feel connected with everyone and everything—they feel a sense of unity.

In a new line of research, Newberg has peered inside the minds of meditating Sufi mystics. The work on Sufis is in its early and exploratory stages—Newberg has studied only two thus far—but it may shed additional light on the neurological underpinnings of mystical states. During meditation, the brains of the Sufis showed a decrease in activity in the frontal lobe, which is responsible for conscious decision-making and giving an individual a sense of control over his environment and actions. If the frontal lobe has dramatically less neuronal inputs than usual, then the logical, controlling part of our mind shuts down, and we feel a sense of surrender.

THOUGH THE TRANSCENDENT moment, as William James pointed out, will eventually end, it can leave an indelible mark on the psyche. People can fundamentally transform after the experience of self-loss. Consider the story of the former astronaut Jeff Ashby. Jeff was just a kid when the first American, Alan Shepard, flew into space. It was May 1961. NASA had been created three years earlier. The Soviets had sent the first man into space just a month prior. And Ashby, at the tender age of six, started dreaming about going into space himself.

It was an exciting time to be a young boy with dreams of space exploration. Within a decade of Shepard's flight with Project Mercury, the United States sent *Apollo 8* into space to orbit the moon. It was a watershed moment in history and a beacon of hope and optimism in an otherwise tumultuous year, 1968, which saw the assassinations of Martin Luther King Jr. and Robert Kennedy. Never before had astronauts ventured beyond a low Earth orbit. Never before had they orbited another body in space.

A fourteen-year-old Ashby tuned in with the rest of the world to watch the live televised broadcast of the mission on Christmas Eve. The crew circled the moon ten times and took turns reading from the Book of Genesis: "In the beginning God created the heaven and the earth. And the earth was without form, and void; and darkness was upon the face of the deep. And the Spirit of God moved upon the face of the waters. And God said, Let there be light: and there was light."

The *Apollo 8* crewmembers also took dazzling photographs, the most famous of which was called *Earthrise*. Seeing a picture of the earth from space would change how humanity understood itself. From thousands of miles away, our planet appeared tiny and fragile. On December 25, 1968, a day after the photograph was taken, the poet Archibald MacLeish wrote in the *New York Times*: "To see the earth as it truly is, small and blue and beautiful in that eternal silence where it floats, is to see ourselves as riders on the earth together, brothers on that bright loveliness in the eternal cold—brothers who know now they are truly brothers."

In the decades since the first human beings went into space, fewer than six hundred astronauts, cosmonauts, and taikonauts have had the chance to see the whole earth from this elevated perspective. Jeff is one of them. In 1999, when he was forty-five years old, he realized his boyhood dream, traveling to space as a pilot for the first female shuttle commander, Eileen Collins. Their mission was to deploy a large telescope called Chandra, a complement to the Hubble telescope that would take pictures of high energy events, like black holes, exploding stars, and colliding galaxies. Ashby and Collins were scheduled to lift off on the thirtieth anniversary of the moon landing. The time from liftoff to space was 8 minutes—8 minutes from being on the earth to being 150 miles above it in orbit. Talk about breaking the roof.

From space, Ashby saw the earth as a sphere suspended precariously in the black void. The atmosphere was "strikingly thin," he said, "like a piece of paper covering a basketball." All of human existence rested behind a diaphanous veil. "You realize that all of humankind is on that little layer on the surface of that rock," he said. "You realize how close we are to potential extinction from the vacuum of space. You realize that the planet is really small. You could circle it in just 90 minutes. With one or two minor exceptions, you don't see the boundaries between countries. You just see one contiguous mass of land and water. I got this sense that what happens on one side of the planet affects the other side. So I got this sense of connectedness—that we are all connected in some way."

Making it into space requires years of training and hard work at the highest levels of academia, military, and government. Those who succeed become part of an elite group of heroes and heroines celebrated by contemporary culture and lionized in history books. So it's no surprise that most astronauts, Ashby included, are driven by ambition and achievement.

The glory of spaceflight motivated Ashby for many years. But after that first mission, Ashby felt that he had fundamentally changed. He started looking for a deeper path to fulfillment, one centered around the greater good rather than his personal goals. Other astronauts who have traveled into space report a similar transformation. Their values, according to one study, shift from self-focused ones like achievement, enjoyment, and self-direction to self-transcendent ones, like unity with nature, belief in God, and world peace. "You develop an instant global consciousness, a people orientation, an intense dissatisfaction with the state of the world," another astronaut has said, "and a compulsion to do something about it. From out there on the moon, international politics looks so petty. You want to grab a politician by the scruff of the neck and drag him a quarter of a million miles out and say, 'Look at that, you son of a bitch.' " Scientists have dubbed this dramatic shift in perspective the Overview Effect.

Ashby flew two more missions to help build the International Space Station. Then, at fifty-four years old, he left NASA. Like many other astronauts who have experienced the Overview Effect, he decided he wanted to contribute his experience and talent toward something bigger. Ron Garan, for example, established Manna Energy Ltd., an environmental organization that brought potable water to villages in Rwanda and Kenya, and Edgar Mitchell founded the Institute of Noetic Sciences, which researches human consciousness.

Based on his experience in space, Ashby spent a lot of time thinking about the future of humankind and the earth. "You cannot view the thin blue arc of our atmosphere from space," he has said, "without developing a great concern for the protection of that fragile band of life and a desire to contribute to its preservation."

Given that the planet will one day perish or become uninhabitable, he realized, humankind will need to move to another one in order to survive. "Maybe it's one within the solar system," he said, "but eventually, since our sun has a finite life, we would have to move to a planet around another star and start a civilization there." Ashby now works for a company called Blue Origin, founded by Jeff Bezos, the CEO of Amazon.com. At Blue Origin, Ashby is collaborating with his colleagues to develop the technology to affordably fly people into space. Their long-term goal is to help get people off the planet in the event that Earth becomes uninhabitable. But in the short run, they want to enable ordinary people to travel safely into space so that those people can experience the Overview Effect and, perhaps, come back changed.

FEW OF US will ever fly in a spaceship. But even here on Earth, we can all experience transcendence by turning to the world around us. Perhaps no one understood that better than John Muir, the nineteenth-century naturalist who championed the national park system and was the first president of the Sierra Club.

Muir was born in the seaside town of Dunbar, Scotland. It was there that he first fell in love with the natural world, taking walks as a toddler with his grandfather. Once he was old enough to get around on his own, he spent his free time by the shore of the North Sea or in nearby meadows. When his family immigrated to the United States in 1849, the eleven-year-old Muir found another wilderness playground in the Wisconsin farm where they settled. Its birds, insects, squirrels, flowers, and ferns all filled him with wonder.

Muir's love of nature deepened as he grew older. He enrolled at the University of Wisconsin when he was in his early twenties and studied botany for the first time. The subject sent him "flying to the woods and meadows in wild enthusiasm," as he would later put it. "Like everybody else," he wrote, "I was always fond of flowers, attracted by their external beauty and purity. Now my eyes were opened to their inner beauty, all alike revealing glorious traces of the thoughts of God, and leading on and on into the infinite cosmos."

If those flowers excited him, then the Sierra Nevada mountains of California threw him into an ecstatic frenzy. Muir moved to the Golden State in 1868, and he spent the summer of the following year in what is today Yosemite National Park, where he "bounded over rocks and up mountain sides, hung over the edge of terrifying precipices, his face drenched in the spray of waterfalls, waded through meadows deep in lilies, laughed at the exuberant antics of grasshoppers and chipmunks, stroked the bark of towering incense cedars and sugar pines, and slept each night on an aromatic mattress of spruce boughs." This nineteenth-century John the Baptist was impressed by the unity and harmony he perceived in nature. "When we try to pick out anything by itself," he wrote, "we find it hitched to everything else in the universe."

Muir's reverence for nature was influenced by Transcendentalism, a philosophical movement that flourished in New England around the time of his birth. One of the seminal works of that movement was Ralph Waldo Emerson's 1836 essay "Nature." For Emerson, the beauty we find in nature is a reflection of divine beauty; nature itself is a manifestation of and portal to God. But most people, Emerson thought, fail to appreciate that splendor. They are too distracted, as his friend Henry David Thoreau lamented, by the tasks of daily living—a problem that was only getting worse with the quickening pace of life occasioned by industrialization and the advent of trains. "To the dull mind," wrote Emerson, "all nature is leaden. To the illuminated mind the whole world burns and sparkles with light."

Muir had such an illuminated mind. For Muir, being in nature was a transcendent experience. When he ventured into the wild, he did not just see mountains, streams, and meadows; he saw the face of God and was humbled by it. "Why should man value himself as more than a small part of the one great unit of creation?" he wrote. In "Nature," Emerson used different language to describe the same feeling. In the woods, he wrote, "I feel that nothing can befall me in life,—no disgrace, no calamity, (leaving me my eyes,) which nature cannot repair. Standing on the bare ground,—my head bathed by the blithe air, and uplifted into infinite space,—all mean egotism vanishes. I become a transparent eye-ball. I am nothing. I see all. The currents of the Universal Being circulate through me; I am part or particle of God."

Muir and Emerson had the same experience in nature that Jeff Ashby had in space and that Cory Muscara had at the monastery in Burma. But all they had to do in order to break the roof was walk outside. "If this is mysticism," as Emerson's biographer writes, "it is mysticism of a commonly occurring and easily accepted sort."

In a study published in 2015, the psychologist Paul Piff and his colleagues investigated the effect an awe-inspiring encounter with the natural world would have on their research subjects. Would they feel, as Emerson did, like a transparent eyeball after a walk in the woods? To find out, the researchers led ninety undergraduates, one at a time, into a towering grove of eucalyptus trees. Half of the students spent one minute staring up at the two-hundred-foot-tall trees, while the others looked at a tall building a few yards away for the same amount of time.

The students did not know the purpose of the study—they had been told the researchers were studying visual perception. Even so, that single minute beneath the towering grove was transformative.

After the students spent some time looking at either the tree or the building, an experimenter approached each one with a box of pens and a questionnaire to fill out. Then the experimenter "accidentally" dropped the pens on the ground. Piff and his associates hypothesized that being awe-inspired would lead the students to focus less on their own individual concerns and more on others and the world at large. That turned out to be the case: people who had focused on the trees were more helpful, picking up significantly more pens than those in the control condition. The questionnaire they later completed offered a reason why. The awe-inspired people, researchers found, felt a diminished sense of their own importance compared to others, and that likely led them to be more generous. As with Emerson, their mean egotism vanished. They abandoned the conceit, which many of us have, that they were the center of the world. Instead, they stepped outside of themselves to connect with and focus on others.

THE SELF-LOSS FELT during a transcendent experience is sometimes called "ego death," and it prepares us for the final loss of self we will all experience: death itself. "When many people think about death," writes the psychologist Mark Leary, "they think about the fact that this conscious thing—the self that seems most central to their existence—will no longer exist." The demise of the self in death is a terrifying prospect for most people. But the person who has already experienced ego death during a transcendent experience is far better prepared to face and accept that loss.

Take the case of Janeen Delaney, who was diagnosed with terminal leukemia in 2005. Janeen had grown up in a Christian household in Michigan, but she eventually drifted away from the faith. In her adulthood, she considered herself vaguely spiritual and derived inspiration from Buddhism, but she had no formal religious or contemplative practice. When she received her diagnosis, the lack of religion in her life suddenly seemed like a hole. "I didn't have a belief system in place," she said, "and that bothered me."

There is never a good time to receive a cancer diagnosis, but for Janeen, the timing was especially hard. Two years earlier, in 2003, she had undergone open-heart surgery. On the heels of surviving that trauma, learning that she had incurable leukemia was an even harsher blow. "Every huge challenge I've ever been faced with, you know, I've always come back." But after the diagnosis, she continued, "I had moments when I just thought, 'man, how many times can you just keep coming back?' " She felt disconnected, but she wasn't sure from what. It was like "being in the wasteland."

In 2008, Janeen found out about a study that was being conducted at Johns Hopkins University. The researchers were interested in whether a transcendent experience, occasioned by the drug psilocybin, would have therapeutic effects on individuals facing imminent death. Psilocybin, the active ingredient in so-called magic mushrooms, can facilitate mystical experiences and feelings of awe and rapture in users, and like many hallucinogens, it has a long history of religious use. "From the moment I read about the study," Janeen said, "I knew, before I dialed the number, I knew that it was exactly what I needed to do."

Since ancient times, mystics, seekers, and shamans all across the world have consumed hallucinogens as part of their rituals. Many indigenous peoples of North America consumed peyote and "divine mushrooms," for example, and there's reason to believe that hallucinogens were involved in the religious ceremonies of the Aryan peoples of modern India and Iran, and also in the Eleusinian mysteries of ancient Greece. These plants were highly sacred and revered, and they were thought to offer users a direct portal into a realm of spirits and gods. Those who consumed them broke into a transcendent world where they saw visions and heard voices that they interpreted as divine. The Aztecs called magic mushrooms *teonanácatl,* or "God's flesh."

Roland Griffiths, the principal investigator on the study, doesn't ascribe any divine properties to the drug. But his personal twenty-year practice of meditation had made him curious about mysticism and how it fit into his secular worldview as a psychopharmacologist. Could a transcendent experience reduce the fear and anxiety that Janeen and others like her felt upon receiving a terminal diagnosis?

To find out, the researchers prepared each participant extensively. For each dose, they put the participant in a comfortable, private room and equipped him or her with an eye mask and a headset. The eye mask was meant to block visual disturbances from interfering with the inner experience. The headset played songs programmed by the researchers that corresponded to the peaks and valleys of the drug-induced experience of transcendence. Subjects had been told what they might feel after taking the drug, and during the sessions, two members of the study staff remained in the room with each volunteer to provide support if needed. All in all, the researchers did everything they could to ensure that the participants felt safe and secure—that they wouldn't have a "bad trip."

The process was so rigorous in part because Griffiths and his team wanted to avoid the fate of the charismatic psychologist and icon of the 1960s counterculture Timothy Leary. Leary, an academic psychologist at Harvard University, had heard of the use of "divine mushrooms" in Mexico. In the summer of 1960, he traveled to Mexico and tried them with some friends at a villa in Cuernavaca. At the time, Leary was on the cusp of a midlife crisis. Nearing forty, he complained, "I was a middle-aged man involved in the middle-aged process of dying. My joy in life, my sensual openness, my creativity were all sliding downhill." But his transcendent experience—complete with psychedelic visions—zapped him back to life. "In four hours by the swimming pool in Cuernavaca," he writes in his autobiography, "I learned more about the mind, the brain, and its structures than I did in the preceding fifteen [years] as a diligent psychologist." The veil, he explained, had been drawn from his eyes, and he was a "changed man."

By the time he returned to Harvard, Leary was convinced that hallucinogens were a force for good. He started the Harvard Psilocybin Project to determine "the conditions under which psilocybin can be used to broaden and deepen human experience"—and also began to publicly promote the use of psychedelics. But Leary's enthusiasm for such drugs led to flaws in his research methodology. And once LSD became popular recreationally, there was a backlash against both Leary and the drugs. He was dismissed from Harvard in 1963, and hallucinogenic drugs were made illegal nationwide several years later. Richard Nixon called Leary "the most dangerous man in America."

Over fifty years later, Griffiths and his research associates are cautiously paving the way forward on this kind of research with the approval of the federal government. Their studies have looked at the effects psilocybin can have on four groups of research participants: healthy volunteers, anxious or depressed cancer patients with a life-threatening diagnosis, people interested in quitting smoking, and religious professionals like clergymen. Their findings have again and again confirmed just how powerful transcendent experiences can be in building meaning—a fact that Janeen would soon learn.

After taking the capsule, Janeen remained in the session room for about eight hours, lying on a sofa and listening to the researchers' soundtrack. During that time, she had a classic mystical experience. She felt time stop; she felt connected to something vast that lay beyond the realm of ordinary experience; feelings of awe flooded her. "There was not one atom of myself that did not merge with the divine," she said of the experience. "You think about these things, you have some experiences that are transcendent, but then the big one comes along, and it's like *oh—my—fucking—god.*"

The most dramatic moment came during Samuel Barber's "Adagio for Strings," which played when Janeen was peaking. She was focused on how beautiful the piece was when she realized that her breath was following the melody. As the music came to its climax, the notes started getting higher and higher. When she reached the top of the ascent, she held her breath. "And then the song was over and, in that moment," she said, "I realized it was ok not to breathe anymore. It was a strange revelation. Being aware that it was ok to stop breathing—that was huge for me."

As was the case for many of the other cancer patients Griffiths has studied, Janeen's anxiety dissolved. She was less afraid of death. "When you have that experience," she said, "you lose your fear." She went on: "It doesn't mean that I wasn't fearful when my kidney came out, or of how aggressive this cancer was. But I just had to remind myself of what I said: That when you get to the end, it's ok not to breathe."

"If you hold the strong materialistic worldview that everything ends with the body's death, with no meaning or hope beyond that," Griffiths explained, "then death seems like a pretty dismal prospect." But, he added, if "you have an experience of transcendence, when one has a sense of the interconnectedness of all things and a stunning appreciation of life and consciousness, whether or not you come out believing in heaven or karma or an afterlife, you can recognize the depth of our ignorance in the astounding mystery of what it is to be alive and aware." In Janeen's case, that experience with mystery allowed her to make peace with the fact that she would die.

"I'm sitting on my back porch right now," Janeen said in 2014, "watching my plants grow, and everything that my eyes fall upon, that's the universe. You are the universe, you are part of the greater whole." Realizing that she was a piece of something much larger was reassuring to her. It helped her reframe her death as just one step in a bigger cycle.

Buddhists, Janeen said, use the example of a cloud to illustrate this point. Does a cloud that disappears from the sky die? "Sooner or later," writes the Buddhist monk Thich Nhat Hanh, "the cloud will change into rain or snow or ice. If you look deeply into the rain, you can see the cloud. The cloud is not lost; it is transformed into rain, and the rain is transformed into grass and the grass into cows and then to milk and then into the ice cream you eat." The cloud did not die. It was always in the universe in one way or another. In a similar way, the transcendent experience helped Janeen see that she, too, would always be in the universe in one way or another—which is why, when the time came, it was okay for her to stop breathing. Janeen passed away in 2015.

6

Growth

"HOW OFTEN DO YOU DREAM OF HER?" SARAH asked. "Is it, like, she comes to you and says, 'It's all going to be okay'?"

"Oh yeah. I've had dreams like that. But also more ordinary ones. Like once," Christine said, "I dreamt that she was doing the dishes and I walked over to her and said, 'Don't worry about doing the dishes. I'll take care of them.' And that was it. Brief. But another time, I dreamt that I was sitting on a bench and she walked over and sat down next to me. She put her hand on my hand and said, 'Everything is going to be okay.' It was intense. I could *feel* her hand on my hand, *physically.*" Christine put one of her hands on the other.

"And then," she continued, "I woke up and thought, 'I'm never going to see my mother again.' It just hits me every now and then. Like I'm walking down the street and something happens in my day and I think, 'Oh, I should tell my mom about this.' But then I remember I can't. Because she's dead." Christine moved some of the food around on her plate with her fork. "She was just *here*. I could see her coming into the room. And now," she said, shaking her head and looking down, "I won't see her again."

"I haven't had a dream like that yet," Sarah said, "about my dad."

I was sitting at a small square dinner table in Sarah's apartment in Washington Heights, in Upper Manhattan. There were five of us at the table—Sarah and her boyfriend Raúl, Christine, another young woman named Sandy, and me. By the time Sarah and Christine spoke about dreaming and not dreaming of their dead parents, it was about 8 p.m. on a crisp Sunday night in October. Christine, Sandy, and I had arrived two and a half hours earlier, bringing wine, chips and guacamole, and an apple pie. Sarah had made moussaka, and once we arrived, Raúl stirred up some cocktails; his infused tequilas sat on a side table in mason jars. The lights were dim. In the background, soft instrumental indie music was playing. Every now and then, one of the two cats in the apartment darted across the floor.

Welcome to The Dinner Party, a national community of young adults who have experienced the unexpected death of a close loved one. In cities all across the United States, dinner partiers like Sarah, Christine, Sandy, and Raúl get together regularly to break bread and talk about how their loss has affected their lives. Though this was my first time meeting the other four, they had all been gathering for a few weeks for dinner parties at Sarah and Raúl's. I haven't experienced a loss like theirs, but I was invited to join them, to see how people can come together to forge meaning and grow through suffering.

We all carry emotional baggage of some kind—baggage that can bring with it fear, hurt, guilt, and insecurity. For most of us, there is at least one specific source of pain that lives inside of us and colors the way we see the world. The memory of an alcoholic mother or an abusive father, the pain of being bullied at school, the horror of losing a child, the trauma of being raped, the helplessness of being held hostage by depression, cancer, addiction, or other ailments of the mind and body: these experiences of suffering can be tremendously difficult to overcome.

They also pose serious threats to finding meaning in life. They can shatter our fundamental assumptions about the world—that people are good, the world is just, and our environment is a safe and predictable place. They can breed cynicism and hatred. They can throw us into despair and even drive us to want to end our lives. They can lead us to have troubled relationships, to lose our sense of identity and purpose, to abandon our faith, to conclude that we don't matter or that life is senseless—that it is all, as Shakespeare's Macbeth says, "sound and fury, signifying nothing."

But this is an incomplete picture of adversity. Traumatic experiences can leave deep, sometimes permanent, wounds. Yet struggling through them can also push us to grow in ways that ultimately make us wiser and our lives more fulfilling. We do so by relying on the pillars of belonging, purpose, storytelling, and transcendence. If those pillars are strong, we'll be able to lean on them when adversity strikes. But if the pillars crumble or fall as a result of a shattering trauma, we can rebuild them to be even stronger and more resilient. This is what I saw Sarah, Christine, Sandy, and Raúl doing as we sat around the dinner table on that autumn evening in New York.

THE DINNER PARTY started when two women, Lennon Flowers and Carla Fernandez, met in Los Angeles in 2010 and soon realized that they each had recently lost a parent. Carla's father had died of brain cancer, and Lennon's mother of lung cancer. Each woman was twenty-one at the time, and they formed an instant connection over their shared experience, especially because neither felt they could talk to their other friends about the loss. Their friends would get uncomfortable when the death came up. Not knowing how to respond, they would say they were sorry and then quickly change the subject. It wasn't their fault—they didn't know any better, as Lennon told me when we met in New York—but their reactions left her and Carla feeling alone. So it was a relief for each of them to have someone to rely on as they went through the ups and downs of grief.

Carla pulled together a list of a few other twentysomethings who had lost loved ones and invited them to a dinner party at her apartment. Five women showed up. They ended up talking until 2 a.m., as if they were best friends. Lennon and Carla realized that they had created a special community that evening, and they eventually started thinking about ways to spread that community across the country.

By 2016, what began as an informal dinner at Carla's apartment had transformed into a national nonprofit organization and movement. Thanks to Carla and Lennon, bereaved young people are now gathering together at tables in more than sixty cities worldwide—from San Francisco and Washington, DC, to Vancouver and Amsterdam—for intimate dinners like the one I attended in Washington Heights. Lennon and Carla have also organized retreats for Dinner Party hosts like Sarah and have put on events in New York and San Francisco that explore how people cope with grief. But the organization's focus is the dinner parties themselves. Each table hosts about six to ten people, and when it fills up, it's not uncommon for a waiting list to develop or for another table to pop up in the same city.

At dinner, there's no agenda or theme. The Dinner Partiers,

as they call themselves, can talk about whatever they want, like relationship problems or the media's beauty standards, as at the dinner I went to. But they eventually come around to the topic of the death of their loved ones. How do I live my life when the person I loved the most is dead? What am I supposed to do now that the person who always cheered me on and gave me advice is no longer here? How do I cope with the guilt of not treating them as well as they deserved when they were alive? Are they ashes-and-dust dead, or are they still watching over me? How do I make sense of this sudden and unexpected loss? These are some of the questions that come up again and again at the tables.

Christine's mother passed away five years before the dinner party, when Christine was a junior studying engineering at the University of Michigan. Her mother had been walking home from work when a truck came barreling down the road and hit her as she crossed the street. She died instantly.

Christine and her mother were very close. They got together regularly to watch movies and make dinner. Before Christine's mother died, a terrible car accident caused her to stop driving, so Christine reorganized her college schedule so that she could come over from Ann Arbor most days of the week and chauffeur her mother around. One reason that Christine decided to study engineering was so that she could find a good job when she graduated to support her mother.

Christine's focus on school was so intense that she had no social life to speak of. Though her mother never pressured her academically, Christine would often sacrifice spending time with her mom to study: "There were times where I just couldn't pull myself away from my school work, so I would call her and say, 'Mom, I can't. I have to work.' And she would say, 'Oh, that's okay.' She was so understanding."

The night her mother died, Christine was on a date at an art museum, an uncharacteristic break from her studying schedule. She told her mother that she wouldn't be able to pick her up as she usually did. It was not a problem, her mom said; she could take the bus home. Later that evening, Christine noticed her phone was ringing. It was her mom.

"I don't like talking on the phone in museums," Christine said. "So when I saw she was calling, I told myself I'd call her back."

Christine didn't check her phone again until the end of the night. "I saw ten missed calls and voicemails from numbers I didn't recognize," she said. "That's never good. I called back and someone at the hospital said, 'Your mom got into an accident. You need to come immediately.' I asked, 'Is she okay? What happened?' and she said, 'You need to come immediately. Someone needs to drive you.'

"I still can't make sense of this," Christine said about her mother's sudden death. "I'm the kind of person who tries to understand why things happen. The logic of it. But I just can't here."

"There doesn't have to be meaning," said Raúl. "Sometimes shit just happens. Part of it is just being able to let go. Accepting that life has a lot of chaos embedded in it. The human struggle is reconciling that life is chaotic but we've managed to control almost all uncertainty. But then one day, a person who is irresponsible runs into our mother."

"I mean," Christine said, "she was killed by an idiot. Someone who was being irresponsible and stupid. He doesn't even know that he ruined a whole family's life, caused so much destruction. How come he gets to go on and live and my mother is dead? I just felt so hopeless after; nothing made sense. She was just gone. How? And I'm torn between this anger and this part of me that wants to let go and live my life. Move forward." Slamming her hands down on the table, she said, "I hate humans so much. At the same time, you have to live your life. Move it forward."

"That's what nihilism is for," said Raúl.

Earlier in the night, Raúl said he lost his faith in humanity after the death of his friend. At the time, Raúl was attending college in Alaska. He was swimming with his friend in a gravel pond in Fairbanks when both of them started cramping up in the cold water. Raúl's friend started to drown. Raúl tried to save him, but he soon exhausted himself. He called to the people on shore for help, but no one came. They thought the two young men were playing a practical joke. Raúl nearly drowned as his friend pushed him underwater to stay afloat. Raúl eventually realized that if he didn't swim back to shore, he would die. Worn out from struggling, the only stroke Raúl could muster was the backstroke. As he swam on his back to safety, he saw his friend fight to stay above water and then sink—and then fight then sink, and fight then sink—until he finally drowned.

When Raúl finally got to shore, he was nearly delirious. The first people he saw were a mother and her child, who was playing with a raft. In a daze, Raúl asked if he could take the raft because his friend was drowning. They didn't believe him. The mother said, "Then why don't you go out there and save him." But it was too late to send anyone out to save him. The authorities found the body three days later. For Raúl, it was hard to imagine how the death of his friend was anything other than senseless.

"I flirted with that philosophy," Christine said of nihilism, "but I didn't find it very productive."

Instead, Christine finished college and moved to New York,

where she abandoned her plans to be an engineer. There, she chose to pursue what she thought was her true calling: being a pastry chef. "I wouldn't have done that if my mom hadn't died," she said. "After an event like that," she went on, "you think about your life and who you are and what you want to do. Ninety-five percent of the decisions I make now are influenced by the fact that she died. So, yeah, pastry."

I was struck, sitting there and watching them speak—sometimes angrily, sometimes sadly, sometimes with deep remorse and guilt—by how, with every sentence, they were struggling to understand their loss and what it meant for their lives now. Some of them were further along the road to recovery and growth than others. But each of them was leaning on some of, if not all, the pillars of meaning. They were forming a community. They were figuring out what their purpose was in light of their loss. They were trying to make sense of what had happened. And they were participating in a ritual that helped them step outside of the hustle and bustle of their daily lives to find peace.

This is why Carla and Lennon founded The Dinner Party: they wanted to bring meaning to people whose lives had been thrown into disarray by grief. "We want to create a movement," Lennon said, "where people are living bigger and stronger versus being derailed and devastated by the loss."

THE IDEA THAT we can grow to lead deeper and more meaningful lives through adversity is an ancient one in literature, religion, and philosophy—as Nietzsche famously wrote, "What does not kill me makes me stronger." But it is a relatively new idea in mainstream psychology. Until recently, many psychologists considered trauma primarily a catastrophic stressor. One of the characteristics of trauma, they believed, was that it damaged a person psychologically and physically, sometimes to the point of incapacitation. In 1980, the American Psychiatric Association added post-traumatic stress disorder to the *Diagnostic and Statistical Manual of Mental Disorders,* used by psychologists and psychiatrists to diagnose mental illness. Since then, PTSD has received a great deal of attention from psychologists, the media, and ordinary people trying to understand what happens to people after a crisis.

The story of Bob Curry, a Vietnam War veteran from Milwaukee, Wisconsin, is a good example of exactly what psychologists were talking about. Curry grew up in a blue-collar neighborhood in Wisconsin, the kind of place, he said, where people eat a lot of apple pie and watch a lot of John Wayne movies. As a child, he took to heart the lesson of John F. Kennedy's "ask not" inaugural address. "Whatever your country asks of you," Curry remembers thinking, "you do it."

When he was a teenager, the protests against the Vietnam War were at their height. Even so, Curry felt a strong call to serve his country. So he joined the army as soon as he graduated from high school. "I thought that I was doing the right thing, what I needed to do with my life," he said. "That was an honorable period of my life. Anything that I was asked, I would do. And I thought what I was doing was saving or helping save people further down the line."

During the war, Curry flew reconnaissance missions over North Vietnam and Laos. It was a harrowing experience, he said. His plane was often bombarded by enemy fire and he nearly died on several occasions. The terror of his war experiences never left him, nor did the guilt of surviving the war when so many others—including his friends—had died. Curry returned home in 1971 a different man. He tried to ease into leading a relatively normal life, and at first he succeeded. He started a family, bought a home, and worked for IBM. He had some flashbacks, but he largely managed to bury his guilt and fear.

When the Gulf War started in 1991, though, Curry's fragile hold on life started to slip away. He couldn't escape the depictions of war plastered all over the television sets he watched and newspapers he read. Those images brought him right back to Vietnam. His flashbacks got worse, and he started having nightmares about his plane going down. He scared his wife by slamming his hand on the backboard of their bed in the middle of the night, as if he were reaching for the handle of the plane's eject lever over his head. He also started to drink heavily. But it didn't help. After the 9/11 attacks, which once again threw war into the national spotlight, his flashbacks intensified, and so did his drinking.

One day in 2002, Curry was in a drugstore near Milwaukee waiting to pick up a prescription for his wife when he started looking through a magazine and saw something that shocked him. The remains of two men with whom he had served, and who were thought to be missing in action, had been found in Laos. Learning that his old friends were dead sent him on a bender. The next thing he remembers is waking up in a hospital with two police officers at his bed. They told him that he had been in a car accident. Then they told him that he had hit and killed a man.

After the accident, Curry went to trial on a homicide charge. He was acquitted after being diagnosed with post-traumatic stress disorder and was sent to a state mental institution. There, he ruminated on how much destruction he had caused. Over the course of the trial, he and his wife lost their house and his daughter had to leave college for financial reasons. Curry considered ending his life. He had, after all, destroyed not only his own family, but also the family of the man he had killed. "I should be in prison," he thought when his trial ended. "I should be done. I should have killed myself." But he had been given a second chance. "How do I go forward," he wondered, "with all the damage that I have done?"

He thought about an experience he had during the trial. His Alcoholics Anonymous sponsor, a fellow Vietnam War veteran, had taken him out to lunch at a VFW post. Curry was struck by how cathartic the experience was. They were having burgers and Diet Cokes, and they were surrounded by memorabilia that reminded him of the war but was not arousing negative flashbacks. It was, in fact, reminding him of the reason he signed up for the military in the first place: the desire to serve a country he loved.

In this safe space, he could bond with people who had endured similar experiences during the war and who were dealing with similar consequences after it. They didn't judge him, either, and that was huge after living for three decades with the burden of fighting in a war that many people hated. When he returned home from Vietnam in 1971, protesters at the airport threw eggs at him and the other veterans while chanting "Baby Killers!" Feeling like an outsider in his own country, Curry later realized, had exacerbated his guilt and stress, which inflamed his PTSD.

When he visited the VFW, he realized that his peers there understood him. "Finding people who are going through the same struggle you are makes you less crazy," he said. Curry started thinking about ways to re-create that bonding experience for his fellow veterans. Though he knew of many existing veterans organizations, those groups tended to appeal to an older crowd, and the social life revolved around drinking—

which was dangerous for veterans who, like Curry, struggled with PTSD or substance abuse. Curry wanted something more modern and alcohol-free.

So in 2008, he and some friends launched Dryhootch, a community center for veterans that takes the form of a coffee shop. It is run by vets and offers live music, reading groups, art classes, and therapy sessions for veterans and their families. There is chess club on Wednesday mornings, and a group of veterans gathers Fridays before lunch for mindfulness meditation. Nonveterans are welcome, too, and their presence helps the veterans integrate back into civilian life. "The idea was that instead of a bar, you have a coffeehouse where people in the services could come and hang out with each other every day," Curry said. "Good coffee and peer groups. That's what I wanted to offer."

Initially Curry didn't have enough money for a shop, so he ran Dryhootch out of an old red-painted popcorn truck that he converted into a mobile coffeehouse. Then, in 2009, he opened his first brick-and-mortar location in Milwaukee. In 2012, the White House recognized Curry as a "champion of change" for his service to veterans. By 2014, Dryhootch had expanded across the Midwest, with two locations in Milwaukee, one in Madison, and two in the Chicago area.

The drunk-driving accident forced Curry to turn inward—to figure out what he could contribute to the world. "Service is the only thing that makes sense after what happened," he said. "I can't undo time, but I can make a difference, and that's what drives me forward. When a vet tells me of the difference Dryhootch made in his life, that's when it all comes together."

After a traumatic experience, many people feel a strong

drive to help those who have suffered as they have. Psychologists and psychiatrists sometimes call this drive "survivor mission." A survivor, in the words of the psychiatrist Robert Jay Lifton, "is one who has been exposed to the possibility of dying or has witnessed the death of others yet remained alive." Survivors, Lifton continues, feel "a sense of debt to the dead, a need to placate them or carry out their wishes in order to justify their own survival."

Today, the term "survivor" has been expanded to include victims of nonfatal traumas, too, and their mission is often tied to making sure others don't have to go through what they've endured. Survivors of sexual assault, for example, have become abuse therapists. Survivors of mass shootings have lobbied for tougher gun laws. Parents who have lost children to leukemia have devoted themselves to raising awareness and support for cancer research and prevention. Survivors of Hiroshima and Nagasaki have worked to reduce stockpiles of nuclear arms. These acts of purpose help survivors cope after their trauma. When people who have suffered help others, they report less depression, anxiety, and anger, and more optimism, hope, and meaning in life.

Curry, for his part, wants to help younger veterans avoid making the mistakes he made abusing alcohol. "I can't go back in time and change the things I did," he said, "but I can help prevent vets today from going down my path." By pursuing his purpose, Curry has benefited not only a new generation of vets, but himself, too. His mission has played an indispensable role in putting his life back on track. Curry has been sober since 2002.

* * *

MOST PEOPLE HAVE heard about how post-traumatic stress disorder can unravel a person. Fewer have heard about post-traumatic growth, the process that lifted Curry out of his despair and into his new role as a leader in the veteran community. As Curry's story shows, these two responses to trauma are not directly opposed to one another or mutually exclusive; someone who experiences one can experience the other, and most people will experience some of the symptoms of PTSD after a trauma, like nightmares or flashbacks, without developing the disorder. But researchers have found that anywhere from half to two-thirds of trauma survivors report post-traumatic growth, while only a small percentage suffer from PTSD.

Richard Tedeschi and Lawrence Calhoun of the University of North Carolina at Charlotte are two of the leading experts on post-traumatic growth, which they define as "positive change that occurs as a result of the struggle with highly challenging life crises." Tedeschi and Calhoun, who coined the term "post-traumatic growth" in the mid-1990s, came to this idea after studying how people develop wisdom. They interviewed individuals who had endured hardships, thinking those conversations might shed light on how people gained perspective and depth. Maybe these people, they reasoned, learned something from their adversity that made them see the world in a new way. After speaking to many trauma survivors, Tedeschi and Calhoun found that suffering could help people transform in fundamentally positive ways—and that these transformations were both more profound and more common than either of them expected.

"We'd been working with bereaved parents for about a decade," Tedeschi has said. "They'd been through the most shattering kind of loss imaginable. I observed how much they helped each other, how compassionate they were toward other parents who had lost children, how in the midst of their own grief they often wanted to do something about changing the circumstances that had led to their child's death to prevent other families from suffering the kind of loss they were experiencing. These were remarkable and grounded people who were clear about their priorities in life."

After studying a wide array of survivors, Tedeschi and Calhoun identified five specific ways that people can grow after a crisis. First, their relationships strengthen. One woman diagnosed with breast cancer, for example, said she realized her relationships "are the most important things you have." Many people respond to trauma by actively building this pillar of meaning. James, whom we met in the chapter on belonging, turned to his community at the Society for Creative Anachronism for support after struggling with suicidal thoughts. The bereaved parents told Tedeschi and Calhoun that losing a child had made them more compassionate: "I've become more empathetic towards anybody in pain and anybody in any kind of grief," one said.

Second, they discover new paths and purposes in life. Sometimes, these are related to a particular survivor mission. Tedeschi and Calhoun heard from one person, for example, who became an oncology nurse after losing her child to cancer. Other times, the crisis becomes the catalyst for a more general reconsideration of priorities, as Christine discovered in the aftermath of her mother's death.

Third, the trauma allows them to find their inner strength. When Carlos Eire suddenly found himself living in poverty in the United States, he developed survival skills by drawing on a well of tenacity he didn't know he had. The common thread among those Tedeschi and Calhoun studied is a "vulnerable yet stronger" narrative. That paradoxical outlook defined the attitude of a rape survivor who admitted that the world now seemed more dangerous to her but that, at the same time, she felt more resilient as a result of the inner strength she built after the assault.

Fourth, their spiritual life deepens. That could mean that their faith in God is renewed, as it was for Carlos, or it could mean that they grapple with existential questions more broadly, coming to know certain deep truths about the world or themselves, as Emeka Nnaka did after his spinal cord injury.

Finally, they feel a renewed appreciation for life. Rather than taking for granted a stranger's kindness or the vivid colors of autumn leaves, they savor the small moments of beauty that light up each day. After coming to terms with her terminal diagnosis, Janeen Delaney felt a regular connection to the natural world, which led her to focus on what really mattered to her. "I think I recognize trivial things as trivial now," said a survivor of an airplane crash. "It reinforced the importance of doing the right thing, not the expedient or politically smart thing, but the right thing."

Tedeschi and Calhoun use the metaphor of an earthquake to explain how we grow in the wake of crisis. Just as a city has a certain structure before a major earthquake, so too do we have certain fundamental beliefs about our lives and the world. Trauma shatters those assumptions. But out of the rubble comes an opportunity to rebuild. In the aftermath of an earthquake, cities aim to erect buildings and infrastructure that are stronger and more resilient than what now lies in ruins. Similarly, those who are able to rebuild psychologically, spiritually, and otherwise after a crisis are better equipped to deal with future adversity, and they ultimately lead more meaningful lives.

Tedeschi and Calhoun wanted to know why some people grow after trauma while others do not. The nature and severity of the trauma, they discovered, was less important than one might think. According to another researcher who has studied post-traumatic growth, "It is not the actual trauma that is causing the change. It is how people interpret what happens, how what they believe about themselves and life and the world gets shaken up, not the trauma itself, that forces people to experience growth." When Tedeschi and Calhoun probed more deeply into their data, they found that the difference between the two groups lay in what they call "deliberate rumination," or introspection. The participants whom Tedeschi and Calhoun studied spent a lot of time trying to make sense of their painful experience, reflecting on how the event changed them. Doing so helped them make the life changes associated with post-traumatic growth.

One way to jump-start the process of deliberate rumination is through writing. Social psychologist James Pennebaker of the University of Texas at Austin studies how people use language to interpret their experiences. He began his research on trauma in the 1980s. Based on previous work, he knew that individuals who had endured a traumatic event were more depressed and emotionally volatile than those who had not, and that they died of heart disease and cancer at higher rates. But he did not know why trauma would have such negative effects on health.

Then, one day, he was poring over data when he found an interesting correlation: people who said that they had experienced a major trauma in their childhood but had kept it a secret were significantly more likely to report health problems as adults than those who had spoken to others about the experience. This sparked a question: Would encouraging the secret-keepers to anonymously open up about the event improve their health?

For the past thirty years, Pennebaker has been trying to answer this question by asking people to come into his lab and spend fifteen minutes each day, for three or four days in a row, writing about "the most upsetting experience in your life." He encourages his subjects to "really let go and explore your very deepest emotions and thoughts" about the experience and how it has affected them. In the studies he has run, people have written about being raped, being mugged, losing loved ones, and attempting suicide. It's not uncommon, Pennebaker told me, for research subjects to leave the writing room in tears.

Pennebaker has found that those who wrote down their thoughts and feelings about the trauma went to the doctor less often. They also reported better grades after the experiment, displayed fewer symptoms of anxiety and depression, registered lower blood pressure and heart rates, and enjoyed better-functioning immune systems. Expressive writing, in other words, is healing. But why was writing about a trauma in this specific way so powerful?

When he analyzed the writing of his research subjects across his various studies, Pennebaker found that those in the expressive writing condition didn't just recount what happened to them during the trauma or use the exercise to blow off steam and vent their emotions. Rather, they were actively working to make sense of what had happened to them—and that search for meaning helped them overcome the traumatic experience both physically and emotionally.

The writing exercise helped Pennebaker's subjects forge meaning in several ways. First, by probing into the causes and consequences of the adversity, the subjects eventually grew wiser about it. They used more of what Pennebaker calls "insight words"—words and phrases like "realize," "I know," "because," "work through," and "understand"—in their narratives. A father might realize, for example, that his son's suicide was not his fault—and understanding that could bring him some closure.

Second, over the course of the three or four days, they showed a shift in perspective, which Pennebaker measured through their pronoun use. Instead of writing about what happened to *me* and what *I* am going through, they started writing about why *he* abused me or why *she* divorced me. In other words, they stepped away from their own emotional turmoil and tried to get inside the head of another person. The ability to look at the trauma from different perspectives, Pennebaker said, indicates that the victim has put some distance between himself and the event, which allows him to understand how it shaped him and his life.

The third characteristic that set the sense-makers apart was their ability to find a positive meaning in their traumatic experience. Pennebaker gave me one example: "Let's say that I have been mugged in an alley. Someone hit me with a tire iron and took all my money and it's really shattered my trust in the world. I could write, 'This was a horrible experience. I don't know what to do,' and so forth. So I'm talking about the event, and may even be coming up with meaning: 'I now realize that the world is a dangerous place and I have to be careful.' Or I might say, 'This event was shattering for me in many ways, but it also made me realize how lucky I had been in the past, and fortunately, I have some stable close friends who have been able to help me through it.'" The second interpretation, Pennebaker said, leads to better health outcomes. Other research has shown that those who find some good that resulted from their trauma, though they continue to have intrusive thoughts about the experience, are less depressed and report higher well-being.

Consider a story that the Holocaust survivor and psychiatrist Viktor Frankl tells about consoling an elderly doctor whose wife had died two years earlier. The doctor dearly loved his wife, and losing her led him to fall into a severe depression that he was unable to lift himself out of. Frankl encouraged the doctor to change his perspective. "What would have happened, Doctor," Frankl asked him, "if you had died first, and your wife would have had to survive you?" The doctor responded: "Oh, for her this would have been terrible; how she would have suffered!"

Frankl then pointed out the benefit of the doctor surviving his wife: "You see, Doctor, such a suffering has been spared her, and it was you who have spared her this suffering—to be sure, at the price that now you have to survive and mourn her." After Frankl said this, the doctor rose from his chair, shook Frankl's hand, and left his office. Frankl helped this doctor find a positive meaning in his wife's death, and that gave him peace.

In Pennebaker's research, the subjects who benefited the most after the experiment were those who demonstrated the greatest progress in sense-making over time. These were people whose initial responses were emotionally raw and their stories disjointed, but whose narratives became smoother and more insightful as each day passed. Venting raw emotions and falling back on platitudes, he has found, does not lead to health benefits. But sustained and thoughtful writing does. It helps us move beyond our initial emotional reactions to something deeper.

In fact, Pennebaker found that expressive writing is uniquely healing—subjects asked to express their emotions about a traumatic experience through dance didn't benefit as much as the writers did. Pennebaker argues that's because writing, unlike many other forms of expression, allows people to systematically process an event, bringing order to it. Through writing, they discover new insights and come to understand how the crisis fits into the broader mosaic of their lives. Sense-making and narrative are thus effective ways to make meaning from trauma and, ultimately, overcome it. But they are not the only tools we have to recover from difficult experiences—as a growing body of research on human resilience has shown.

THE QUESTION RESILIENCE researchers ask is why—why do some people handle adversity better than others, and go on to lead normal lives despite their negative life experiences, while others are derailed by them? In the early 1990s, the psychologist Gina Higgins tried to answer that question. In her book *Resilient Adults,* she profiles individuals who have experienced profound trauma and come out remarkably whole.

One of those people is Shibvon. Shibvon grew up in dire poverty and her parents had a fraught relationship. Though her father loved his children, he was a remote figure. He suffered from mental illness and attempted suicide when Shibvon was seven. Her mother, meanwhile, was a terror. A large woman with a booming voice, she regularly beat Shibvon and her three younger siblings and tied them to their beds at night. Twice, she sent them to orphanages to get rid of them, though she later took them back. And when Shibvon was nine years old, the abuse became even more nightmarish. Shibvon's mother allowed her boyfriend to rape Shibvon on a regular basis. He threatened to kill Shibvon's father if she told anyone—so Shibvon stayed quiet.

The word Shibvon uses to describe her childhood is "chaos." She remembers "a lot of screaming, a lot of yelling, getting thrown across the room." She has no memories of receiving love or affection from her mother, who constantly thundered that Shibvon was "stupid" and "rotten." On multiple occasions, her mother told Shibvon that she had tried to abort her—and that the only reason she married Shibvon's father was that she got pregnant with Shibvon. "I felt like it was another way of saying how much she hated me," Shibvon said of her mother's role in her sexual abuse, "and how much I just was a piece of excrement, a sacrificial lamb."

It should go without saying that the consequences of this kind of abuse are devastating. Childhood trauma is one of the most difficult forms of adversity to overcome, and it can also leave lasting psychological and physical scars on the victim. When children experience severe and unpredictable stress, their brains and bodies rewire in a way that makes them hypersensitive to other stressors later in life and more susceptible to disease. Childhood adversity has been linked to heart disease, obesity, and cancer in adults. And adults who faced serious stressors as children are also more likely to abuse drugs and alcohol, suffer from depression, develop learning problems, commit violent crimes, and be arrested.

This is what makes Shibvon's story so remarkable. Though she struggled at times with depression and anxiety as an adult, she was ultimately resilient. Her life was not shattered by the perpetual stress and chaos of her childhood. Shibvon went on to have a career as a pediatric nurse, working in a neonatal intensive care unit. When she was twenty-one, she married a man she deeply loved, with whom she had three sons. Together, they built a happy family.

Systematic research on resilience began around 1970 with the study of children like Shibvon. Initially, psychologists and psychiatrists were interested in understanding the origins of mental illness. Because childhood adversity was one of the predictors of psychological disorders, they began studying children who were experiencing poverty or living in troubled households. As the researchers tracked the at-risk children over time, they made an unexpected discovery: While many struggled or fell apart psychologically, a subset emerged that beat the odds and did not experience significant mental health problems. They were emotionally healthy, formed strong relationships, and did well in school. What set them apart?

Over the years, researchers have answered that question by closely studying children and adults who manage to lead healthy and productive lives after their experiences of adversity, stress, and trauma. Steven Southwick of the Yale School of Medicine and Dennis Charney of the Icahn School of Medicine at Mount Sinai, two experts on resilience, have spent the last three decades studying people who have endured traumas like abduction, rape, and captivity as prisoners of war—and emerged from them bent but not broken, as they put it. These resilient people not only bounced back, but some actually grew: "In fact," the two psychiatrists write of the prisoners of war they studied, "many of them reported having a greater appreciation of life, closer connections with family, and a newfound sense of meaning and purpose because of their prison experience." After extensive interviews with such individuals, Southwick and Charney found ten characteristics that distinguish the resilient from the rest.

One was purpose, which the researchers defined as "having a worthy goal or mission in life." Another, related to purpose, was having a moral compass tied to altruism—or selflessly serving others. Each of these themes played a role in Shibvon's story. When her mother sent her and her siblings to the orphanage, ten-year-old Shibvon helped the nuns in the nursery care for babies who had been abandoned. There, the nuns and the babies showed her affection and care, which was healing for her, as was thinking more broadly about her life's purpose. "I pretty much thought I was going to become what the nuns at the orphanage were, and that's how I would take care of kids: come back and help these little kids who have had their bad troubles and make their lives better," she said, "so that was my first goal in life." Reflecting on and planning for that future gave her hope for a better life. She realized that she could help others by cultivating love and warmth around her instead of the hatred and hurt that was her mother's currency. "I don't have much to offer," she would think, "but I have myself."

Beyond purpose, another critical predictor of resilience is social support. For children, especially, a healthy relationship with an adult or caregiver can be a buffer against the harmful effects of adversity. Though Shibvon's mother rejected her and made her feel like she "didn't belong," Shibvon received love from her father and from a paternal aunt who lived nearby. Her relationship with her aunt, she said, was especially important, even though they didn't see each other very often. But Shibvon remembers that her aunt "always" came to visit her and her siblings when they lived at the orphanages and took them out to dinner. When they were home with their mother, she brought them food and clothes, and when Shibvon visited her aunt's house, her aunt made Shibvon feel secure, safe, and valued. "She really made me feel like I mattered," Shibvon said. The love and care of her aunt gave Shibvon the strength to muddle through her horrible circumstances and, in time, overcome them.

Transcendent sources of meaning also play a role in helping people cope with trauma. For example, Southwick and Charney studied Vietnam War veterans who were held as prisoners of war, some up to eight years. These men were tortured, starved, and lived in horrendous conditions. But one of the things that kept them going was a connection to God. Some prayed regularly in their cells and others found strength in remembering that God was by their side, which meant, "We can handle this thing together," in the words of one former POW. The prisoners also gathered together for religious and patriotic services at the infamous prison camp nicknamed the Hanoi Hilton. Not all of these men were devout, Southwick and Charney found, but many of them relied on spirituality to help them endure their ordeal. In the words of one, "If you can't tap into a source of strength and power greater than yourself, you're probably not gonna last."

Research has shown that some people naturally resist adversity better than others; scientists now know that our capacity for resilience is determined, in part, by our genetic makeup and early life experiences. But the good news is that resilience is not a fixed trait. Though some people are inherently more sensitive to stress than others, all of us can learn to adapt to stress more effectively by, Charney has said, developing a set of psychological tools to help us cope with stressful events.

The fact that resilience can be taught was revealed in two studies published in 2004 by Michele Tugade of Vassar College and Barbara Fredrickson of the University of North Carolina at Chapel Hill. Tugade and Fredrickson invited research subjects into the lab and recorded their baseline heart rate, blood pressure, and other physiological indicators. Next, the participants were presented with a stressful task. Each participant was asked to quickly prepare and deliver a three-minute speech on why he or she is a good friend. They were told that the speech would be videotaped and evaluated.

Even though the participants in this study were presented with a minor stressor compared to the ones we've covered in this chapter, they still became anxious—their heart rate and blood pressure spiked. But some people in the study returned to their baseline levels more quickly than others. The researchers took note of which people showed more resilience, as measured by their physiological recovery rate, and which showed less. Tugade and Fredrickson then examined how the more resilient and less resilient people approached the task. The naturally resilient people, the researchers found, took a different attitude toward the speech task. They did not view it as a threat the way the nonresilient participants did; they saw it as a challenge.

With that in mind, the researchers conducted a separate experiment to see if they could transform less resilient people into more resilient ones. The researchers invited a new set of subjects into the lab and repeated their earlier experiment. Then Tugade and Fredrickson added a twist. The researchers told some people to see the task as a threat, and they told others to see it as a challenge.

What the researchers discovered is good news for more resilient and less resilient people alike. People who were naturally resilient recovered quickly whether they saw the task as a challenge or a threat. But for those who were less resilient, reframing the task as a challenge erased the gap: those who were told to approach the task as an opportunity rather than as a threat suddenly started looking like resilient people in their cardiovascular measures. They were able to bounce back.

Though it's difficult for researchers to study adverse experiences in the lab, one way they can understand how people cope with long-term stressors is by monitoring them over time during a stressful period of their lives. That's what Gregory Walton and Geoffrey Cohen of Stanford University did in a study published in 2011—they followed a group of college students over three years to see how they handled the difficult but important transition from high school life to adult life. Their findings reveal how the pillars of meaning help people weather adversity more effectively.

When freshmen come to college, they are thrown into a new world, which can be disorienting. They have to figure out what classes they want to take and what groups to join, and they often need to find a new set of friends. As Walton and Cohen point out, that transition can be particularly difficult for African American students. Though all students worry about fitting in at school, black students often feel especially alienated, Walton explained. As minorities on most college campuses and the target of racial discrimination, they might worry about whether "people like me" belong here. Their need to belong becomes threatened—and, as the researchers note, this can change how they interpret their experiences. When they get a bad grade or receive negative feedback, rather than acknowledging these setbacks as a normal part of college life, they might think there's something wrong with them and, even, people like them.

The researchers invited a group of black and white students into the lab and gave them several stories to read. The stories had been written by older students, and they were meant to protect the subjects' sense of belonging. The narrative thread among the stories was that adversity is a common but temporary part of the adjustment process for freshmen. If a student faces setbacks or feels like he does not belong, the participants in the experimental condition of the study learned by reading these stories, that's a natural part of the transition to college; it does not mean that they themselves are flawed in some way, or that people don't like them because of their race or ethnic background. The narrative was meant to change the story students told themselves about college.

The researchers followed up with the participants three years later, toward the end of their college careers, and found that the story-editing intervention had significant consequences—but only for the African American students. Their GPAs rose steadily over the three years, while the GPAs of the black students in the control condition did not change. Their improvement in academic performance was so dramatic that it cut the minority achievement gap in half. Three times as many were in the top 25 percent of their class. The students also reported being healthier and happier, and said they went to the doctor less often. Reading the belonging narrative helped them navigate college life more effectively. When those in the control condition experienced a setback, they doubted themselves and whether they belonged at their school. When those in the experimental condition faced similar stresses, their belonging was not threatened, which helped them weather the challenge successfully.

Walton and Cohen did not see these effects among the white students. In fact, the GPAs of the white students in both the control and experimental groups increased between their freshman and senior years. Reading the narrative had made no difference to their grades or to their physical or psychological well-being. As a majority group on campus, white students didn't attribute their stresses to not belonging, so they didn't need an intervention to help redefine their challenges; the black students did. When they were able to change the story they told themselves about their transition to college, they were better off years later. This kind of intervention is not a magic bullet for inequality, as Walton points out—"it doesn't give people opportunities when they lack them," he said—but it does reveal how a shift in mindset can elevate a traditionally marginalized group.

The pillars of meaning can help people recover from the trauma of abuse, imprisonment, and racism. But these serious hardships are not the only forms of adversity people will face. Daily life is filled with stressors both major and minor, like moving to a new city, finding a job, or completing a difficult assignment for work or school. As is the case with trauma, some people are more resilient to these quotidian sources of stress than others—and here, too, meaning plays a valuable role.

In a study published in 2014, a group of researchers led by James Abelson at the University of Michigan wanted to find out how a meaning mindset might affect an individual's performance during a stressful job interview. In the study, the researchers gave each participant three minutes to prepare a five-minute talk to a selection committee about why he or she was the best applicant for a job. Before the mock interview, the researchers told some participants that rather than focusing on promoting themselves in the interview, they should focus on how the job would enable them to help others and to live out their self-transcendent values. The meaning intervention, it turns out, dampened the body's physiological response to stress.

The benefits of adopting a meaning mindset are not just

short-lived artifacts of a lab experiment—they have lasting results in the real world. Research led by David Yeager and Marlone Henderson at the University of Texas at Austin shows that high school students who wrote about how their schoolwork allowed them to fulfill a life purpose got better grades in math and science several months later. In the same set of studies, college students who thought about their purpose were more likely to persist through a tedious set of math problems, even though they were free to play online games at any time during the experiment. The reason these exercises worked, Yeager and Henderson found, is that the students developed a "purpose for learning." Those who remembered their sources of meaning were able to reframe a tough class—or, in the case of Abelson's study, a nerve-racking interview—as a necessary step toward accomplishing their purpose and living according to their values rather than as an annoyance to be avoided or feared.

Keeping meaning in mind also protects us against the damage stress can do. As Stanford's Kelly McGonigal writes, summarizing a large body of research: "Stress increases the risk of health problems, except when people regularly give back to their communities. Stress increases the risk of dying, except when people have a sense of purpose. Stress increases the risk of depression, except when people see a benefit in their struggles."

In his classic work on grief, *When Bad Things Happen to Good People,* Rabbi Harold Kushner captures the complicated nature of finding meaning in adversity. Writing about his growth after the death of his young son, he explains: "I am a more sensitive person, a more effective pastor, a more sympathetic counselor because of Aaron's life and death than I would ever have been without it. And I would give up all those gains in a second if I could have my son back. If I could choose, I would forgo all of the spiritual growth and depth which has come my way because of our experiences, and be what I was fifteen years ago, an average rabbi, an indifferent counselor, helping some people and unable to help others, and the father of a bright, happy boy. But I cannot choose."

As much as we might wish, none of us will be able to go through life without some kind of suffering. That's why it's crucial for us to learn to suffer well. Those who manage to grow through adversity do so by leaning on the pillars of meaning—and afterward, those pillars are even stronger in their lives.

Some go even further. Having witnessed the power of belonging, purpose, storytelling, and transcendence in their own lives, they're working to bring these wellsprings of meaning into their schools, workplaces, and neighborhoods—and, ultimately, they're hoping to make a change in our society at large. It is to these cultures of meaning that we now turn.

7

Cultures of Meaning

THE INTERIOR OF THE "HOLY BOX," AS ST. MARK'S Cathedral in Seattle is sometimes called, is basic and bare. Patches of the once-white walls are dirty and gray where the paint has worn away; the lightbulbs are out in some of the chandeliers. There are no stained-glass scenes from the Bible, no baroque crucifixes at the altar. And on the October morning that I visited the Episcopal church for the Sunday service, it smelled like wet dog. That Sunday happened to be the feast day honoring Saint Francis of Assisi, the medieval monk who loved nature. In his honor, the church encouraged the congregants to bring their pets to the morning service. There were dogs sitting on the pews and pacing around the back of the church—and every few minutes, one of them would let out a series of restless, high-pitched yelps.

By nighttime, though, the cathedral had transformed into a sanctuary of peace and stillness. The church was completely silent when I entered and took my seat. Except for a few dimly lit lanterns above and some candles flickering on the altar, the space was dark. There was a woman with a service dog sitting nearby, a monk with a rope around his waist, and several families with children. Beyond those of us sitting in the crowded pews were dozens of people gathered on the benches along the walls of the church and some sitting and lying right on the floor. Others had made themselves comfortable beside the pulpit. All of us had gathered to listen in silence to an ancient monastic prayer service called Compline.

Compline, from the Latin *completorium* (complete), originated around the fourth century. Made up of psalms, prayers, hymns, and anthems chanted before bedtime, it completes the cycle of fixed-hour prayers that monastics pray each day. Compline is a plea to God for protection from the unknown and unseen terrors of the night—and a plea, too, for peace in the face of death.

It's rare to hear Compline outside of monasteries, which is what makes St. Mark's, and the handful of other churches that offer it regularly, unique. When Compline began at St. Mark's in 1956, it marked the first time that the service had been chanted for the public in the United States. In its early years, it attracted only a few people, but by the 1960s, word had spread, and hundreds of hippies yearning for a "direct, unmediated experience of the Divine Presence" descended on the church on Sunday nights. Like a mass, Compline follows a specific order, though there are no sermons or priests—just a choir of singers who fill the cathedral with the holy sounds of chant.

Nearly fifty years after the Summer of Love, the countercultural spirit was still alive and well at St. Mark's. Some congregants near the altar had hair dyed in fluorescent colors. Some of them had tattoos and piercings. Many were young—younger than you'd expect to find at an Episcopal church on a Sunday night in a city like Seattle. They brought blankets and cushions—and in a few cases, even sleeping bags—and lay down on the ground, staring straight up at the wood-beamed ceiling, waiting for the service to begin. One goateed man sat with his legs crossed like the Buddha, chin to chest, meditating. A college-aged woman leaned against one of the church's massive white columns. She pulled her knees into her chest and gazed ahead contemplatively with her arms wrapped around her legs.

An all-male choir stood in the back corner of the church, hidden from the congregants. One voice broke the silence: "The Lord Almighty grant us a quiet night and a perfect end." A chorus joined him, chanting: "Glory be to the Father, and to the Son, and to the Holy Ghost. As it was in the beginning, is now, and ever shall be, world without end." Their disembodied voices filled the cathedral. "What is man," they chanted from Psalm 8, "that you should be mindful of him? the son of man that you should seek him out?" They also sang a mystical anthem composed by the twentieth-century musician Francis Poulenc, using the words of Saint Francis of Assisi: "Lord, I beg you, let the burning and tender power of your love consume my soul and remove from it all that is beneath the heavens. And so I may die through love for your love, as you submitted yourself to die through love for my love."

At the end of the service, a great silence descended on the church. Some listeners filed out quietly. Others lingered in their seats. A woman and a man near the altar stood up and hugged before gathering their blankets to go. Some formed small groups outside the church, speaking to each other in hushed voices. The service was only thirty minutes long, but people were visibly different afterward—calmer, softer, gentler.

Like those who gathered here in the 1960s for Compline, many of the congregants at St. Mark's today are anti-establishment. There were certainly Christians there, but many were agnostics and atheists, some of them overtly hostile to organized religion. That just makes Compline all the more remarkable. There is something spiritually powerful that happens inside the walls of the church each Sunday night that attracts believers and nonbelievers alike.

"It transports me out of my own mind," said Emma, a twenty-year-old college student, on the steps outside of the cathedral. She has been attending Compline semiregularly for several years. "I was raised Jewish, so I don't agree with the sentiment," she said, "but there is something about the music that gets you in a holy space. It's like taking a spiritual shower. It washes away a lot of your smaller concerns. Feeling the presence of a higher power makes you realize how superficial the little problems are."

Emma was with two friends, Dylan and Jake. Dylan, a twenty-five-year-old freelancer, had tied his hair back in a ponytail. Like Emma, he was moved by the music. "Music isn't a community thing like it used to be," he said. "People have their headphones on all the time. But here, you are in a space with tons of other people listening to the same thing. The voices of the choir are resonating all over—"

"It's like the whole church is singing," Jake interrupted.

"Yeah. Their voices sound bigger than just normal human voices," Dylan added. "It reminds you that music goes beyond the self."

"It makes your ego feel smaller," Jake said; "a bit quieter."

What happens at St. Mark's is unique. People in our society are growing increasingly alienated from mystical and transcendent sources of meaning. As awe researchers Paul Piff and Dacher Keltner have written, "Adults spend more and more time working and commuting and less time outdoors and with other people. Camping trips, picnics and midnight skies are forgone in favor of working weekends and late at night. Attendance at arts events—live music, theater, museums and galleries—has dropped over the years." Even when we do seek out mystery at a church service, in a museum, or in the woods, experiencing transcendence often requires attention, focus, and stillness, qualities that are difficult to cultivate in our distracted age. That became clear one Friday in 2007, when the master violinist Joshua Bell stood in a Washington, DC, Metro station at rush hour to play some of the most difficult and dazzling pieces in all of classical music, from Schubert's "Ave Maria" to Bach's "Chaconne." He had been convinced to do this by a *Washington Post* journalist who wanted to know if people would stop and make time for beauty on their commute to work, or if they'd merely trudge along as usual. Sure enough, most of the commuters, living their busy lives, did not stop to listen to the music. Over a thousand people rushed by Bell that morning. Only seven stopped to watch him play.

Compline attracts people seeking refuge from the white noise of daily life. They find meaning by coming together in a community and surrendering themselves to the music, to the silence, to the divine. Compline makes you feel "connected to something *greater than*—whatever that ultimately means for you," says Jason Anderson, the director of the Compline Choir.

So FAR, this book has focused on the individual—what each of us can do personally to lead a more meaningful life. But meaning seekers face an uphill battle in our culture. The "work-and-spend" mentality that characterizes life today, as the author Gregg Easterbrook has written, alienates people from what really matters. In neighborhoods and offices, social connections are becoming less and less frequent. The fast pace of modern life, with all of its distractions, makes introspection almost impossible. And in a world where scientific knowledge is supreme, transcendent experiences are looked upon with suspicion.

These trends have left many people unsatisfied and yearning for something more. Now they're starting to push back and looking for a deeper way to live. All across the country, medical professionals, business leaders, educators, clergymen, and ordinary people are using the pillars of meaning to transform the institutions in which we live and work, creating communities that value and build connections, celebrate purpose, provide opportunities for storytelling, and leave space for mystery. Their efforts are part of a larger shift in our society toward meaning. As Easterbrook writes, "A transition from material want to meaning want is in progress on an historically unprecedented scale—involving hundreds of millions of people—and may eventually be recognized as the principal cultural development of our age."

Ronald Inglehart, a political scientist at the University of Michigan, directs the World Values Survey, which has tracked people's values, motivations, and beliefs since 1981. In his research, Inglehart discovered that postindustrial nations such as the United States are in the middle of a major cultural transformation. They are moving from a focus on "materialist" values emphasizing economic and physical security to "postmaterialist" values emphasizing self-expression and "a sense of meaning and purpose." The late Robert William Fogel, who was a Nobel Prize–winning economist at the University of Chicago, detected a similar trend. He wrote that we are in the middle of a "fourth great awakening," which is defined by an interest in "spiritual" concerns like purpose, knowledge, and community over "material" ones like money and consumer goods.

Unfortunately, not all of the cultures of meaning that have arisen to fill the existential vacuum are admirable ones. Cultures of meaning can be good or evil depending on their values and aims. Just like positive cultures of meaning, evil ones—like cults and hate groups—use the four pillars to attract individuals who are searching for more. The Islamic State, for example, offers adherents a community of fellow believers, a purpose thought to be divinely sanctioned, an opportunity to play a part in a heroic narrative, and the chance to get as close as possible to God. Many educated Westerners are attracted to its message and have joined its ranks. Others will continue to seek fulfillment within such groups if our society does not offer better alternatives.

The cultures of meaning highlighted in this book use the four pillars to amplify positive values and goals. Their members recognize and respect the dignity of each individual. They promote virtues like kindness, compassion, and love rather than fear, hatred, and anger. They seek to lift others up, not to inflict harm on them. Rather than sowing the seeds of destruction and chaos, these cultures contribute positively to the world.

POSITIVE CULTURES OF meaning help us all grow, but they may be especially important for adolescents. Many teenagers are unsure of their path in life, which can make them vulnerable to the lure of gangs and other negative influences. Having something to believe in and work toward helps inoculate them against those threats.

That's the idea behind The Future Project. Founded by Andrew Mangino and Kanya Balakrishna, the organization has a goal to unlock the "limitless potential of every young person."

Mangino and Balakrishna have put together an all-star team of advisers to advance their mission, including researchers like Stanford's William Damon, the University of Pennsylvania's Angela Duckworth, and Stanford's Carol Dweck. Damon, Duckworth, and Dweck are known for their groundbreaking work on purpose, "grit," and "growth mindset," respectively, and Mangino and Balakrishna use their scientific findings to help young people find their purpose and work to achieve it.

The fruits of their labor all came together on a wintry Saturday morning in 2014, at the Edison Ballroom in Times Square. Nearly seven hundred teenagers were dancing in the glow of baby blue pin lights to the music of Kanye West, Jay Z, and Alicia Keys being spun by a charismatic DJ at the front of the room. The kids were standing on chairs, climbing on stage, and hanging over the balcony above as they moved their bodies in sync with the music, which was blasting from the speakers around the room. Two boys with wild hair did the robot while a girl in a hijab moved her hips like Elvis. The whole place was shaking like a nightclub.

The roaring music, the dancing and cheering teenagers, the adults running around keeping everything under control—it all seemed appropriate to the mission of the day. The teenagers in the Edison Ballroom had traveled from some of the roughest neighborhoods in cities like New Haven, Detroit, Newark, and Philadelphia to attend DreamCon, the daylong event where all seven hundred of them would present their dreams, and the progress they had made on achieving them over the past few months, to a panel of adult judges.

Teenagers spend most of their waking hours at school. But most schools are designed to teach kids to solve algebra problems and write essays, not to help them discover what their individual callings might be. As a result, many students graduate without a real sense of what they want to do. Others drop out because school feels pointless. Mangino and Balakrishna want to change that. They want to catch teens—especially at-risk teens—at this critical moment in their lives and help them find their purpose.

Every school, Mangino and Balakrishna believe, should have a Dream Director, a person like a guidance counselor who sits down with kids and encourages them to think big about the contribution they want to make to society. Then they help each student create a step-by-step plan to achieve that goal. Plenty of people have dreams, after all, but many do nothing to actually accomplish them. The Future Project has placed Dream Directors in dozens of public schools across the United States. In the years since the organization's founding, those Dream Directors have helped thousands of students get on a purposeful path.

At DreamCon, I met one young woman from New York who dreamed of becoming a cop in order to bring safety and order to communities like her own. Her Dream Director suggested that she do some more research about the different law enforcement roles that she could pursue. After she looked into it further, she decided that she wanted to become an FBI investigator and is now researching the steps she needs to take, in terms of education and additional training, to reach that goal. I also met a high school senior from New Haven who was a single father. The mother of his baby daughter, he told me, "wasn't really around." His dream, he said as he showed me pictures of his little girl on his cellphone, is to create a community of single dads to support each other as they transition into fatherhood. He's currently organizing meetings in New Haven with single fathers he knows. The next step is to expand that community to other cities and create a national network.

Mangino and Balakrishna have found that when students pursue their purpose, the benefits spill over into other aspects of their lives. Students who worked with Dream Directors became more excited about learning, had higher attendance at school, and reported higher levels of empathy and leadership. Four out of five said that they "accomplished something they did not think was possible," and nearly all of the alumni of the program report still being positively affected by it and say that they are thriving in college, a career, or an entrepreneurial endeavor. They also reported a stronger sense of purpose. At the conference, one high school freshman told me that pursuing his purpose made him more confident. Another said that working with his Dream Director to pursue his calling as an artist kept him off the streets, where he would have been selling drugs. A girl who wanted to become a doctor said pursuing her dream helped her get better grades and inspired her younger brother to take his studies more seriously, too.

Mangino and Balakrishna's efforts are part of a broader turn in our culture. Over the last two hundred years, society's interest in purpose, as measured by one social scientist, has never been stronger than it is today. This preoccupation with purpose has taken root not only in education, but also in business, where companies are increasingly defining their missions in terms of contributing to society rather than merely making a profit.

One such company is Life is Good, an apparel brand founded by brothers Bert and John Jacobs in 1994. As Bert and John tell it, the story of Life is Good begins not with the company's founding but in their childhood. The boys, who were the two youngest of six children, grew up in Needham, Massachusetts, a suburb of Boston. Life in the Jacobs household was, by many people's standard, hard. The second floor of their small home had no heat. Their dad had a temper. And they couldn't always afford basic necessities. Their mom, Joan, joked that she bought them food they didn't like so that it would last longer.

Despite all of this, Joan was a resilient and cheerful woman who focused on the positive. Every night at the dinner table, she asked all six children to share one good thing that happened to them that day. As the kids talked about finding a Rolling Stones CD at the dump, hearing a funny joke, or learning something cool in school, the energy of the room transformed. Everyone started laughing and smiling. Joan's optimism lifted them all up. "I like running out of money," she would tell them, because "then I don't have to worry about what I need to buy." From her, the boys learned that joy comes from your mindset, not just your circumstances. That lesson eventually inspired Bert and John's vision for Life is Good.

In 1989, when they were in their twenties, Bert and John started a business designing printed T-shirts, which they sold on the streets of Boston. They also traveled up and down the East Coast, selling the shirts door-to-door on college campuses, each time making barely enough money to fund the next road trip. They slept in their van, ate peanut butter and jelly sandwiches, and showered where they could.

On the road, they spent a lot of time talking. During one trip, they discussed the way the media inundates the culture with stories of murder, rape, war, and suffering day after day. Though bad things happen and it's important to know about them, they agreed, the world is also full of good news. They thought of Joan and her ability to turn a light on in a dark room. They decided they wanted to promote her values in their work, to create a symbol that would serve as an antidote to the cynicism they saw in the culture—a superhero whose power was optimism.

John sketched a grinning stick figure on a T-shirt. He called the character Jake. When they got back to Boston, they threw a party and pinned the new T-shirt on a wall. Their friends loved it. One of them wrote on the wall next to the T-shirt, "This guy's got life figured out," with an arrow pointing to Jake, who would become the main symbol of Life is Good.

The brothers distilled that phrase to three words: "Life is good." Then they printed the image of Jake and the phrase on forty-eight T-shirts. When they set up their stand on a sidewalk in Cambridge, they sold all of the shirts in less than an hour—a first for them. That was in 1994. At the time, they had $78 to their names. Today, they run a $100 million lifestyle brand.

As the business got going, the brothers declared that its purpose was to leave a positive mark on the lives of others, the way Joan had on them. Then something unexpected happened. They started receiving letters and emails from people who had faced and were facing difficult life circumstances, including cancer, the loss of a loved one, homelessness, and natural disasters. They wrote about how they wore Life is Good apparel to get through chemotherapy or an amputation, or, in the case of one woman, the loss of her husband in 9/11, a firefighter whose personal motto had been "Life is good." They wrote about how moved they were by the Life is Good message, and how they had emerged from their adversity with a deeper appreciation of and gratitude for life.

Bert and John did not know what to do with these letters at first. "I don't think we quite understood the depth of our message when we first created it," John said. As they tried to keep their small business afloat, they read and savored the letters—but then stashed them in a drawer. Then, in 2000, they decided to share the letters at staff meetings and company-wide gatherings so that everyone could see that their hard work was making a tangible difference in the lives of others. The letters remind all of the employees that their efforts serve the larger purpose of spreading optimism. "When the daily grind of activities begins to obscure the value of our work," Bert and John write, "these inspiring stories lift us up and remind us we are members of a much bigger tribe."

Since 2010, Life is Good employees have had another source of meaning to tap into. That year, the company launched a non-profit arm called the Life is Good Kids Foundation, devoted to children who are living with illnesses, violence, abuse, poverty, and other adversities. The primary program of the foundation is called Playmakers, an initiative that offers training and enrichment workshops to childcare providers like teachers, social workers, and hospital workers. During these programs, they learn about research on optimism and resilience, and how they can apply that research to improving the lives of the children they care for. Every year, Life is Good donates 10 percent of its net profits to help kids in need. Since its founding, the foundation has trained over 6,000 Playmakers who are working to improve the lives of over 120,000 kids every day.

The commitment to helping kids means that employees at all levels are working not just to spread the power of optimism to their customers, but to help children facing adversity live better lives. Everyone in the company knows, Bert explained, that the quarterly and annual sales goals are tied not only to profitability and growth as a company, but to helping kids who really need it.

"I spend most of my time unloading boxes from a truck

and doing other manual labor," said Ian Mitchell, who works at the Life is Good warehouse in New Hampshire, "and I know that just by doing my job well, I am helping the kids." Craig Marcantonio, a graphic designer based at the company's Boston headquarters, felt the same way. "Sometimes you'll get caught up in your daily tasks," he said, "and then you'll hear about what Playmakers is doing at one of our monthly design meetings, and it reminds you that your work is pushing the needle forward on spreading optimism and being a beacon of hope for others." Allison Shablin, the Life is Good receptionist, said that even when she's fielding calls and greeting visitors, she knows she's part of something bigger. "I work for a company that does so much good for other people, and that makes me feel very proud," she said.

Life is Good is part of what entrepreneur Aaron Hurst has called "the new purpose economy." Just as the agrarian economy gave way to the industrial economy in the nineteenth century, the information economy is today giving way to an economy focused on purpose, argues Hurst, the founder of the Taproot Foundation, a multibillion-dollar marketplace that connects marketers, designers, and other professionals with nonprofits that could use their help. The purpose economy, Hurst writes, "is defined by the quest for people to have more purpose in their lives. It is an economy where value lies in establishing purpose for employees and customers—through serving needs greater than their own, enabling personal growth, and building community." Beyond niche companies like the New Belgium Brewing Company, The Container Store, and Virgin Atlantic, which call purpose the backbone of their business operations, traditional companies like Pepsi, Deloitte, and Morgan Stanley are rebranding themselves around purpose, too.

That might come as a surprise, but there's a good reason for corporations to embrace these ideas—by pursuing purpose, companies are also helping the bottom line. In their book *Conscious Capitalism,* John Mackey of Whole Foods and Raj Sisodia of Babson College point out that purpose-driven firms that create cultures of meaning among their employees, customers, and society at large are on the rise, and they are financially outperforming their peers. That's in part because consumers are seeking them out. As Sisodia has written with his colleagues, "People are increasingly looking for higher meaning in their lives, rather than simply looking to add to the store of the things they own." But it's also because, as Bert and John found, having a purpose-driven culture actually makes companies work better.

Today, about 70 percent of all employees either are "not engaged" in their work—that is, they feel uninvolved, uncommitted, and unenthusiastic about it—or are "actively disengaged" from it, and less than half of all workers feel satisfied with their jobs. But when people have meaning at work, they are more engaged, more productive, and far likelier to stay at their organizations. They realize that their daily tasks, no matter how menial, are making a positive difference in the world—and that, research has found, is a very potent motivating force. As research by Teresa Amabile of Harvard Business School has found, "Of all the events that can deeply engage people in their jobs, the single most important is making progress in meaningful work."

CULTURES OF MEANING can also have dramatic consequences for our health. This becomes especially clear when turning to those over the age of sixty-five, a rapidly growing segment of the population. Sadly, though, as older adults enter the last decades of their lives, they often find themselves shunted to the side—or worse. Research shows that elder abuse and neglect are serious problems, especially at long-term-care facilities like nursing homes. In one study, for example, 40 percent of nursing home staff members admitted to committing psychological abuse like swearing and yelling at residents, depriving them of food, or subjecting them to "inappropriate isolation." In another, about 4 in 10 nursing home residents reported that they had been abused or seen someone else be abused.

I still viscerally remember the first time I visited a nursing home. The place was depressing. There were layers of filth on the floors and the surfaces. The food trays that were delivered to the patients were dirty. And a rank odor hung in the air. This grim environment was a reflection of the grim health of the patients themselves. They were helpless, confused, and aimless. Most of them received no visitors, and their cognitive and physiological health seemed to be in decline. There was no reason, after all, for them to remain sharp.

It doesn't have to be this way. Healthy aging is possible, even in a nursing home, but it requires a radically different culture from the one many of us are used to. In the 1970s, two researchers, Ellen Langer and Judith Rodin, conducted what has become a classic psychology experiment that sheds light on what that culture might require.

After a life of independent living, elderly people often have a difficult time transitioning to a nursing home, where they're often seen as helpless. As the months and years wear on, they predictably lose their zest for life. Langer and Rodin wanted to see if they could reverse that trend. They selected a group of nursing home residents and gave each of them a houseplant for their rooms. Half the subjects were told that the nurses on their floor would care for the plant, while the rest were given full control over the plant. Each in that second group was allowed to pick out the plant, choose where in the room to put it, and decide when to water it. It was their job to care for the plant.

After a year and a half, the psychologists followed up with both groups of people. They found that those who cared for a plant did remarkably better than those who did not. They were more social, alert, cheerful, active, and healthy. Most surprising to the researchers was that those who took care of a plant actually lived longer. Over the eighteen months of the experiment, fewer of them had died compared with the other group. A very small intervention had made a big difference in the lives of the individuals Langer and Rodin studied.

What was it about looking after a plant? The patients in the nursing home were responsible for their plant, which made them feel in control of their circumstances. The plant gave them a "thing," as Camus might put it—a purpose in their otherwise monotonous lives, and this motivated them. More recent research bears this out: older people who report having more purpose in life live longer than those who report having less. They have a reason to get out of bed in the morning—a reason, even, to go on living.

Indeed, a growing body of research suggests that meaning can protect against numerous ailments. Having meaning in life, for example, has been associated with longevity, better immune functioning, and more gray matter in the brain. Purpose, in particular, has been shown to have a wide range of health benefits. It decreases the likelihood of mild cognitive impairments, Alzheimer's disease, and strokes. Among those who have heart disease, having purpose diminishes the chances of having a heart attack—and people who lack purpose are at higher risk for cardiovascular disease.

It's unclear why exactly meaning and health have such a strong relationship, but some psychologists speculate that people leading meaningful lives may take better care of themselves. Research finds that they're less likely to smoke cigarettes and drink alcohol, have better exercise and sleep habits, and maintain better diets. They are also more likely to use preventive health services. "If you invest in life," as meaning researcher Michael Steger has put it, "you invest in health." These findings have policy implications in a world where healthcare costs are rising, the population is rapidly aging, and people are living longer than ever. According to the World Health Organization, the proportion of individuals over 60 in the world will double by the middle of this century—and, in the United States, one fifth of the population will be over sixty-five years old by 2050.

Unfortunately, as people age, research finds that their sense of purpose declines. With retirement, their primary identities—mother, Little League coach, doctor, supervisor—weaken or vanish, and they often struggle to replace their old roles with new ones. Can cultures of meaning help these people live healthier lives? Many innovators think so. Marc Freedman, for example, is the founder of an organization called Encore.org, which does for older adults what The Future Project does for teenagers—inspiring them to craft a new purpose for themselves during retirement.

Many think of retirement as a vacation, a time when they can golf, spend time at the beach, or travel unburdened by the responsibilities of their younger years. That attitude is certainly understandable. After a busy life of going to school, raising children, and working, it's natural to want a break. The problem, though, is that this mindset kills meaning. Purpose arises from having something to do. "Nothing is so insufferable to man as to be completely at rest, without passions, without business, without diversion, without study," wrote the French philosopher Blaise Pascal in his *Pensées*. "He then feels his nothingness, his forlornness, his insufficiency, his dependence, his weakness, his emptiness. There will immediately arise from the depth of his heart weariness, gloom, sadness, fretfulness, vexation, despair." When the elderly believe they still have a part to play in society, though, they maintain a strong sense of purpose.

Freedman wants to radically reframe retirement from a time of leisure to a time when people use the skills and experiences they've accumulated over a lifetime to improve society. Encore creates opportunities for them to do so by matching retirees to organizations that have a social purpose for yearlong fellowships. Former engineer Pam Mulhall, for example, did her Encore Fellowship at an organization called Crossroads for Women in Albuquerque, where she used her technology skills to build a database to help women struggling with addiction and homelessness find housing and jobs. After the fellowship, many fellows move into part- or full-time jobs with their host organizations or find new roles using their skills in the nonprofit sector.

In addition to its fellowship program, Encore also maintains a story bank of people who have moved into "encore careers"—and these stories, Encore hopes, will help change our culture's narrative of retirement and inspire others to adopt new purposes in their later years. Tom Hendershot, whose story is featured on the Encore website, for example, is a retired police officer who now creates dinosaur art and builds exhibitions for museums. People like Mulhall and Hendershot are actively engaged in the "second act" of their lives, as Freedman puts it—and though their second acts can be wildly different from their first, there is usually some connection between their early career and their encore one.

Cultures of meaning can also be created with the help of public policy. In 2006, the World Health Organization launched the Global Age-Friendly Cities project to encourage city leaders to design communities that foster positive aging. One of the cities to have taken up the WHO's cause is New York, and it has become a model for other communities hoping to make life more enriching for their older citizens. The president of the New York Academy of Medicine, Dr. Jo Ivey Boufford, helped to establish the WHO criteria for an age-friendly city and advocated to implement the model in New York. "Age-Friendly New York City" was launched in 2007 as a partnership between the academy, the mayor's office, and the city council. Its goal is to enhance the health and well-being of older adults by making the city a more inclusive and humane home for them. "From the city's standpoint," said Lindsay Goldman of the academy, who directs the project, "this makes good financial sense. If you promote health and well-being, you'll have fewer people who are becoming dependent and in need of social insurance programs and city services."

When the project first launched, officials held community forums and focus groups across the five boroughs to hear from older New Yorkers about what they liked and didn't like about the city. A few topics came up again and again, but one overarching theme united many of their comments. Like most people, they simply wanted to lead good, fulfilling lives. But as they've grown older, there have been more and more obstacles getting in the way of that goal. Some of their concerns were practical, like pedestrian safety and the lack of affordable housing. Others said they wanted to be as engaged with the community as they were when they were younger, but worried about being, or had been, marginalized or disrespected because of their age. "I'd like to do something that I can be proud of," one New Yorker said. "I don't mind getting old. I just want to be doing something."

Over the last decade, program leaders have continued the dialogue, and they've enacted many initiatives to address the concerns older New Yorkers have raised. For example, the Department of Transportation installed more bus shelters throughout the city and ensured they had seating and transparent walls so that seniors would feel comfortable and safe inside of them. They added more benches throughout the city to promote walking, and some city pools have implemented special senior hours so that the adults don't have to worry about being overrun by young children. These changes are small but significant. In a fast-paced city that can be exhausting to navigate, these enhancements make life a little bit easier for older New Yorkers and give them the chance to participate more fully in their communities, helping to bolster their sense of belonging. "People socialize," said one woman during senior hours at a pool: "And being around people their own age—our age, I should say—you are not self-conscious of who's looking."

These age-friendly initiatives are designed not only to provide assistance and support, but also to give seniors an opportunity to use their strengths to give back to the community—to live with purpose. Success Mentor, for example, is an initiative that connects older individuals with at-risk school-aged children. Through Success Mentor, dozens of adults are mentoring and tutoring students at schools all across the city. As a result of such programs, students perform better academically and experience fewer disciplinary problems. But there are also benefits for the adults: studies show that when adults volunteer in their communities as mentors to kids, their physical and mental health improves.

Nursing homes where neglect and abuse run rampant may soon become relics of a bygone era as cultures of meaning emerge that redefine the role elderly people play in society. From Encore's Marc Freedman to bureaucrats in New York, more and more people are realizing that older adults can contribute a great deal to the community, and should be supported in their desire to do so. "It's hard to have a life of meaning and purpose," said Lindsay Goldman, "when you can't do all of those things you've loved to do throughout your life." By expanding opportunities for older adults, New York is now trying to change that.

TRANSCENDENCE AND PURPOSE are not the only pillars that institutions rely upon to create cultures of meaning. Age-friendly New York City is working to enhance belonging among older New Yorkers by emphasizing that they are valued members of the community. At St. Mark's and DreamCon, people come together over shared interests and form a unique community. And likewise, the staff at Life is Good are a tight-knit tribe of optimists—and Bert and John have crafted a compelling story that explains the origin and significance of the brand. The pillars of belonging and storytelling also define the mission of another organization that is dedicated to creating a culture of meaning in our society—StoryCorps, an oral history project founded by journalist Dave Isay.

Isay got hooked on storytelling as a young man. After graduating from New York University, the twenty-two-year-old was planning to attend medical school when a walk through the East Village changed his life. He passed by a storefront that looked interesting, went inside, and met the married proprietors—Angel and Carmen Perez. Their shop, full of self-help books, was for people recovering from addiction. As he spoke to them, Isay learned that they had been heroin addicts, that Carmen had HIV, and that they dreamed of opening a museum of addiction before Carmen died. "They showed me scale models of the building," Isay wrote, "which they'd constructed out of tongue depressors and plywood. They had blueprints for every floor and intricate drawings of each exhibit."

Deeply affected by the conversation, Isay went home and called the local television and radio stations, suggesting they cover Angel and Carmen's story. No one was interested except for a community radio station called WBAI. The station didn't have a reporter on hand, so the news director told Isay to put the story together himself. "When I went back to their store, and sat with them and hit record on my recorder," Isay said, "I knew that this is what I would be doing with the rest of my life."

Over the next two decades, Isay worked as a radio producer and documentary maker telling the stories of, as he has put it, "underdogs in hidden corners of the country." He focused on the people whom society has traditionally overlooked: prisoners, drug addicts, the homeless, and the poor—people like Carmen and Angel. During the process of interviewing these individuals, he learned that the simple act of listening to another person could make that person feel valued, respected, and dignified. It kindled belonging. As he asked the people he interviewed his standard questions—how they would like to be remembered, who matters to them, what they are proud of—he saw their backs straighten and eyes light up. Isay realized that no one had ever asked them about their lives like that before; no one had ever taken a genuine interest in hearing their stories.

When one of his radio documentaries, which was about the last flophouses in New York, turned into a book, he took the proofs of it to the homeless men he had interviewed. "One of the men," Isay wrote, "looked at his story, took it in his hands, and literally danced through the halls of the old hotel shouting, 'I exist! I exist!'" Isay couldn't believe what he was seeing. "I realized as never before," he wrote, "how many people among us feel completely invisible, believe their lives don't matter, and fear they'll someday be forgotten." Listening, Isay realized, is "an act of love"—a way to make people feel like they and their stories matter. Research confirms this: sharing stories strengthens the bond between the listener and the storyteller and makes people feel that their lives are meaningful and have dignity and worth.

Isay founded StoryCorps in 2003 to give ordinary people the opportunity to tell their stories and be heard. In the StoryBooth, he created an intimate space where two people could come together and honor one another through the act of listening. He opened the first StoryBooth in Grand Central Terminal in New York. Though the Grand Central booth closed in 2008, there are other booths today in New York, Atlanta, Chicago, and San Francisco, as well as a mobile booth that travels around the country to record stories. What happens inside is the same today as it was back then. Two people who care about one another meet in the booth, which looks like a metal capsule, where they have an intimate and uninterrupted conversation for forty minutes. One person in the booth assumes the role of the interviewer, while the other speaks about some aspect of his or her life. A facilitator in the booth records the interview.

After the interview, the participants receive a recording of the conversation. With participant permission, a copy of the recording is sent to the American Folklife Center at the Library of Congress, where it is archived, giving participants some measure of immortality. The sessions are free: anyone can make an appointment to record one—and tens of thousands have. By collecting a wide variety of stories from people across the country, Isay hopes StoryCorps will preserve the "wisdom of humanity."

But StoryCorps also has a more radical aim. It sees storytelling as a way to combat certain harmful aspects of our existing culture, like materialism, which research shows leads people to be more self-oriented and is associated with having less meaning in life. In 2008, StoryCorps launched an initiative called the National Day of Listening to encourage Americans to record stories with family members, friends, and loved ones on Black Friday, the pre-Christmas shopping bonanza that occurs the day after Thanksgiving. This act of resistance against consumer culture was rebranded as the Great Thanksgiving Listen in 2015. Working with schools across the nation, StoryCorps asked students to record the story of an older relative on an app on their phone—taking a technology that can separate and isolate individuals and using it to foster human connection. "We want to shake people on the shoulders and remind them of what's important," Isay said.

In October of 2015, I traveled to the StoryCorps office in Chicago to speak to people about the experience of sharing their stories. As I waited for one couple to come out of the booth, a facilitator named Yvette approached me to say that there was a woman who had made an appointment and needed a partner to interview her. This woman's friend, who had agreed to come with her, could no longer make it. Would I be willing to step in?

The woman's name was Mary Anna Elsey, and she was a fifty-one-year-old schoolteacher from South Carolina who was visiting Chicago for the weekend. Mary Anna and I shook hands and chatted for a few minutes before we stepped inside of the booth, taking our seats across from each other at a small table. Yvette positioned the microphone in front of us and then closed the door of the booth, sealing us into the quiet wood-paneled room, away from the noises and distractions of the outside world. The lights were dim and the room was bare. We turned our cellphones off. All Mary Anna and I had to focus on in this almost sacred space was each other. Yvette fiddled with the recording equipment. Then she gave us a silent cue that it was time to begin the conversation.

Before we entered the booth, Mary Anna had told me that she had been adopted when she was a baby. Inside the booth, I asked her to tell me the story of her adoption. "My parents realized that they couldn't have children together," she began in her Southern twang. "This was back in the late fifties and early sixties. Their doctor told them that if they wanted to get divorced because of this, that would be an acceptable reason. But they said no, they'd rather adopt." They adopted Mary Anna's older brother and sister, and then welcomed Mary Anna into their home in 1964, when she was only eighteen days old.

You can take being adopted in one of two ways, Mary Anna said. Either you are grateful that your adoptive parents wanted you, or you are angry that your biological parents didn't. Mary Anna fell into the first camp. "I never questioned anything about my adoption because I loved my mom and dad so much," she said. As she got older, though, Mary Anna felt a yearning to find out more about her birth parents. While she remembers her childhood as full of warmth, she also recalls keeping to herself and feeling lonely quite a bit. She always had many friends at school, but she nonetheless felt isolated from others. She also struggled with depression. Tracking down her biological parents, she thought, might help her understand herself—and her emotional turmoil—a bit better.

After she gave birth to her second child, Mary Anna wrote to the state asking them to send her any information they could about her biological parents. Seven days later, she knew her biological mother's name. She learned that Effie had been the salutatorian of her high school class. She learned that Effie had been working as a nurse and was unmarried when she got pregnant with Mary Anna in 1963. And she learned that, over the course of their lives, she and Effie had been at a wedding and a funeral together without realizing it.

She also learned that Effie was now living in Charleston. When Mary Anna told her husband, he suggested that they call his uncle Donald, a child psychologist in Charleston, and ask if he knew her. "And so he called Donald," Mary Anna said of her husband, "and he said, 'Donald, have you ever heard of a nurse by the name of Effie?' And Donald said, 'Yeah, she's standing right here, do you want to talk to her?' My husband said, 'Donald, that's Mary Anna's mother.' And he said 'Effie?' and she turned and looked at him."

Mary Anna met Effie a few weeks later in Charleston. They had a cordial lunch. Mary Anna assured her she had led a good life. Effie told her about her two sons. She also explained that she put Mary Anna up for adoption because she thought she'd have a better life. Afterward, the two women parted ways and never saw each other again.

The meeting helped Mary Anna gain a new perspective on herself and on her relationship with her own three daughters. "You can only imagine," Mary Anna said, "what Effie was feeling as she was expecting a baby, knowing she can't keep it, making a decision to give a child away. How much of my personality—of my temperament—was affected by my in utero experience?" She wondered if spending her first seventeen days on earth in a foster home, with no consistent and strong bond with a caregiver, contributed to her loneliness and depression. She thought about the "hard" and "courageous" decision Effie made to give her up so she could lead a better life. She realized that it was a decision she could never have made.

Motherhood was much on Mary Anna's mind in the booth. She and her husband were about to become empty nesters. One of their daughters was in pharmacy school. Another was heading to law school. And the youngest was getting ready to graduate from high school. For a woman who defined her identity primarily in terms of being a mother—in large part because she never knew her own biological mother—letting go of her children was a deeply painful process.

"What does it mean to you to be a mom?" I asked.

Mary Anna's lips tightened and she started fanning her face with her fingers. "You're going to make me cry, Emily!" she said, laughing.

Your goal as a mother, she explained, is to prepare your children to face the world on their own. Her greatest achievement in life has been accomplishing that goal: with her husband, she has raised three strong and independent girls who no longer need her. "That's also the hardest thing about being a mother," Mary Anna said as she started to cry. She could barely get out the next words through her tears: "They don't need you."

"What's going to give my life meaning and purpose," she asked, "now that I've done my most important and challenging job in life?"

The interview ended. Mary Anna and I stepped outside of the booth and continued our conversation. I asked her what the experience was like of telling her story in the booth. It was cathartic: "It made me feel heard," she said, "like someone wanted to listen to me." She said things in the booth, she explained, that she would never have said in an ordinary conversation with friends and loved ones back home. There was something about the booth that made her open up, and that helped her build meaning.

For Mary Anna, the forty minutes in the booth enabled her to gain insight into her past experiences and present relationships. "Part of the reason I feel lonely," she said, "is because I don't tell people things. I hold my thoughts and feelings inside. This taught me that I should make more of a point of talking to others—and not just for me, but for them. When we tell our story, we do two things. We understand ourselves better and we offer support to people going through the same thing that we're going through."

We also leave behind a legacy. The reason Mary Anna came to StoryCorps was that she was attracted to the idea of leaving behind a record of her story for her grandchildren and great-grandchildren to hear. "We live in this world where we seem so little compared to everything that's going on. After a couple of generations, no one even remembers who you are," Mary Anna said. "So this is a way to leave something permanent behind."

Conclusion

DEATH, AS MARY ANNA IMPLIED, POSES A GRAVE challenge to the ability to lead a meaningful life. If our lives will end anyway and we will soon be forgotten, what is the point of anything we do? This is the problem that led Will Durant to write that letter to his friends. In the absence of a definitive belief in an afterlife, the philosopher was in search of "a meaning that cannot be annulled by death."

Is there one?

William Breitbart, the chairman of the Department of Psychiatry and Behavioral Sciences at New York's Memorial Sloan Kettering Cancer Center, specializes in end-of-life care for terminally ill cancer patients. He has devoted the better part of his life to answering the challenge that death poses to meaning. His groundbreaking research shows that while the specter of death often leads people to conclude that their lives are meaningless, it can also be a catalyst for them to work out, as they have never done before, the meaning of their lives. Contemplating death can actually help us, if we have the proper mindset, to lead more meaningful lives and to be at peace when our final moment on earth arrives.

Meaning and death, Breitbart believes, are two sides of the

same coin—the two fundamental problems of the human condition. How should a human being live a finite life? How can we face death with dignity and not despair? What redeems the fact that we will die? These questions roll around Breitbart's mind every day as he works with patients facing life's final challenge.

Breitbart was born in 1951 and grew up on the Lower East Side of Manhattan. His parents, Jews from eastern Poland, narrowly avoided Hitler's death camps. During the war, they hid from the Nazis in the woods, and his father fought in the underground resistance movement. After the war ended, the two of them found themselves in a displaced-persons camp, and it was there that they got married. When they moved to America, they carried their memories of the war years with them. Breitbart's childhood was steeped in that tragic past. Every morning, his mother would ask him at the breakfast table, "Why am I here?" Why, she wondered, did she live when so many others had died?

"I grew up with a sense of responsibility to justify my parents' survival and to create something in the world that would be significant enough to make my life worthwhile. It's no coincidence," he laughed, "that I ended up at Sloan Kettering, where the people wear striped gowns and are facing death."

Breitbart came to Sloan Kettering in 1984 because he wanted to live "at the edge of life and death." It was the height of the AIDS epidemic, and young men Breitbart's age were dying all around him. "They were constantly asking me to help them die," he said. He was also working with terminal cancer patients. "When I walked in the room, they would say, 'I only have three months to live. If that's all I have, I see no value or purpose to living.' This was not an atypical response. They said, 'If you want to help me, kill me.' "

"Everybody said how important it is to have a positive attitude," one woman, a former IBM executive who had been diagnosed with colon cancer, said. "But I'm not Lance Armstrong. I wanted to jump in the grave." If death means nonexistence, Breitbart's patients reasoned, then what meaning could life possibly have? And if life has no meaning, there's no point of suffering through cancer.

By the nineties, physician-assisted suicide was a hot topic in Breitbart's circles and beyond. Dr. Jack Kevorkian, known then as Dr. Death, had helped his first patient end her life in 1990. He claimed he helped another 130 patients end their lives over the next eight years. As the United States debated the ethics of assisted suicide, other countries were taking steps toward normalizing the practice. In 1996, the Northern Territory of Australia legalized assisted suicide, only to later rescind the law. Then, in 2000, the Netherlands became the first nation to make physician-assisted suicide legal. In 2006, the United States took a big step in that direction with the Supreme Court decision in *Gonzales v. Oregon,* which allowed states to make their own decisions on assisted suicide. Today, the practice is legal in California, Vermont, Montana, Washington, and Oregon. In 2014, the *Journal of Medical Ethics* released a report indicating the growth of "suicide tourism." Between 2009 and 2012, the number of people who traveled to Zurich, Switzerland, where assisted suicide is legal, seeking to end their lives, doubled.

As Breitbart heard more and more stories of assisted suicide, he began to wonder what specifically was driving the terminally ill to give up on life. At the time, he was doing a series of research studies on pain and fatigue at the end of life, so he tacked onto those studies some questions that asked his subjects whether they felt a desire for a hastened death. What he discovered surprised him. The assumption had been that the ill chose to end their lives because they were in terrible pain. But Breitbart and his colleagues found that wasn't always the case. Instead, those who desired a hastened death reported feelings of meaninglessness, depression, and hopelessness. They were living in an "existential vacuum." When Breitbart asked patients why they wanted a prescription for assisted suicide, many said it was because they had lost meaning in life.

Breitbart knew he could treat depression—there were medicines and well-developed psychotherapies for that—but he was stumped when it came to treating meaninglessness. Then, in 1995, he began to see a way forward. He was invited to join the Project on Death in America, which aimed to improve the experience of dying. Breitbart and his colleagues on the project—who included philosophers, a monk, and other physicians—had long conversations about death and the meaning of life, "peppered with references to people like Nietzsche and Kierkegaard and Schopenhauer," Breitbart said.

"What I suddenly discovered," Breitbart explained, "was the importance of meaning—the search for meaning, the need to create meaning, the ability to experience meaning—was a basic motivating force of human behavior. We were not taught this stuff at medical school!" Breitbart became convinced that if he could help patients build meaning, he could decrease their suicidal thoughts and urges, protect them from depression, improve their quality of life, and make them more hopeful about the future. In short, he believed he could make their lives worth living even to the very end.

He developed an eight-session group therapy program where six to eight cancer patients come together in a counseling workshop. Each session, in one way or another, helps build a meaning mindset. In the first session they are asked to reflect on "one or two experiences or moments when life has felt particularly meaningful to you—whether it sounds powerful or mundane."

The second session deals with identity "BC and AD"—that is, with who the individuals were *before the cancer diagnosis* and who they are *after the diagnosis*. They are encouraged to respond to the question "Who am I?" to tap into the identities that give them the most meaning. One woman responded saying, "I am a daughter, a mother, a grandmother, a sister, a friend and a neighbor. . . . I'm somebody who can be very private and not always share all my needs and concerns. I also have been working on accepting love and affection and other gifts from other people." She reflected on how the illness was changing who she was: "I don't like to receive care, but I'm beginning to, . . . actually . . . this may be the one thing that my illness has caused me to mull over. That I'm more accepting of people wanting to do things."

In the third and fourth sessions, they share the story of their life with the group. "When you look back on your life and upbringing," they are asked, "what are the most significant memories, relationships, traditions, and so on, that have made the greatest impact on who you are today?" They also discuss their accomplishments and points of pride, and what they still have left to do. They think about lessons that they want to pass along to others. For homework, they are asked to share their story with a loved one.

Session five is one of the most difficult. Here, they confront life's limitations—the greatest limitation of all being death. They talk to each other about what they consider a "good" death: whether they want to die at home or in the hospital, what their funeral will look like, how they hope their families will adapt in the aftermath, and how they want to be remembered by those who love them.

In the next two sessions, they dwell on their "creative" and "experiential" sources of meaning—the people, places, projects, and ideas that helped them express their most important values and "connect to life." They discuss their responsibilities and any "unfinished business" they have and what's preventing them from accomplishing those goals. They're also asked to think about the role that love, beauty, and humor played in their lives. Many people mention their families here. Others discuss work, or hobbies like keeping a garden. The former IBM executive mentioned seeing the statue of winged victory, the *Nike of Samothrace*, at the Louvre in Paris when she was a young woman.

In the final session, the patients consider their hopes for the future and their legacy, the part of them that will go on living even after they are dead. They present a "legacy project" to the group, which is generally something they do or create that represents how they want to be remembered. One man brought in a woodcut of a heart sculpted into a Celtic Trinity. "This is what I will teach my children," he said, "that there is eternal love and that I will be there for them, far beyond my passing."

Breitbart performed three randomized controlled experiments on the meaning-centered psychotherapy, giving it to several hundred patients. When he analyzed the results with his colleagues, Breitbart saw the therapy had been transformative. By the end of the eight sessions, the patients' attitudes toward life and death had changed. They were less hopeless and anxious about the prospect of death. They no longer wanted to die. Their spiritual well-being improved. They reported a higher quality of life. And, of course, they found life to be more meaningful. These effects not only persisted over time—they actually got stronger. When Breitbart followed up with one group of patients two months later, he found that their reports of meaning and spiritual well-being had increased, while their feelings of anxiety, hopelessness, and desire for death had decreased. The time between diagnosis and death, as Breitbart saw, presents an opportunity for "extraordinary growth." The former IBM executive, for example, was initially devastated by her diagnosis—but after enrolling in the therapy program, she realized, "I didn't have to work so hard to find the meaning of life. It was being handed to me everywhere I looked."

Breitbart's ideas are catching on. Doctors in Italy, Canada, Germany, Denmark, and beyond are using his therapeutic methods to infuse the lives of their otherwise hopeless and despairing patients with meaning. "The reaction in the field was explosive," Breitbart said. "They hadn't paid attention to it before, but now everyone and their cousins have suddenly started discovering meaning."

Breitbart developed his meaning-centered psychotherapy for the terminally ill, but the lessons gleaned from his research can help anyone live a better life. No matter how near or far off death may be in each of our individual cases, thinking about death forces us to evaluate our lives as they are and to consider what we would change about them to make them more meaningful. Psychologists call this "the deathbed test." Imagine that you're at the end of your life. Perhaps a freak accident or diagnosis of disease has suddenly shortened your life, or maybe you have lived a long and healthy life, and are now in your eighties or nineties. Sitting on your deathbed, with only days ahead of you to live, reflecting on the way you have led your life and what you have done and not done, are you satisfied with what you see? Did you live a good and fulfilling life? Is it a life you are glad that you led? If you could live your life over again, what would you do differently?

Many people on their actual deathbeds fear that the lives

they led were not meaningful enough. Bronnie Ware, a former palliative-care worker, found that at the end of her patients' lives, their regrets fell into the same basic categories. Their principal regrets included not following their true aspirations and purposes, giving too much of themselves to their careers rather than spending more time with their children and spouses, and not keeping in better touch with their friends. They wish they had spent more time during their lives building the pillars of meaning.

Breitbart has thought a great deal about the challenge death posed to another group of individuals—the victims and survivors of the Holocaust. After Breitbart joined the Project on Death in America, he read the book *Man's Search for Meaning* by Holocaust survivor Viktor Frankl about his experiences in the concentration camps. The book made a powerful impression on Breitbart, as it has on millions of people, and he developed his meaning-centered therapy after reading it. He gives each of the patients who receives his therapy a copy of Frankl's book to read, hoping that though their circumstances may differ, they may find in one man's struggle with suffering a source of wisdom and consolation.

IN SEPTEMBER 1942, Frankl, a Jewish psychiatrist and neurologist in Vienna, was arrested and transported to a Nazi concentration camp with his wife and parents. Three years later, when his camp was liberated, most of his family, including his wife, had perished—but he, prisoner number 119,104, had lived.

In *Man's Search for Meaning*, Frankl describes the importance of finding meaning in suffering. The prisoners in the camps lost everything—their families, their liberty, their former identities, and their possessions. Many, as a result, concluded that they had nothing more to live for and abandoned hope. But some continued to believe their lives were meaningful. Frankl saw that the prisoners who found or maintained a sense of meaning, even in the most horrendous circumstances, were far more resilient to suffering than those who did not. Those who had a reason to live, he argued, were even more "apt to survive" in the face of starvation, sickness, exhaustion, and the general degradation of camp life.

Frankl worked as a therapist in the camps, and in his book he tells the story of two suicidal inmates he counseled there. Like many of the people around them, these two men believed that they had nothing left to live for. "In both cases," Frankl writes, "it was a question of getting them to realize that life was still expecting something from them; something in the future was expected of them." For one man, it was his young child, who was still alive. For the other, a scientist, it was a series of books that he hoped to finish writing. As Frankl observed more and more inmates, he saw that those men and women who knew the "why" for their existence, as Nietzsche put it, could withstand almost any "how."

He was also struck by how some people were able to maintain their dignity despite the dehumanizing conditions by choosing how to respond to the suffering they faced and saw others endure. "We who lived in concentration camps," he wrote, "can remember the men who walked through the huts comforting others, giving away their last piece of bread. They may have been few in number, but they offer sufficient proof that everything can be taken from a man but one thing: the last of the human freedoms—to choose one's attitude in any given set of circumstances, to choose one's own way."

Before his arrest, Frankl had established himself as one of

the leading psychiatrists in Vienna. His interest in psychology and meaning had been intense and precocious. When he was about thirteen years old, one of his science teachers declared to the class, "Life is nothing more than a combustion process, a process of oxidation." But Frankl would have none of it. "Sir, if this is so," he cried, jumping out of his chair, "then what can be the meaning of life?" A couple of years later, he struck up a correspondence with Sigmund Freud and sent Freud a paper he had written. Freud, impressed by Frankl's talent, sent the paper to the *International Journal of Psychoanalysis* for publication. ("I hope you have no objection," Freud wrote the teenager.)

During and after medical school, Frankl distinguished himself even further. Not only did he establish suicide-prevention centers for teenagers—a precursor to his work in the camps—but he also developed his signature contribution to the field of psychology: logotherapy. Frankl believed that people have a "will to meaning," and that this drive to find meaning in life is the "primary motivational force in man." The purpose of logotherapy, then, was to treat the distress and suffering of his patients by helping them find meaning in their lives. By 1941, Frankl's theories had received international attention, and he was working as the chief of neurology at Vienna's Rothschild Hospital, where he risked his life and career by making false diagnoses of mentally ill patients to keep them from being killed by the Nazis.

That same year, Frankl faced a decision that changed his life. With both a rising career and the threat of the Nazis looming over him, Frankl had applied for and was granted a visa to America. By that time, the Nazis had already started taking Jews away to concentration camps, focusing on the elderly first. Frankl knew that it was only a matter of time before the Nazis came to take his parents away. He also knew that once they did, he had a responsibility to be there with them to help them. Still, he was tempted to leave for America, where he would find both safety and professional success.

Frankl was at a loss for what to do, so he set out for St. Stephen's Cathedral in Vienna to clear his head. Listening to the organ music, he repeatedly asked himself, "Should I leave my parents behind? . . . Should I say goodbye and leave them to their fate?" Where did his responsibility lie? He was looking for a "hint from heaven."

When he returned home, he found it. A piece of marble was sitting on the table. His father explained that it was from the wreckage of one of the synagogues that the Nazis had destroyed. The marble contained the fragment of one of the Ten Commandments—the one about honoring your father and your mother. With that, Frankl decided to stay in Vienna and forgo whatever opportunities for safety and career advancement awaited him in the United States. He put aside a life of comfort to serve his family and, later, other prisoners in the camps.

During his three years in the concentration camps, Frankl began many of his mornings in more or less the same way. He woke up before the sun rose and marched for miles to a dismal work site, where he and his fellow inmates were forced to dig ditches in the frozen ground as Nazi guards loomed over them with rifles and whips. During the march, the winter wind would cut through their threadbare clothing. They were starving and exhausted, and those who were too weak to walk on their own held themselves up against the men next to them. In the darkness, they tried their best to not fall over the rocks standing in their way as the Nazis shoved them along with the ends of their rifles. If they fell out of line, the guards beat and kicked them.

One day, Frankl managed to transcend the indignity of this morning routine. As he was marching along, an inmate next to him turned to him and whispered: "If our wives could see us now! I do hope they are better off in their camps and don't know what is happening to us." That remark led Frankl to think about his wife, Tilly, who had been sent to a different concentration camp. Frankl did not know where she was or even if she was alive, but he held the thought of her in his mind that morning, and this brought him hope. "I heard her answering me," he recalled later; "saw her smile, her frank and encouraging look. Real or not, her look was then more luminous than the sun which was beginning to rise."

Then Frankl had an epiphany. On that cold and grim march, with nothing except the warm memory of Tilly to bring him comfort, he realized that he understood the meaning of life. "For the first time in my life," he explained, "I saw the truth as it is set into song by so many poets, proclaimed as the final wisdom by so many thinkers." That truth, he writes, was "that love is the ultimate and the highest goal to which man can aspire. Then I grasped the meaning of the greatest secret that human poetry and human thought and belief have to impart: *The salvation of man is through love and in love.*"

As he turned these thoughts over in his mind, an ugly scene unfolded before him. An inmate had tripped and fallen, leading other inmates to fall like dominoes behind him. A Nazi guard ran over and started whipping them. But not even this image of cruelty, nor any other horror he had experienced up to that point or would experience before he was finally freed, could shake the faith he now had that the meaning of life lay in love.

"I understood," he wrote, "how a man who has nothing

left in this world still may know bliss, be it only for a brief moment, in the contemplation of his beloved. In a position of utter desolation, when man cannot express himself in positive action, when his only achievement may consist in enduring his sufferings in the right way—an honorable way—in such a position man can, through loving contemplation of the image he carries of his beloved, achieve fulfillment. For the first time in my life I was able to understand the meaning of the words 'The angels are lost in perpetual contemplation of an infinite glory.' "

Love, of course, is at the center of the meaningful life. Love cuts through each of the pillars of meaning and comes up again and again in the stories of those I have written about. Think of when the SCA members organized a fundraiser for their sick friend. Or when Ashley Richmond enhanced the lives of the giraffes at the Detroit Zoo. Or when Emeka Nnaka emerged from his accident to serve others. Or when Jeff Ashby dedicated himself to helping people experience the Overview Effect. Or when Shibvon resolved to make the lives of vulnerable children better than hers had been.

The act of love begins with the very definition of meaning: it begins by stepping outside of the self to connect with and contribute to something bigger. "Being human," Frankl wrote, "always points, and is directed, to something, or someone, other than oneself—be it a meaning to fulfill or another human being to encounter. The more one forgets himself—by giving himself to a cause to serve or another person to love—the more human he is."

That's the power of meaning. It's not some great revelation. It's pausing to say hi to a newspaper vendor and reaching out to someone at work who seems down. It's helping people get in better shape and being a good parent or mentor to a child. It's sitting in awe beneath a starry night sky and going to a medieval prayer service with friends. It's opening a coffee shop for struggling veterans. It's listening attentively to a loved one's story. It's taking care of a plant. These may be humble acts on their own. But taken together, they light up the world.

Acknowledgments

That this book exists is a testament to the generosity of the people I've been lucky enough to call family, friends, and colleagues over the years. They've sustained, supported, and inspired me—and to the extent that this book has anything valuable to say, their guidance has made it so.

My parents modeled what it means to live meaningfully, taught me the central place that love and compassion play in a life that matters, and helped me to find beauty and goodness in the ordinary—those little moments of meaning that light up the world. I'm also eternally grateful for the many sacrifices they've made for me, for their guidance and support over all the years of my life, and for nurturing my curiosity and encouraging me to think creatively and independently. They knew me better than I knew myself, and helped me find my path when I was lost. I'm enormously grateful, also, to my brother Tristan, who was always willing to help me out by answering my many (sometimes annoying) questions—"Do you have a sense of purpose?" "What makes your life meaningful?" "Do you ever think about your legacy?" etc.—and sharing his valuable insights about meaning. He inspired much of the chapter on purpose and gave me an emerging adult's perspective on the search for meaning.

This book would not exist without my incredible agents, Bridget Wagner Matzie and Todd Shuster. Bridget and Todd saw potential where I did not, and helped to translate my mess of ideas into a coherent book proposal. They not only shepherded me through the publishing process, but also were always there to brainstorm ideas, answer questions, and provide comments on the numerous proposal and book drafts I sent. I couldn't ask for more zealous agents, or for more supportive friends.

Rachel Klayman is the editor of my dreams: brilliant, creative, engaged, and kind. She poured her love and care into this book with enthusiasm and craftsmanship—and has been this book's number one champion in innumerable ways. Associate editor Emma Berry's thoughtful letters, comments, and editorial suggestions brought this book to another level. It's been a privilege to work with both of them.

The team at Crown worked tirelessly to bring this book out into the world, and I'm grateful to publicity director Rachel Rokicki, associate marketing director Lisa Erickson, art director Chris Brand, and editorial assistant Jon Darga. Thanks also to Kevin Callahan, Lauren Dong, Lance Fitzgerald, Wade Lucas, Mark McCauslin, Sarah Pekdemir, Annsley Rosner, Courtney Snyder, Molly Stern, and Heather Williamson. Judith Kendra, Nicole Winstanley, Nick Garrison, Regine Dugardyn, and my other international publishers introduced this work to a global audience.

Jonathan Haidt and Martin Seligman, both of whom mentored me throughout this book-writing process, have been intellectual guides and inspirations. Jon taught me to think in new ways about old topics. Marty championed this book from the very start, and was always there to answer an email, read a draft, or push back against my faulty reasoning. I'm also indebted to Adam Grant, who not only taught me about the roles meaning and purpose play in organizations and beyond, but also introduced me to a number of fascinating paragons of meaning, one of whom is profiled in this book. And I wouldn't have had the courage to pursue writing as a career had it not been for Jeffrey Hart, Marlene Heck, and David Wykes. Thanks also to Julia Annas, Roy Baumeister, Paul Bloom, William Damon, Ed Diener, Angela Duckworth, Jane Dutton, Barbara Fredrickson, Emily Garbinsky, Veronika Huta, Scott Barry Kaufman, Laura King, Anthony Kronman, Matt Lieberman, Dan McAdams, Darrin McMahon, Russell Muirhead, Andrew Newberg, Ken Pargament, James Pawelski, Judy Saltzberg, Michael Steger, Roger Ulrich, Kathleen Vohs, Susan Wolf, Paul Wong, and Amy Wrzesniewski for their wisdom and time.

Over the years, I've had colleagues who have encouraged and inspired me. James Panero gave me my first writing job, was a committed mentor, and is a generous friend. Tunku Varadarajan taught me the value of an idiosyncratic mind—and of the finer things in life. Chris Dauer magnanimously supported my development and ideas. Roger Kimball gave me a home and a second college education at *The New Criterion*. David Yezzi, Cricket Farnsworth, Eric Simpson, Brian Kelly, Rebecca Hecht, Mary Ross, and Rebecca Litt made day-to-day life more fun and stimulating. Susan Arellano, Melanie Kirkpatrick, Eric Kraus, Paul and Emma Simpson, and Marisa Smith all opened doors for me and made a career in writing possible. And *The Atlantic*'s James Hamblin helped spark this book, which grew out of an article I wrote for him called "There's More to Life Than Being Happy."

Friends cheered me along and were always willing to talk meaning, especially Jennifer Aaker, Catherine Amble, Dan

Bowling, Anne Brafford, Leona Brandwene, Eleanor Brenner, Emily Brolsma, Lauren Caracciola, Meghan Danton, Taylor Dryman, Jordan and Samara Hirsch, Kian and Lexi Hudson, Liz Kahane, Willie Kalema, Zak Kelm, Taylor Kreiss, Amita Kulkarni, Emily Larson, Cory Muscara, Emma Palley, Lucy Randall, Mike Schmidt, Bit Smith, Carol Szurkowski, Ali Tanara, Layli Tanara, Paolo Terni, Dan Tomasulo, Emily Ulrich, Marcy Van Arnam, Christine Wells, and David Yaden. My whole extended family has provided love, support, and encouragement for this project.

Jennifer Aaker, Adam Grant, Charlie Hill, Roger Kimball, Darrin McMahon, James Panero, Lucy Randall, Reb Rebele, Judy Saltzberg, Martin Seligman, and David Yaden all took the time to read drafts of this book. Their comments made me a better thinker and writer.

The transcendence chapter wouldn't have been the same without Ginny and Mark Dameron, who said I'd find mystery and beauty at the McDonald Observatory and in Marfa, Texas, and were right. My conversations with them also made me think deeper about cultures of meaning—and their support, enthusiasm, and joyfulness for this project has helped to carry it along. I won the in-laws lottery.

I would also like to acknowledge the many people who opened up to me about their lives, their life's work, and their sources of meaning—from researchers in psychology labs to ordinary people leading extraordinary lives. Not all of them appear in this book by name, but all of them shaped and inspired some aspect of it. The best part of writing this book was meeting and getting to know and learn from them. Many of them also took the time to confirm facts from their lives and research. Any remaining errors or omissions are mine.

Finally, Charlie Dameron. Charlie was the angel on my

shoulder from the beginning to the end. He read every proposal draft, commented on each book draft, and was there with me in Fort Davis, Tangier, Cleveland, and beyond. We went in search of meaning all over the world together, but the most meaningful thing I did while writing this book was marrying this amazing and awe-inspiring man. He has pushed me to grow as a writer and as a person, taught me to love better and deeper, and gave me confidence when I was full of doubt. Every day with him is richer and fuller than the one before.

Notes

Introduction

1 **darvishes:** Readers may be more familiar with the spelling "dervish," as in a whirling dervish. "Darvish" is the Persian transliteration.

2 **"Ever since I was":** This is from the Sufi poem "The Masnai." It was always sung in Farsi at the meetinghouse, but this is a translation of it courtesy of my parents, Tim and Fataneh Smith.

2 **"Since love," he writes:** Farid ud-Din Attar, *The Conference of the Birds,* translated by Afkham Darbandi and Dick Davis (New York: Penguin Classics, 1984), 30.

2 **Those on the path are on:** For more on Sufism, see Javad Nurbakhsh, *Discourses on the Sufi Path* (New York: Khaniqahi Nimatullahi Publications, 1996) and *The Path: Sufi Practices* (New York: Khaniqahi Nimatullahi Publications, 2003); Seyyed Hossein Nasr, *The Garden of Truth* (PT Mizan Publika, 2007); Robert Frager and James Fadiman, *Essential Sufism* (New York: HarperCollins, 1999).

4 **great work of human literature:** Thanks to psychology researcher and meaning expert Michael Steger for pointing out the connection between Gilgamesh's story and the search for meaning.

4 **The first question addresses:** Though distinct, these questions are related. Knowing the meaning of life can help people find meaning within life, and living meaningfully can make life, on the whole, feel more significant. For example, living a meaningful life, many religious and cultural traditions say, will bring people closer to and help them understand the meaning *of* life, defined as something like God or Love or Being. And not knowing what the meaning of life is, some would say, makes it almost impossible to lead a meaningful life.

4 **no longer commands the authority:** In *A Secular Age* (Cambridge: Belknap Press, 2007), Charles Taylor addresses how, over the course of Western history, the unchallenged authority of religion eventually gave way to secularization, where religious practice became a choice—one path among many to lead a meaningful life.

5 **fewer people . . . important component:** Tobin Grant, "Graphs: 5 Signs of the 'Great Decline' of Religion in America," Religion News Service, August 1, 2014. Grant writes: "Religiosity in the United States is in the midst of what might be called 'The Great Decline.' Previous declines in religion pale in comparison. Over the past fifteen years, the drop in religiosity has been twice as great as the decline of the 1960s and 1970s. . . . 2013 had the lowest level of religiosity of any year we can measure." See Tobin Grant, "The Great Decline: 61 Years of Religiosity in One Graph, 2013 Hits a New Low," Religion News Service, August 5, 2014. For a more in-depth and academic treatment of religion's decline, see Tobin J. Grant, "Measuring Aggregate Religiosity in the United States, 1952–2005," *Sociological Spectrum* 28, no. 5 (2008): 460–76.

5 **one path among many . . . adrift:** Taylor, *A Secular Age*. "There is a generalized sense in our culture," as Taylor writes, "that with the eclipse of the transcendent, something may have been lost," 107.

5 **philosophy had largely abandoned:** Though this was true when I was a college student—and continues to be true in many philosophy departments today—there has been a renaissance over the last decade of work on meaning, the good life, and the virtues in academic philosophy. See, for example, the work of Julia Annas, Susan Wolf, Kristján Kristjánsson, Nancy Snow, and Franco Trivigno. The broad point of philosophy (and the humanities more generally) abandoning the question of meaning is addressed in Anthony T. Kronman, *Education's End: Why Our Colleges and Universities Have Given Up on the Meaning of Life* (New Haven: Yale University Press, 2007). The social scientist Jonathan Haidt, who writes about philosophy and psychology in his book *The Happiness Hypothesis* (New York: Basic Books, 2006), has elsewhere written that he went to college "committed to figuring out the meaning of life, and I thought studying philosophy would help. I was disappointed. Philosophy addressed many fundamental questions of being and knowing, but the question 'What is the meaning of life?' never came." Quoted in Susan Wolf, *Meaning in Life and Why It Matters* (Princeton: Princeton University Press, 2010), 93.

6 **education to be instrumental:** See this article for two visions of

what college is for—utility or the development of the soul: Kwame Anthony Appiah, "What Is the Point of College?" *New York Times,* September 8, 2015.

6 **American Freshman survey has:** John H. Pryor, Sylvia Hurtado, Victor B. Saenz, José Luis Santos, and William S. Korn, "The American Freshman: Forty Year Trends" (Los Angeles: UCLA Higher Education Research Institute, 2007).

6 **a strong yearning for meaning:** See Alexander W. Astin, Helen S. Astin, J. A. Lindholm, A. N. Bryant, K. Szelényi, and S. Calderone, "The Spiritual Life of College Students: A National Study of College Students' Search for Meaning and Purpose" (Los Angeles: UCLA Higher Education Research Institute, 2005).

6 **Educating students about:** The next few paragraphs are drawn mostly from Kronman, who in *Education's End* argues that the topic of life's meaning "has been expelled from our colleges and universities, under pressure from the research ideal and the demands of political correctness," 46. Some of the material also came from Alex Beam, *A Great Idea at the Time: The Rise, Fall, and Curious Afterlife of the Great Books* (New York: PublicAffairs, 2008).

8 **The research ideal dealt a blow:** The growth of political correctness, multiculturalism, and moral relativism were some of the other reasons why the search for meaning was banished from the academy, according to Kronman and Beam.

8 **beyond their purview:** There are exceptions to the trend described in this paragraph, of course. Some schools continue to offer students an education grounded in the humanities. See, for example, Columbia's Core Curriculum, Yale's Directed Studies program, and the curriculum of St. John's College. For more on how educational reformers tried to resist the research ideal's weakening of the humanities-oriented curriculum, see Beam's and Kronman's books.

8 **"consensus in the academy":** Mark W. Roche, "Should Faculty Members Teach Virtues and Values? That Is the Wrong Question," *Liberal Education* 95, no. 3 (Summer 2009): 32–37.

8 **Meaning has regained:** See Dan Berrett, "A Curriculum for the Selfie Generation," *The Chronicle of Higher Education,* June 6, 2014. I also conducted an interview with Yale professor Miroslav Volf—the director of the Yale Center for Faith and Culture and founder of the Life Worth Living Program within that center—about this resurgence of interest in meaning on campus (on September 24, 2014). The question of the good life has regained some

traction in philosophy and literature, too. See, e.g.: James O. Pawelski and D. J. Moores (editors), *The Eudaimonic Turn: Well-Being in Literary Studies* (Madison, New Jersey: Fairleigh Dickinson University Press, 2013).

9 **called positive psychology:** Not all of the new research in well-being is occurring within positive psychology. Some of it is in psychology more broadly, economics, and other fields. It's also important to note that a number of psychologists were studying well-being before positive psychology came around, and some of them were drawing on the humanities for guidance. See, for example, Carol D. Ryff and Corey Lee M. Keyes, "The Structure of Psychological Well-Being Revisited," *Journal of Personality and Social Psychology* 69, no. 4 (1995): 719–27; and Alan S. Waterman, "Two Conceptions of Happiness: Contrasts of Personal Expressiveness (Eudaimonia) and Hedonic Enjoyment," *Journal of Personality and Social Psychology* 64, no. 4 (1993): 678–91. See also Richard M. Ryan and Edward L. Deci, "Self-Determination Theory and the Facilitation of Intrinsic Motivation, Social Development, and Well-Being," *American Psychologist* 55, no. 1 (2000): 68–78. There were also researchers studying meaning, like Roy Baumeister, Laura King, Brian Little, Dan McAdams, and Paul Wong.

9 **rich tradition of the humanities:** The founding of positive psychology and the development of its vision not only involved social scientists but philosophers, including Robert Nozick and Daniel Robinson. A great example of the melding of the humanities and science in positive psychology is Christopher Peterson and Martin E. P. Seligman, *Character Strengths and Virtues: A Handbook and Classification* (New York: Oxford University Press, 2004). See also the work of James Pawelski.

9 **Positive psychology was founded by:** For good reviews of what positive psychology is about and its development, see Martin E. P. Seligman, *Authentic Happiness: Using the New Positive Psychology to Realize Your Potential for Lasting Fulfillment* (New York: Free Press, 2002) and *Flourish: A Visionary New Understanding of Happiness and Well-Being* (New York: Free Press, 2011); and Seligman and Mihaly Csikszentmihalyi, "Positive Psychology: An Introduction," *American Psychologist* 55, no. 1 (2000): 5–14.

9 **Some researchers studied:** For good overviews of the research on happiness, I recommend Sonja Lyubomirsky, *The How of Happiness: A New Approach to Getting the Life You Want* (New York: Penguin Books, 2008) and *The Myths of Happiness: What Should*

Make You Happy, but Doesn't, What Shouldn't Make You Happy, but Does (New York: Penguin Books, 2014).

9 **over 10,000 per year:** Ed Diener, a pioneer in happiness research, sent me a graph by email showing the growth of research on happiness (which researchers called subjective well-being) on April 16, 2014.

9 **Major media outlets:** For a book that discusses the happiness zeitgeist more fully, see John F. Schumaker, *In Search of Happiness: Understanding an Endangered State of Mind* (Westport, Connecticut: Praeger, 2007). For a brief history of the idea of happiness and how, in America, the pursuit of happiness took off as a cultural phenomenon, see Shigehiro Oishi, Jesse Graham, Selin Kesebir, and Iolanda Costa Galinha, "Concepts of Happiness across Time and Cultures," *Personality and Social Psychology Bulletin* 39, no. 5 (2013): 559–77.

9 **According to *Psychology Today*:** Carlin Flora, "The Pursuit of Happiness," *Psychology Today,* January 1, 2009.

10 **since the mid-2000s:** From my own analysis as measured by Google Trends in 2013.

10 **"The shortcut to anything":** Rhonda Byrne, *The Secret* (New York: Atria Books, 2006), 100.

10 **we're more miserable than ever:** See chapter 1 for a discussion of the rise of depression and suicide, and chapter 2 for one on the rising rates of social isolation and the consequences of that.

10 **actually makes people unhappy:** See Iris B. Mauss, Maya Tamir, Craig L. Anderson, and Nicole S. Savino, "Can Seeking Happiness Make People Unhappy? Paradoxical Effects of Valuing Happiness," *Emotion* 11, no. 4 (2011): 807–15. Mauss also led research showing how the pursuit of happiness begets loneliness: Iris B. Mauss, Nicole S. Savino, Craig L. Anderson, Max Weisbuch, Maya Tamir, and Mark L. Laudenslager, "The Pursuit of Happiness Can Be Lonely," *Emotion* 12, no. 5 (2012): 908. For more on how actively trying to pursue happiness makes you unhappy, see section four of Jonathan W. Schooler, Dan Ariely, and George Loewenstein, "The Pursuit and Assessment of Happiness Can Be Self-Defeating," in Isabelle Brocas and Juan D. Carrillo (editors), *The Psychology of Economic Decisions: Volume 1: Rationality and Well-Being* (Oxford: Oxford University Press, 2003), 41–70. For a discussion of the benefits of happiness, along with the cons of valuing it above all, see June Gruber, Iris B. Mauss, and Maya Tamir, "A Dark Side of Happiness? How, When, and Why Happiness Is Not Always Good,"

Perspectives on Psychological Science 6, no. 3 (2011): 222–33. In another paper, reporting on the findings from two studies, social scientists pointed out that "the culturally-pervasive value placed on attaining happiness can represent a risk factor for symptoms and a diagnosis of depression": Brett Q. Ford, Amanda J. Shallcross, Iris B. Mauss, Victoria A. Floerke, and June Gruber, "Desperately Seeking Happiness: Valuing Happiness Is Associated with Symptoms and Diagnosis of Depression," *Journal of Social and Clinical Psychology* 33, no. 10 (2014): 890–905.

10 **"a human being dissatisfied":** John Stuart Mill, *Utilitarianism* (Indianapolis: Hackett Publishing Company, 2001), 10.

10 **Harvard philosopher Robert Nozick:** This quote is from Robert Nozick, *The Examined Life: Philosophical Meditations* (New York: Touchstone, 1989), 100. The remaining information about the experience machine is drawn from *The Examined Life,* 99–108, and from Nozick, *Anarchy, State, and Utopia* (New York: Basic Books, 2013), 43–45.

11 **as a majority of us do:** See Ed Diener and Shigehiro Oishi, "Are Scandinavians Happier than Asians? Issues in Comparing Nations on Subjective Well-Being," in Frank Columbus (editor), *Asian Economic and Political Issues: Volume 10* (Hauppauge, New York: Nova Science, 2004), 1–25; Shigehiro Oishi, Ed Diener, and Richard E. Lucas, "The Optimum Level of Well-Being: Can People Be Too Happy?" *Perspectives on Psychological Science* 2, no. 4 (2007): 346–60; and Schumaker, *In Search of Happiness.*

11 **we recoil:** The analysis in this paragraph comes mostly from Nozick, *The Examined Life.* There, he writes, "We care about what is actually the case. . . . We want to be importantly connected to reality, not to live in a delusion." In *Anarchy, State, and Utopia,* he gives three related reasons for not plugging in. First, "we want to *do* certain things"; second, "we want to *be* a certain way"; and third, "plugging into an experience machine limits us to . . . a world no deeper or more important than that which people can construct," 43.

12 **distinction between:** See, e.g., Richard M. Ryan and Edward L. Deci, "On Happiness and Human Potentials: A Review of Research on Hedonic and Eudaimonic Well-Being," *Annual Review of Psychology* 52, no. 1 (2001): 141–66; Veronika Huta and Alan S. Waterman, "Eudaimonia and Its Distinction from Hedonia: Developing a Classification and Terminology for Understanding Conceptual and Operational Definitions," *Journal of Happiness Studies*

15, no. 6 (2014): 1425–56; and Corey L. M. Keyes and Julia Annas, "Feeling Good and Functioning Well: Distinctive Concepts in Ancient Philosophy and Contemporary Science," *The Journal of Positive Psychology* 4, no. 3 (2009): 197–201.

Researchers also point out that our motivations differ—some people are motivated by the pursuit of happiness and others by the pursuit of meaning, which has implications for how they behave and feel. For more on our differing orientations to well-being, see Christopher Peterson, Nansook Park, and Martin E. P. Seligman, "Orientations to Happiness and Life Satisfaction: The Full Life Versus the Empty life," *Journal of Happiness Studies* 6, no. 1 (2005): 25–41; Veronika Huta, "The Complementary Roles of Eudaimonia and Hedonia and How They Can Be Pursued in Practice," in Stephen Joseph (editor), *Positive Psychology in Practice: Promoting Human Flourishing in Work, Health, Education and Everyday Life,* second edition (Hoboken, New Jersey: John Wiley & Sons, 2015), 159–68; Veronika Huta, "An Overview of Hedonic and Eudaimonic Well-Being Concepts," in Leonard Reinecke and Mary Beth Oliver (editors), *Handbook of Media Use and Well-Being,* chapter 2 (New York: Routledge, 2015); and Veronika Huta, "Eudaimonic and Hedonic Orientations: Theoretical Considerations and Research Findings," in Joar Vittersø (editor), *Handbook of Eudaimonic Well-Being* (Dordrecht, Netherlands: Springer, 2016).

12 **two paths to the good life:** Much of the material in this paragraph draws from Darrin M. McMahon, *Happiness: A History* (New York: Grove Press, 2006). I also interviewed McMahon and exchanged a number of emails with him throughout 2014–2016.

12 **footsteps of Sigmund Freud:** Sigmund Freud, *Civilization and Its Discontents* (New York: W. W. Norton & Company, 1989), 25. Freud himself didn't believe that happiness was the purpose of life, but he thought most people did.

12 **Aristippus wrote:** Quoted in Michael F. Steger, Todd B. Kashdan, and Shigehiro Oishi, "Being Good by Doing Good: Daily Eudaimonic Activity and Well-Being," *Journal of Research in Personality* 42, no. 1 (2008): 22–42.

12 **"Nature has placed mankind":** Quoted in McMahon, *Happiness,* 218.

13 **One tool commonly used:** There are a number of ways social scientists measure happiness. One of the most common tools is called the Subjective Well-Being Scale, which is understood to be a mea-

sure of hedonic happiness by researchers, as pointed out in Ryan and Deci, "On Happiness and Human Potentials"; and Todd B. Kashdan, Robert Biswas-Diener, and Laura A. King, "Reconsidering Happiness: The Costs of Distinguishing between Hedonics and Eudaimonia," *The Journal of Positive Psychology* 3, no. 4 (2008): 219–33. The Subjective Well-Being Scale consists of two subscales. One is called the PANAS (or the Positive Affect Negative Affect Schedule), which measures your emotional or affective state. The second is the Satisfaction with Life Scale, which asks individuals to rate items like "the conditions of my life are excellent" and "so far I have gotten the important things I want in life." For other ways to measure happiness, see Sonja Lyubomirsky and Heidi S. Lepper, "A Measure of Subjective Happiness: Preliminary Reliability and Construct Validation," *Social Indicators Research* 46, no. 2 (1999): 137–55; Daniel Kahneman, Alan B. Krueger, David A. Schkade, Norbert Schwarz, and Arthur A. Stone, "A Survey Method for Characterizing Daily Life Experience: The Day Reconstruction Method," *Science* 306, no. 5702 (2004): 1776–80; Daniel Kahneman, "Objective Happiness," in Daniel Kahneman, Edward Diener, and Norbert Schwarz (editors), *Well-Being: The Foundations of Hedonic Psychology* (New York: Russell Sage Foundation, 1999), 3–25; and Mihaly Csikszentmihalyi and Jeremy Hunter, "Happiness in Everyday Life: The Uses of Experience Sampling," *Journal of Happiness Studies* 4, no. 2 (2003): 185–99. These measures of happiness are hedonic, but other researchers define happiness more broadly. For example, in *Authentic Happiness,* Seligman argues that happiness arises from three pillars: positive emotions, engagement, and meaning. Later, he expanded his definition of a good life to also include the pillar of relationships and achievement, and called this new model "well-being theory" or "flourishing" rather than "authentic happiness" (see Seligman, *Flourish*). Interestingly, when psychologists expand their definition of well-being beyond positive states and emotions, they tend to call the construct something other than happiness—like flourishing or psychological well-being.

13 **Meaning is the other path:** Some people might say that the distinction between hedonia and eudaimonia is really between two forms of happiness, one grounded in pleasure and one grounded in meaning. However, because our common cultural understanding of happiness is a state of good feeling, positive emotions, and pleasure, while eudaimonia, or living a meaningful life, is something that we

do, and can be stressful and full of negative emotions, I've chosen to draw a distinction between the two. Also, I use the terms "meaning" and "eudaimonia" interchangeably since my definition of meaning essentially encompasses the various aspects of eudaimonia as defined in the various sources I cite throughout this section.

13 **Aristotle:** For the section on Aristotle, I relied on Aristotle, *The Nicomachean Ethics,* translated by David Ross (Oxford: Oxford University Press, 2009); *Stanford Encyclopedia of Philosophy* entry "Aristotle's Ethics," plato.stanford.edu/entries/aristotle-ethics/; author interview with philosopher Julia Annas on September 23, 2014, and subsequent email exchanges; and McMahon, *Happiness.*

13 **gets translated as "happiness":** As Julia Annas pointed out to me in an interview, philosophers tend to think that the word "happiness" is not adequate for discussing what Aristotle meant by *eudaimonia.* See also Rosalind Hursthouse, *On Virtue Ethics* (Oxford: Oxford University Press, 1999), where she writes, "'[F]lourishing' is a better translation of eudaimonia than 'happiness,'" 10.

13 **pretty harsh words:** Aristotle, *The Nicomachean Ethics,* 6.

13 **requires cultivating the best:** Aristotle also believed that certain external conditions—like having money, friends, luck, and health—had to be minimally satisfied before someone could flourish.

14 **Aristotle's distinction:** See, for example, Ryan and Deci, "On Happiness and Human Potentials"; Huta and Waterman, "Eudaimonia and Its Distinction from Hedonia"; Carol D. Ryff, "Psychological Well-Being Revisited: Advances in the Science and Practice of Eudaimonia," *Psychotherapy and Psychosomatics* 83, no. 1 (2013): 10–28; and Steger et al., "Being Good by Doing Good."

14 **defined as "feeling good":** Specifically, psychologists define it as pleasure, positive feelings, comfort, the absence of distress and negative emotions, and enjoyment.

14 **as "being and doing good":** See Steger et al., "Being Good by Doing Good."

14 **"seeking to use and develop":** Veronika Huta and Richard M. Ryan, "Pursuing Pleasure or Virtue: The Differential and Overlapping Well-Being Benefits of Hedonic and Eudaimonic Motives," *Journal of Happiness Studies* 11, no. 6 (2010): 735–62.

14 **"The more directly one aims to":** Richard M. Ryan, Veronika Huta, and Edward L. Deci, "Living Well: A Self-Determination Theory Perspective on Eudaimonia," in Antonella Delle Fave (editor), *The Exploration of Happiness: Present and Future Perspectives* (Dordrecht, Netherlands: Springer Science+Business Media, 2013), 119.

14 **according psychologists, when people say:** See Michael F. Steger, "Meaning in Life: A Unified Model," in Shane J. Lopez and Charles R. Snyder (editors), *The Oxford Handbook of Positive Psychology,* third edition (Oxford: Oxford University Press, in press); and Roy Baumeister, *Meanings of Life* (New York: The Guilford Press, 1991).

14 **some social scientists are skeptical:** See, for example, Kashdan et al., "Reconsidering Happiness."

14 **can't be conflated so easily:** In the following papers, Huta does a wonderful job of drawing out this distinction between meaning and happiness. Both *hedonia* and *eudaimonia*, she points out, relate to psychological health in different ways, and both can be taken to extremes, though the research shows that meaning offers a more elevated and prosocial form of well-being than *hedonia:* Huta, "The Complementary Roles of Eudaimonia and Hedonia and How They Can Be Pursued in Practice"; Huta, "An Overview of Hedonic and Eudaimonic Well-Being Concepts"; and Huta, "Eudaimonic and Hedonic Orientations."

14 **led by Florida State University's:** Roy F. Baumeister, Kathleen D. Vohs, Jennifer L. Aaker, and Emily N. Garbinsky, "Some Key Differences between a Happy Life and a Meaningful Life," *The Journal of Positive Psychology* 8, no. 6 (2013): 505–16.

14 **overlap in certain ways:** The researchers did not measure people who are high on meaning and low on happiness or high on happiness and low on meaning. Instead, they measured how much happiness and meaning each individual reported and then saw what each of those variables correlated with. They write: "Meaningfulness and happiness are positively correlated, so they have much in common. Many factors, such as feeling connected to others, feeling productive, and not being alone or bored contribute similarly to both. Yet the two are distinct, and the focus of this investigation has been to identify the major differences in correlates of happiness (corrected for meaning) and meaningfulness (corrected for happiness)."

15 **can be at odds:** In one analysis of five datasets comprising nearly 3,000 people, Veronika Huta found that 33 percent of respondents were high on happiness and low on meaning, 26 percent were high on meaning and low on happiness, 20 percent were high on both, and 20 percent were low on both—suggesting a real distinction between meaning and happiness. Email to author on October 28, 2014.

15 **of a 2010 study:** Huta and Ryan, "Pursuing Pleasure or Virtue," study 4.

16 **The philosopher John Stuart Mill:** John Stuart Mill, *Autobiography* (London: Penguin Books, 1989), 117.

17 **more fulfilling:** See, as mentioned, Huta and Ryan, "Pursuing Pleasure or Virtue"; Peterson et al., "Orientations to Happiness and Life Satisfaction"; and Steger et al., "Being Good by Doing Good." See also Keyes and Annas, "Feeling Good and Functioning Well," where the findings imply that meaning is a more effective buffer against mental illness than happiness, as Keyes explained to me in an email from March 31, 2016. He also said that *eudaimonia* has been found to be a stronger protector against mortality than *hedonia*. Another study found that *eudaimonia* was associated with a healthier genetic signature than *hedonia*: Barbara L. Fredrickson, Karen M. Grewen, Kimberly A. Coffey, Sara B. Algoe, Ann M. Firestine, Jesusa M. G. Arevalo, Jeffrey Ma, and Steven W. Cole, "A Functional Genomic Perspective on Human Well-Being," *Proceedings of the National Academy of Sciences* 110, no. 33 (2013): 13684–89. Also, as discussed, the pursuit of happiness can make people unhappy. Meanwhile, there's research showing that meaningful pursuits like doing acts of kindness, expressing gratitude, setting important goals, and nurturing social relationships boost happiness. For a summary of that research, see Lyubomirsky, *The How of Happiness*.

1: The Meaning Crisis

19 **historian and philosopher Will Durant:** For the biographical sketch of Durant, I relied on Will Durant, *Fallen Leaves: Last Words on Life, Love, War, and God* (New York: Simon & Schuster, 2014); *On the Meaning of Life* (Dallas, Texas: Promethean Press, 2005); *Transition: A Mental Autobiography* (New York: Touchstone, 1955); and Will and Ariel Durant, *A Dual Autobiography* (New York: Simon & Schuster, 1977).

22 **risen dramatically:** Martin E. P. Seligman, *The Optimistic Child: A Proven Program to Safeguard Children Against Depression and Build Lifelong Resilience* (Boston: Houghton Mifflin, 2007).

22 **antidepressants rose 400 percent:** Laura A. Pratt, Debra J. Brody, and Qiuping Gu, "Antidepressant Use in Persons Aged 12 and Over: United States, 2005–2008," National Center for Health Statistics Data Brief No. 76, October 2011.

22 **According to the World Health Organization:** Cited in T. M. Luhrmann, "Is the World More Depressed?" *New York Times,* March 24, 2014.

22 **the incidence of suicide among:** David M. Cutler, Edward L. Glaeser, and Karen E. Norberg, "Explaining the Rise in Youth Suicide," in Jonathan Gruber (editor), *Risky Behavior Among Youths: An Economic Analysis* (Chicago: University of Chicago Press, 2001), 219–70.

22 **nearly thirty years . . . 40 percent:** Sabrina Tavernise, "U.S. Suicide Rate Surges to a 30-Year High," *New York Times,* April 22, 2016. Today, the suicide rate is 13 per 100,000. As context, the suicide rate reached its highest point in the United States in 1932 during the Great Depression (22.1 per 100,000) and its lowest point in 2000 (10.4 per 100,000). See also "CDC: US Suicide Rate Hits 25-Year High," Associated Press, October 8, 2014; Feijun Luo, Curtis S. Florence, Myriam Quispe-Agnoli, Lijing Ouyang, and Alexander E. Crosby, "Impact of Business Cycles on US Suicide Rates, 1928–2007," *American Journal of Public Health* 101, no. 6 (2011): 1139–46; and Tony Dokoupil, "Why Suicide Has Become an Epidemic—And What We Can Do to Help," *Newsweek,* May 23, 2013.

22 **forty thousand Americans:** "Suicide: Facts at a Glance," Centers for Disease Control, cdc.gov/violenceprevention/pdf/suicide_factsheet-a.pdf.

22 **closer to a million:** The World Health Organization estimates that over 800,000 take their lives each year. See "Suicide Data," who.int/mental_health/prevention/suicide/suicideprevent/en/.

22 **Shigehiro Oishi . . . and Ed Diener:** Shigehiro Oishi and Ed Diener, "Residents of Poor Nations Have a Greater Sense of Meaning in Life than Residents of Wealthy Nations," *Psychological Science* 25, no. 2 (2014): 422–30.

23 **suicide rate of Japan:** The suicide rates are from WHO, "Suicide Rates Data by Country," http://apps.who.int/gho/data/node.main.MHSUICIDE?lang=en.

23 **strange relationship between:** Maia Szalavitz, "Why the Happiest States Have the Highest Suicide Rates," *Time,* April 25, 2011.

24 **a satisfying life purpose:** These findings are from a study the CDC supported of a nationally representative sample of U.S. adults. The researchers found that a quarter of Americans strongly disagreed, moderately disagreed, or were neutral about the statement "I have a good sense of what makes my life meaningful." And 40 percent

strongly disagreed, moderately disagreed, or were neutral about the statement "I have discovered a satisfying life purpose." See Rosemarie Kobau, Joseph Sniezek, Matthew M. Zack, Richard E. Lucas, and Adam Burns, "Well-Being Assessment: An Evaluation of Well-Being Scales for Public Health and Population Estimates of Well-Being among US Adults," *Applied Psychology: Health and Well-Being* 2, no. 3 (2010): 272–97.

24 **"Everyone at times":** Huston Smith, *The World's Religions* (New York: HarperCollins, 1991), 276.

24 **Russian novelist Leo Tolstoy:** I drew on the following sources for information about Tolstoy's life: Leo Tolstoy, *Confession,* as translated by David Patterson (New York: W. W. Norton & Company, 1983); Rosamund Bartlett, *Tolstoy: A Russian Life* (New York: Houghton Mifflin Harcourt, 2011); A. N. Wilson, *Tolstoy* (New York: W. W. Norton & Company, 1988); and Gary Saul Morson, "Leo Tolstoy," Britannica.com.

25 **perhaps with some exaggeration:** In his biography of Tolstoy, Wilson cautions that we should take Tolstoy's reflective assessment of his life in *A Confession* with a grain of salt. Clearly, Tolstoy wrestled with questions of meaning and morality prior to his breakdown—yet, equally clearly, he really did have some sort of crisis of meaning around this point in his life.

29 **intellectual Albert Camus:** For Camus's story and ideas, I relied primarily upon Robert Zaretsky, *A Life Worth Living: Albert Camus and the Quest for Meaning* (Cambridge, Massachusetts: Belknap Press, 2013); Olivier Todd, *Albert Camus: A Life* (New York: Carroll & Graf, 2000); and Albert Camus, *The Myth of Sisyphus and Other Essays* (New York: Vintage International, 1991).

31 **search for it particularly urgent:** As pointed out by Terry Eagleton, cited in Zaretsky, *A Life Worth Living.*

33 **As Sartre wrote:** John-Paul Sartre, *Existentialism and Human Emotions* (New York: Citadel, 1987), 49.

35 ***The Little Prince*:** Antoine de Saint-Exupéry, *The Little Prince,* translated by Richard Hough (Boston: Mariner Books, 2000). The quotes are presented out of order. First the prince and fox meet, and the prince tames the fox as the fox teaches the prince why taming something is valuable. Then he tells the prince that if he returns to the roses, he'll see why the prince's original rose was special. When the prince comes back, the fox tells him that you are responsible forever for what you have tamed. But the prince had, in effect, already learned that lesson by the time he saw the roses.

36 **the "IKEA effect":** Michael I. Norton, Daniel Mochon, and Dan Ariely, "The 'IKEA Effect': When Labor Leads to Love," *Journal of Consumer Psychology* 22, no. 3 (2012): 453–60.

38 **skyrocketed during the Great Depression:** Gene Smiley, "Great Depression," from the *Concise Encyclopedia of Economics,* econlib.org/library/Enc/GreatDepression.html.

38 **suicide rates tend to rise:** Luo et al., "Impact of Business Cycles on US Suicide Rates, 1928–2007."

38 **it's easy to understand why:** The link between unemployment and suicide has been well established. For some examples of research studies on this topic, see Glyn Lewis and Andy Sloggett, "Suicide, Deprivation, and Unemployment: Record Linkage Study," *British Medical Journal* 317, no. 7168 (1998): 1283–86; Stephen Platt, "Unemployment and Suicidal Behaviour: A Review of the Literature," *Social Science & Medicine* 19, no. 2 (1984): 93–115; and A. Milner, A. Page, and A. D. Lamontagne, "Cause and Effect in Studies on Unemployment, Mental Health and Suicide: A Meta-analytic and Conceptual Review," *Psychological Medicine* 44, no. 5 (2014): 909–17.

39 ***Life* magazine undertook:** David Friend and the Editors of *Life, The Meaning of Life: Reflections in Words and Pictures on Why We Are Here* (Boston: Little, Brown and Company, 1991).

2: Belonging

43 **Tangier Island, Virginia:** I visited Tangier twice: May 27, 2013, and November 15–16, 2014. This write-up collapses both of those experiences into a single narrative. I interviewed Edward Pruitt on September 8, 2015. I also drew on these sources for my write-up of Tangier: Kirk Mariner, *God's Island: The History of Tangier* (New Church, Virginia: Miona Publications, 1999); Kate Kilpatrick, "Treasured Island," *Aljazeera America,* May 11, 2014; "As Bones of Tangier Island's Past Resurface, Chesapeake Bay Islanders Fret about Their Future," Associated Press, April 23, 2013; and Harold G. Wheatley, "This Is My Island, Tangier," *National Geographic,* November 1973.

50 **most important driver of meaning:** Nathaniel M. Lambert, Tyler F. Stillman, Joshua A. Hicks, Shanmukh Kamble, Roy F. Baumeister, and Frank D. Fincham, "To Belong Is to Matter: Sense of Belonging Enhances Meaning in Life," *Personality and Social Psychology Bulletin* 39, no. 11 (2013): 1418–27.

50 **two conditions have been satisfied:** Roy F. Baumeister and Mark R. Leary, "The Need to Belong: Desire for Interpersonal Attachments as a Fundamental Human Motivation," *Psychological Bulletin* 117, no. 3 (1995): 497–529.

50 **many influential psychologists and physicians:** The material from this section comes from Deborah Blum, *Love at Goon Park: Harry Harlow and the Science of Affection* (New York: Basic Books, 2011), 31–60; Robert Karen, *Becoming Attached: First Relationships and How They Shape Our Capacity to Love* (Oxford: Oxford University Press, 1998), 13–25; and René Spitz, *Grief: A Peril in Infancy,* a 1947 video, canal-u.tv/video/cerimes/absence_maternelle_et_traumatisme_de_l_enfance.10347. For more on John Watson's *Psychological Care of Infant and Child,* see Ann Hulbert, "He Was an Author Only a Mother Could Love," *Los Angeles Times,* May 11, 2003.

52 **What was going on?:** A handful of doctors and psychologists did recognize children's need for emotional care. One of them was pediatrician Harry Bakwin, who headed the pediatric unit at Bellevue Hospital in New York in the 1930s, where he instituted some changes that would have dramatic consequences on the health of the infants in his charge. He put up signs encouraging affection—"Do not enter this nursery without picking up a baby," read one (see Karen, *Becoming Attached,* 20)—and under his leadership of the unit, "nurses were encouraged to mother and cuddle the children, to pick them up and play with them, and parents were invited to visit. The results of this change in policy were dramatic: despite the increased possibility of infection, the mortality rate for infants under 1 year of age fell sharply from 30–35 per cent to less than 10 per cent," quoted in Frank C. P. van der Horst and René van der Veer, "Loneliness in Infancy: Harry Harlow, John Bowlby and Issues of Separation," *Integrative Psychological and Behavioral Science* 42, no. 4 (2008): 325–35. It would be many years before the ideas Bakwin championed became mainstream. That they did is in large part thanks to René Spitz.

52 **Spitz published the results:** See René A. Spitz, "Hospitalism: An Inquiry into the Genesis of Psychiatric Conditions in Early Childhood," *The Psychoanalytic Study of the Child* 1 (1944): 53–74; and René A. Spitz, "Hospitalism: A Follow-up Report," *The Psychoanalytic Study of the Child* 2 (1946), 113–17. As Karen explains in *Becoming Attached,* Spitz's methodology was flawed in this study, as was the methodology of most psychological research in those

days—but later research by people like John Bowlby and Harry Harlow confirmed the negative effects of a lack of care and affection on the young.

53 **Spitz showed his colleagues video:** You can watch this heartbreaking video online: canal-u.tv/video/cerimes/absence_maternelle_et_traumatisme_de_l_enfance.10347.

54 **chronic loneliness, scientists have found:** John T. Cacioppo and William Patrick, *Loneliness: Human Nature and the Need for Social Connection* (New York: W. W. Norton & Company, 2008).

55 **20 percent of people consider loneliness:** Cacioppo and Patrick, *Loneliness,* 5.

55 **Americans 45 and older:** "Loneliness among Older Adults: A National Survey of Adults 45+," a report prepared by Knowledge Networks and Insight Policy Research for *AARP: The Magazine,* September 2010.

55 **common response was three:** Specifically, they asked how many people the respondents discussed important matters with over the last six months. Miller McPherson, Lynn Smith-Lovin, and Matthew E. Brashears, "Social Isolation in America: Changes in Core Discussion Networks over Two Decades," *American Sociological Review* 71, no. 3 (2006): 353–75. The researchers believe that the data may be overestimating the rise in social isolation, but, even still, they later found a "70 percent increase in social isolation from 1985 to 2004," quoted in McPherson, Smith-Lovin, and Brashears, "Models and Marginals: Using Survey Evidence to Study Social Networks," *American Sociological Review* 74, no. 4 (2009): 670–81. Some researchers have questioned the degree of isolation found by McPherson and his colleagues, but sources largely agree that sociality is in decline. See Robert D. Putnam, *Bowling Alone: The Collapse and Revival of American Community* (New York: Simon & Schuster, 2000).

56 **close relationships as our most important:** See Nathaniel M. Lambert, Tyler F. Stillman, Roy F. Baumeister, Frank D. Fincham, Joshua A. Hicks, and Steven M. Graham, "Family as a Salient Source of Meaning in Young Adulthood," *The Journal of Positive Psychology* 5, no. 5 (2010): 367–76; Peter Ebersole, "Types and Depth of Written Life Meanings," in Paul T. P. Wong and Prem S. Fry (editors), *The Human Quest for Meaning: A Handbook of Psychological Research and Clinical Applications* (Mahwah, New Jersey: Lawrence Erlbaum Associates, Publishers, 1998); and Dominique Louis Debats, "Sources of Meaning: An Investigation of Sig-

nificant Commitments in Life," *Journal of Humanistic Psychology* 39, no. 4 (1999): 30–57.

56 **their lives are less meaningful:** See Tyler F. Stillman, Roy F. Baumeister, Nathaniel M. Lambert, A. Will Crescioni, C. Nathan DeWall, and Frank D. Fincham, "Alone and Without Purpose: Life Loses Meaning Following Social Exclusion," *Journal of Experimental Social Psychology* 45, no. 4 (2009): 686–94.

56 **Durkheim explored the question:** Émile Durkheim, *Suicide: A Study in Sociology* (New York: Free Press, 1971).

57 **Shigehiro Oishi and Ed Diener:** Oishi and Diener, "Residents of Poor Nations Have a Greater Sense of Meaning in Life than Residents of Wealthy Nations."

58 **with religiosity leading the pack:** The effect of religion on meaning was so strong that, in the case of a few countries, the general trend of the study—that wealthier countries have lower meaning rates—was reversed. Some rich countries, such as the United Arab Emirates, rated relatively high on meaning and some poor countries, such as Haiti, rated relatively low on meaning based on how religious their inhabitants reported being. That said, if you look at two equally religious people living in two different countries, the one in a poorer country will still likely report higher levels of meaning in life than the one in a richer country, and vice versa, because of the other social factors mentioned.

58 **driving the increase in mental illness:** Jean M. Twenge, Brittany Gentile, C. Nathan DeWall, Debbie Ma, Katharine Lacefield, and David R. Schurtz, "Birth Cohort Increases in Psychopathology among Young Americans, 1938–2007: A Cross-Temporal Meta-analysis of the MMPI," *Clinical Psychology Review* 30, no. 2 (2010): 145–54.

58 **several measures of individualism:** Richard Eckersley and Keith Dear, "Cultural Correlates of Youth Suicide," *Social Science & Medicine* 55, no. 11 (2002): 1891–1904. The association between individualism and youth suicide was especially strong among males and weaker among females.

58 **"privatizing our leisure time":** Putnam, *Bowling Alone,* 283.

58 **moves eleven times in his life:** Mona Chalabi, "How Many Times Does the Average Person Move?" FiveThirtyEight, January 29, 2015.

58 **many will change jobs:** Carl Bialik, "Seven Careers in a Lifetime? Think Twice, Researchers Say," *Wall Street Journal,* September 4, 2010.

59 **I traveled to Cleveland, Ohio:** September, 26, 2015.

59 **Society for Creative Anachronism:** The information from this section derives from a number of interviews I conducted while at the event in Cleveland, including with Howard Fein and a man whom I call James (who asked that I not reveal his name or identifying information about him). I also conducted several interviews in the fall of 2015 with SCA members in Ann Arbor, including Kay Jarrell on September 11, 2015, and Carol and Matt Lagemann on September 21, 2015. I interviewed SCA member Kat Dyer, who lives in the Chicago area, by phone on September 16, 2015, and Diana Paxson, one of the founders of the SCA, on September 23, 2015.

61 **people naturally grow to like others:** See Roy F. Baumeister and Brad J. Bushman, *Social Psychology and Human Nature: Brief Version* (Belmont, California: Thomson Wadsworth, 2008), chapter 10.

61 **share common experiences and values:** See Baumeister and Bushman, *Psychology and Human Nature,* in particular chapter 10; and Angela J. Bahns, Kate M. Pickett, and Christian S. Crandall, "Social Ecology of Similarity: Big Schools, Small Schools and Social Relationships," *Group Processes & Intergroup Relations* 15, no. 1 (2012): 119–31. There are also other determinants of friendship formation, such as opening up to another person. See Karen Karbo, "Friendship: The Laws of Attraction," *Psychology Today,* November 1, 2006.

62 **with dignity and respect:** Most of their peers, anyway. One SCA member told me a story of one member who was consistently rude to other people within the SCA. That member was eventually expelled from the organization.

64 **"High quality connections":** Information on high quality connections from Jane E. Dutton, *Energize Your Workplace: How to Create and Sustain High-Quality Connections at Work* (San Francisco: Jossey-Bass, 2003); Jane E. Dutton and Emily D. Heaphy, "The Power of High-Quality Connections," in Kim S. Cameron, Jane E. Dutton, and Robert E. Quinn (editors), *Positive Organizational Scholarship: Foundations of a New Discipline* (San Francisco: Berrett-Koehler, 2003), 263–78; and author interview with Jane Dutton on April 2, 2014. Dutton's work focuses on high quality connections at work, but such connections can occur outside of work, too.

64 **Jonathan Shapiro, an entrepreneur:** Jonathan, a friend and classmate of mine in the positive psychology program at Penn, told this story in class one day in 2013. I subsequently interviewed him about it on October 18, 2015.

66 **social exclusion . . . is a threat:** See Stillman et al., "Alone and

Without Purpose"; and Jean M. Twenge, Kathleen R. Catanese, and Roy F. Baumeister, "Social Exclusion and the Deconstructed State: Time Perception, Meaninglessness, Lethargy, Lack of Emotion, and Self-Awareness," *Journal of Personality and Social Psychology* 85, no. 3 (2003): 409–423; and Kristin L. Sommer, Kipling D. Williams, Natalie J. Ciarocco, and Roy F. Baumeister, "When Silence Speaks Louder than Words: Explorations into the Intrapsychic and Interpersonal Consequences of Social Ostracism," *Basic and Applied Social Psychology* 23, no. 4 (2001): 225–43.

66 **undergraduates were brought into the lab:** Twenge et al., "Social Exclusion and the Deconstructed State."

66 **rate their own lives:** Stillman et al., "Alone and Without Purpose."

66 **rejected *and* the rejecter feel alienated:** Kipling D. Williams, *Ostracism: The Power of Silence* (New York, The Guilford Press, 2001). Though, as Williams pointed out to me in an email on April 1, 2016, when people feel motivated and justified in ostracizing another person, being the rejecter might actually be empowering.

67 **the cleaning and janitorial staff:** Jane E. Dutton, Gelaye Debebe, and Amy Wrzesniewski, "Being Valued and Devalued at Work: A Social Valuing Perspective," in Beth A. Bechky and Kimberly D. Elsbach (editors), *Qualitative Organizational Research: Best Papers from the Davis Conference on Qualitative Research*, volume 3 (Charlotte, North Carolina: Information Age Publishing, 2016).

67 **powerful role that belonging plays:** This study was specifically measuring "being socially valued." Dutton draws a distinction between belonging and being valued, arguing that the former is related to feeling like part of the group, while the latter refers to feeling a sense of worth. My definition of belonging includes both concepts: you feel belonging not only when you feel part of a group or relationship, but also when people treat you like you matter and have worth.

69 **relationship to their work changed:** See also Amy Wrzesniewski and Jane E. Dutton, "Crafting a Job: Revisioning Employees as Active Crafters of Their Work," *Academy of Management Review* 26, no. 2 (2001): 179–201.

71 **Buddha offers an instructive parable:** This information is from PBS documentary *The Buddha,* a film by David Grubin, which aired on April 8, 2010; and Sister Vajirā and Francis Story, *Last Days of the Buddha: Mahaāparinibbāna Sutta* (Kandy, Sri Lanka: Buddhist Publication Society, 2007). Note that in the quotes, I changed "Nibhana" to "Nirvana."

3: Purpose

73 **Ashley Richmond:** Interview with author, October 8, 2015.

75 **zoo community as "enrichment":** Beyond the interview with Ashley, information from this section came from an author interview with Scott Carter, Chief Life Sciences Officer at the Detroit Zoo, on October 8, 2015; an author interview with Ron Kagan, Executive Director and CEO of the Detroit Zoo, on October 7, 2015; and Vicki Croke, *The Modern Ark: The Story of Zoos: Past, Present, and Future* (New York: Simon & Schuster, 2014).

77 **zookeepers have an unusually strong:** Stuart J. Bunderson and Jeffery A. Thompson, "The Call of the Wild: Zookeepers, Callings, and the Double-Edged Sword of Deeply Meaningful Work," *Administrative Science Quarterly* 54, no. 1 (2009): 32–57.

77 **purpose has two important dimensions:** William Damon, Jenni Menon, and Kendall Cotton Bronk, "The Development of Purpose during Adolescence," *Applied Developmental Science* 7, no. 3 (2003): 119–28. The authors mention a third dimension as well: "Unlike meaning alone (which may or may not be oriented towards a defined end), purpose is always directed at an accomplishment towards which one can make progress" (121). In my opinion, the first dimension of purpose—that it is a long-term goal—implies this third dimension.

78 **Teens who help:** Eva H. Telzer, Kim M. Tsai, Nancy Gonzales, and Andrew J. Fuligni, "Mexican American Adolescents' Family Obligation Values and Behaviors: Links to Internalizing Symptoms across Time and Context," *Developmental Psychology* 51, no. 1 (2015): 75–86.

78 **their lives are more meaningful:** This paper examines the connection between goals, purpose, and living a meaningful life: Robert A. Emmons, "Personal Goals, Life Meaning, and Virtue: Wellsprings of a Positive Life," in Cory L. M. Keyes and Jonathan Haidt (editors), *Flourishing: Positive Psychology and the Life Well-Lived* (Washington, DC: American Psychological Association), 105–28. See also David S. Yeager and Matthew J. Bundick, "The Role of Purposeful Work Goals in Promoting Meaning in Life and in Schoolwork during Adolescence," *Journal of Adolescent Research* 24, no. 4 (2009): 423–52.

78 **more satisfying:** In this study, living a meaningful life was associated with life satisfaction. The researchers measured meaning by

asking participants purpose-related questions like "My life serves a higher purpose" and "I have the responsibility to make the world a better place": Peterson et al., "Orientations to Happiness and Life Satisfaction: The Full Life versus the Empty Life," 31.

78 **more resilient . . . their goals:** Todd B. Kashdan and Patrick E. McKnight, "Origins of Purpose in Life: Refining Our Understanding of a Life Well Lived," *Psychological Topics* 18, no. 2 (2009): 303–13.

78 **When Damon looked:** He describes this study in William Damon, *The Path to Purpose: How Young People Find Their Calling in Life* (New York: Simon & Schuster, 2009).

78 **more motivated . . . better grades:** David S. Yeager, Marlone D. Henderson, David Paunesku, Gregory M. Walton, Sidney D'Mello, Brian J. Spitzer, and Angela Lee Duckworth, "Boring but Important: A Self-Transcendent Purpose for Learning Fosters Academic Self-Regulation," *Journal of Personality and Social Psychology* 107, no. 4 (2014): 559–80.

78 **risky behaviors like drug use:** Martha L. Sayles, "Adolescents' Purpose in Life and Engagement in Risky Behaviors: Differences by Gender and Ethnicity," PhD dissertation, ProQuest Information & Learning, 1995, cited in Damon et al., "The Development of Purpose During Adolescence."

78 **8 out of 10:** Damon, *The Path to Purpose,* 60. Based on a 2006 analysis of the initial wave of data, Damon and his colleagues found that only 20 percent of the young people he and his colleagues interviewed were purposeful. Twenty-five percent expressed essentially no purpose at all, while the remaining participants were either "dreamers," who had aspirations but did not know how to achieve them, or "dabblers," who tried a number of purposes but did not have a clear sense of why they were doing what they were doing.

78 **"expressing virtually no purpose":** Damon, *The Path to Purpose,* 60.

79 **Coss Marte was:** Interview with author on December 10, 2014, and January 15, 2015.

79 **the crime rate in New York:** This paper shows that most indices of crime were rising from the 1980s until the mid-1990s: Patrick A. Langan and Matthew R. Durose, "The Remarkable Drop in Crime in New York City," paper presented at the 2003 International Conference on Crime (December 3–5), Rome, Italy. Retrieved March 10, 2016, from scribd.com/doc/322928/Langan-rel.

79 **epicenters of the drug trade:** As former police commissioner Howard Safir put it: "Historically, the Lower East Side has had a lot of entrenched drug gangs." John Sullivan, "Once More, Lower East Side Is the Focus of Drug Arrests," *New York Times,* August 7, 1997.

80 **At nineteen years old:** When I asked Coss about how much violence he experienced or participated in, he said: "I never brought up any violence, but violence came with it. People robbed me, tied me up, broke into my houses."

80 **biggest drug busts:** According to the New York City government website, it was a "Significant Case" of 2009.

83 **Defy Ventures:** From the Defy Ventures website: defyventures.org.

84 **self-reflection and self-knowledge:** See, for example, the literature on "self-concordant goals," or goals that align with our values and identity: Kennon M. Sheldon and Andrew J. Elliot, "Goal Striving, Need Satisfaction, and Longitudinal Well-Being: The Self-Concordance Model," *Journal of Personality and Social Psychology* 76, no. 3 (1999): 482–97; and Kennon M. Sheldon and Linda Houser-Marko, "Self-Concordance, Goal Attainment, and the Pursuit of Happiness: Can There Be an Upward Spiral?" *Journal of Personality and Social Psychology* 80, no. 1 (2001): 152–65.

84 **Erik Erikson described identity:** See Erik H. Erikson, *Childhood and Society* (New York: W. W. Norton & Company, 1993); and *Identity: Youth and Crisis* (New York: W. W. Norton & Company, 1968). I'm grateful to William Damon and Dan McAdams for helping me understand Erikson's ideas about identity.

85 **"ego integrity" . . . "despair":** Erikson, *Childhood and Society,* 268.

85 **Researchers at Texas A&M University:** This section was informed by author interviews with researchers Joshua Hicks on February 17, 2015, and Rebecca Schlegel on October 9, 2015.

85 **In one study, a group:** Rebecca J. Schlegel, Joshua A. Hicks, Jamie Arndt, and Laura A. King, "Thine Own Self: True Self-Concept Accessibility and Meaning in Life," *Journal of Personality and Social Psychology* 96, no. 2 (2009): 473–90, study 3. For more on the link between self-knowledge and meaning in life, see also Rebecca J. Schlegel, Joshua A. Hicks, Laura A. King, and Jamie Arndt, "Feeling Like You Know Who You Are: Perceived True Self-Knowledge and Meaning in Life," *Personality and Social Psychology Bulletin* 37, no. 6 (2011): 745–56.

85 **their "true self," as opposed to:** The true self, the researchers write, is "defined as those characteristics that you possess and would like

to express socially, but are not always able to, for whatever reason . . . those traits you are able to express around those people you are closest to." Following a convention in psychology, they refer to the inauthentic self, a bit confusingly, as "the actual self" and define it "as those characteristics that you possess and are often able to express to others in social settings." They also call this the "public self." The idea is that "people only feel comfortable expressing their true selves around close others and keep them hidden during most of their daily activities." Schlegel et al., "Thine Own Self," 475.

85 **subconsciously reminded of their true selves:** In the control condition, students were flashed traits that they had earlier listed to describe their "actual self." Students who were primed with their actual self, as opposed to their true self, did not rate their lives as more meaningful after the task.

85 **Someone whose strengths are:** There are several assessments individuals can take to help determine their strengths, including the Gallup StrengthsFinder and the VIA Survey of Character Strengths. For more on each, see Tom Rath, *StrengthsFinder 2.0* (New York: Simon & Schuster, 2007), and Peterson and Seligman, *Character Strengths and Virtues: A Handbook and Classification.*

85 **use those gifts:** According to Ryan Niemiec of the VIA Institute of Character, your strengths don't pigeonhole you into particular careers. The important thing to remember about your strengths is that you can use them in a variety of work environments (and nonwork environments).

85 **more meaning . . . perform better:** See Claudia Harzer and Willibald Ruch, "When the Job Is a Calling: The Role of Applying One's Signature Strengths at Work," *The Journal of Positive Psychology* 7, no. 5 (2012): 362–37; and Philippe Dubreuil, Jacques Forest, and François Courcy, "From Strengths Use to Work Performance: The Role of Harmonious Passion, Subjective Vitality, and Concentration," *The Journal of Positive Psychology* 9, no. 4 (2014): 335–49.

86 **more satisfied . . . persevere:** Sheldon and Elliot, "Goal Striving, Need Satisfaction, and Longitudinal Well-Being: The Self-Concordance Model." See also Sheldon and Houser-Marko, "Self-Concordance, Goal Attainment, and the Pursuit of Happiness."

86 **story of Manjari Sharma:** Author interview on March 6, 2013, and October 16, 2015.

91 **German thinker Immanuel Kant:** Immanuel Kant, *Groundwork of the Metaphysics of Morals,* edited and translated by Mary Gregor

and Jens Timmermann (Cambridge: Cambridge University Press, 2012), 35. I was inspired to make this point about Kant as a result of an article I read: Gordon Marino, "A Life Beyond 'Do What You Love,'" *New York Times,* May 17, 2014.

92 **as the theologian Frederick Buechner:** Frederick Buechner, *Wishful Thinking: A Seeker's ABC* (New York: HarperCollins, 1993), 119. Buechner, a theologian, has a theistic understanding of vocation and calling. Buechner writes: "The kind of work God usually calls you to is the kind of work (a) that you need most to do and (b) that the world most needs to have done. . . . The place God calls you to is the place where your deep gladness and the world's deep hunger meet." Indeed, the idea of calling has religious origins as discussed in Bunderson and Thompson, "The Call of the Wild." Today, researchers who study calling acknowledge the religious roots of this idea but define it secularly. See Amy Wrzesniewski, Clark McCauley, Paul Rozin, and Barry Schwartz, "Jobs, Careers, and Callings: People's Relations to Their Work," *Journal of Research in Personality* 31, no. 1 (1997): 21–33.

93 **The four most common occupations:** According to the Bureau of Labor Statistics in a press release from March 2015, bls.gov/news.release/pdf/ocwage.pdf.

93 **Amy Wrzesniewski . . . told me:** Author interview, April 18, 2014.

93 **see their work as a calling:** Cited in Ryan D. Duffy and Bryan J. Dik, "Research on Calling: What Have We Learned and Where Are We Going?" *Journal of Vocational Behavior* 83, no. 3 (2013): 428–36.

93 **Grant points out that those:** Adam Grant, "Three Lies About Meaningful Work," *Huffington Post,* May 6, 2015. See also Stephen E. Humphrey, Jennifer D. Nahrgang, and Frederick P. Morgeson, "Integrating Motivational, Social, and Contextual Work Design Features: A Meta-analytic Summary and Theoretical Extension of the Work Design Literature," *Journal of Applied Psychology* 92, no. 5 (2007): 1332–56.

93 **In a survey:** The survey was conducted by the organization PayScale in 2013 and the resulting list of the most meaningful jobs can be found here: payscale.com/data-packages/most-and-least-meaningful-jobs/full-list.

94 **university-call-center fundraisers:** Adam M. Grant, Elizabeth M. Campbell, Grace Chen, Keenan Cottone, David Lapedis, and Karen Lee, "Impact and the Art of Motivation Maintenance: The Effects of Contact with Beneficiaries on Persistence Behavior," *Or-*

ganizational Behavior and Human Decision Processes 103, no. 1 (2007): 53–67.

94 **a coupon-processing factory in Mexico:** Jochen I. Menges, Danielle V. Tussing, Andreas Wihler, and Adam Grant, "When Job Performance Is All Relative: How Family Motivation Energizes Effort and Compensates for Intrinsic Motivation," *Academy of Management Journal* (published online, February 25, 2016).

95 **children can be a source:** S. Katherine Nelson, Kostadin Kushlev, Tammy English, Elizabeth W. Dunn, and Sonja Lyubomirsky, "In Defense of Parenthood: Children Are Associated with More Joy than Misery," *Psychological Science* 24, no. 1 (2013): 3–10.

95 **raising kids makes parents unhappy:** For a summary of the research on parenting and unhappiness, see Lyubomirsky, *The Myths of Happiness*, 85. "Although the evidence is mixed," as Lyubomirksy writes, "a number of studies that simply compare the happiness or satisfaction levels of parents and nonparents drawn from all ages and life circumstances find that parents are less happy." For a good summary of the complicated link between parenting and well-being, I recommend S. Katherine Nelson, Kostadin Kushlev, and Sonja Lyubomirsky, "The Pains and Pleasures of Parenting: When, Why, and How Is Parenthood Associated with More or Less Well-Being?" *Psychological Bulletin* 140, no. 3 (2014): 846–95.

95 **raising children is a powerful:** See, for example, Nelson et al., "In Defense of Parenthood: Children Are Associated with More Joy than Misery"; and Debra Umberson and Walter R. Gove, "Parenthood and Psychological Well-Being Theory, Measurement, and Stage in the Family Life Course," *Journal of Family Issues* 10, no. 4 (1989): 440–62.

95 **As one mother told me:** Author interview with Eleanor Brenner, September 30, 2015.

95 **"The growing good":** George Eliot, *Middlemarch* (Hertfordshire, United Kingdom: Wordsworth Editions Ltd., 1998), 688.

95 **adopted by the janitor:** This story appears in Carolyn Tate, *Conscious Marketing: How to Create an Awesome Business with a New Approach to Marketing* (Milton, Australia: Wrightbooks, 2015), 44.

96 **a roadworker:** Bryan J. Dik and Ryan D. Duffy, *Make Your Job a Calling: How the Psychology of Vocation Can Change Your Life at Work* (Conshohocken, Pennsylvania: Templeton Foundation Press, 2012), 4.

96 **"My job isn't to take":** Thanks to my friend Luis Pineda for this story.

4: Storytelling

97 **Erik Kolbell vividly remembers:** Erik told his story at The Players club at a Moth event on December 9, 2014. This information comes from that story and an author interview on August 26, 2015.

100 **As a young man, George:** Information about The Moth, its origin story, and how it finds and puts on stories from author interview with Green on August 26, 2015; author interview with Catherine Burns on November 18, 2014; the organization's website, themoth .org; and Catherine Burns (editor), *The Moth* (New York: Hyperion, 2013).

102 **Jeffery Rudell told a story:** Jeffery's story is available at *The Moth,* themoth.org/stories/under-the-influence. Details from his story came from this online recording and from information he sent to me via several emails in 2013 and 2014.

103 **"act of creation" . . . "the way":** Mary Catherine Bateson, *Composing a Life* (New York: Grove Press, 2001), 1.

104 **and coherence, psychologists say:** Recall that the definition of meaning from the introduction included coherence. See Michael F. Steger, "Meaning in Life: A Unified Model," and Roy F. Baumeister, *Meanings of Life.* Baumeister compares the meaning of one's life to the meaning of a sentence: the more coherent it is, the more meaningful it is. See also Aaron Antonovsky, "The Structure and Properties of the Sense of Coherence Scale," *Social Science & Medicine* 36, no. 6 (1993): 725–33.

104 **the need to make sense:** For more information on our powerful sense-making drive and its relation to meaning, see Steven J. Heine, Travis Proulx, and Kathleen D. Vohs, "The Meaning Maintenance Model: On the Coherence of Social Motivations," *Personality and Social Psychology Review* 10, no. 2 (2006): 88–110; Jerome S. Bruner and Leo Postman, "On the Perception of Incongruity: A Paradigm," *Journal of Personality* 18, no. 2 (1949): 206–23; and Samantha J. Heintzelman, Jason Trent, and Laura A. King, "Encounters with Objective Coherence and the Experience of Meaning in Life," *Psychological Science* (published online, April 25, 2013).

104 **"Storytelling is fundamental":** Bateson, *Composing a Life,* 34.

104 **when it comes to defining:** Dan P. McAdams, "The Psychology of Life Stories," *Review of General Psychology* 5, no. 2 (2001): 100–22.

104 **Take the story of Emeka Nnaka:** Author interview, September 14, 2015.

107 **McAdams is a psychologist:** Information about McAdams's re-

search on narrative identity, redemptive stories, and meaning comes from Dan P. McAdams, "The Psychology of Life Stories"; *The Redemptive Self: Stories Americans Live* (New York: Oxford University Press, 2005); "The Redemptive Self: Generativity and the Stories Americans Live By," *Research in Human Development* 3, no. 2–3 (2006): 81–100; Jack J. Bauer, Dan P. McAdams, and Jennifer L. Pals, "Narrative Identity and Eudaimonic Well-Being," *Journal of Happiness Studies* 9, no. 1 (2008): 81–104; and author interview on May 20, 2014, and subsequent email exchanges in 2014 and 2015.

107 **"about who we are deep down":** As Jonathan Gottschall writes in *The Storytelling Animal: How Stories Make Us Human* (New York: Mariner Books, 2012), 161.

111 **we can edit, revise, and interpret:** As Gottschall points out in *The Storytelling Animal.*

111 **"life story gone awry":** Michele Crossley, *Introducing Narrative Psychology* (Buckingham, United Kingdom: Open University Press, 2000), 57; quoted in Gottschall, *The Storytelling Animal,* 175.

111 **A review of the scientific literature:** As Gottschall points out in *The Storytelling Animal.* Also see Jonathan Shedler, "The Efficacy of Psychodynamic Psychotherapy," *American Psychologist* 65, no. 2 (2010): 98–109.

111 **Even making smaller story edits:** For more on what the University of Virginia psychologist Timothy Wilson has called "story-editing," see Timothy Wilson, *Redirect: Changing the Stories We Live By* (New York: Back Bay Books, 2015).

111 **Adam Grant and Jane Dutton:** Adam Grant and Jane Dutton, "Beneficiary or Benefactor: Are People More Prosocial When They Reflect on Receiving or Giving?" *Psychological Science* 23, no. 9 (2012): 1033–39.

112 **"When seeing themselves as benefactors":** Email from Jane Dutton on January 28, 2016.

113 **In research published in 2010:** Laura J. Kray, Linda G. George, Katie A. Liljenquist, Adam D. Galinsky, Philip E. Tetlock, and Neal J. Roese, "From What Might Have Been to What Must Have Been: Counterfactual Thinking Creates Meaning," *Journal of Personality and Social Psychology* 98, no. 1 (2010): 106–18. I focus on counter-factual reasoning with respect to positive events in my summary of this paper, but the researchers also probed into negative events.

115 **Carlos Eire, that moment was:** Information from Carlos's story

from Carlos Eire, *Waiting for Snow in Havana: Confessions of a Cuban Boy* (New York: Simon & Schuster, 2004); and author interview on October 9, 2015.

118 **The University of Missouri's Laura King:** Information about King's work comes from Laura A. King and Joshua A. Hicks, "Whatever Happened to 'What Might Have Been'? Regrets, Happiness, and Maturity," *American Psychologist* 62, no. 7 (2007): 625–36; Laura A. King, "The Hard Road to the Good Life: The Happy, Mature Person," *Journal of Humanistic Psychology* 41, no. 1 (2001): 51–72; and author interview on April 2, 2014.

119 **two years after they responded:** For divorced women, King writes, "lost possible self elaboration related to current ego development in interaction with time since the divorce." King and Hicks, "Whatever Happened to 'What Might Have Been'?" 630.

121 **the novel *Life of Pi*:** Yann Martel, *Life of Pi* (Orlando, Florida: Harcourt, 2001).

121 **fiction can help people:** Don Kuiken and Ruby Sharma, "Effects of Loss and Trauma on Sublime Disquietude during Literary Reading," *Scientific Study of Literature* 3, no. 2 (2013): 240–65.

122 **In a study published in 2002:** David S. Miall and Don Kuiken, "A Feeling for Fiction: Becoming What We Behold," *Poetics* 30, no. 4 (2002): 221–41.

123 **"levitate the room":** Burns, *The Moth,* xiii.

5: Transcendence

125 **McDonald Observatory in Fort Davis:** I traveled to the McDonald Observatory twice for this section. The opening description of my journey to the observatory and the interview with William Cochran were from a trip I took March 18 and 19, 2013, where I also interviewed the director of the observatory, Tom Barnes. The star party is from the second trip—July 29, 2014.

128 **early horses and the first elephants:** "The Oligocene Period," University of California Museum of Paleontology, retrieved online: ucmp.berkeley.edu/tertiary/oligocene.php.

129 **the discovery of around 1,000 exoplanets:** If you're interested in contributing to this enterprise, you, too, can examine stellar light data for evidence of planetary transits. The citizen science website planethunters.org allows volunteers to comb through data provided by the Kepler Space Telescope for signs of exoplanets.

131 **In Buddhism, transcendence is:** According to Mircea Eliade, *The*

Sacred and the Profane: The Nature of Religion (Orlando, Florida: Harcourt, 1987), 175–76.

132 **Many people have had:** George H. Gallup Jr., "Religious Awakenings Bolster Americans' Faith," January 14, 2003, gallup.com/poll/7582/religious-awakenings-bolster-americans-faith.aspx.

132 **among the most meaningful and important:** See Roland R. Griffiths, William A. Richards, Una McCann, and Robert Jesse, "Psilocybin Can Occasion Mystical-Type Experiences Having Substantial and Sustained Personal Meaning and Spiritual Significance," *Psychopharmacology* 187, no. 3 (2006): 268–83; Roland R. Griffiths, William A. Richards, Matthew W. Johnson, Una D. McCann, and Robert Jesse, "Mystical-Type Experiences Occasioned by Psilocybin Mediate the Attribution of Personal Meaning and Spiritual Significance 14 Months Later," *Journal of Psychopharmacology* 22, no. 6 (2008): 621–32; and Rick Doblin, "Pahnke's 'Good Friday Experiment': A Long-Term Follow-Up and Methodological Critique," *The Journal of Transpersonal Psychology* 23, no. 1 (1991): 1–28.

132 **with William James:** William James, *The Varieties of Religious Experience* (London: Longmans, Green, and Co, 1905), retrieved online from Google Books; and Dmitri Tymoczko, "The Nitrous Oxide Philosopher," *The Atlantic,* May 1996. Though James claims in *Varieties* that his "constitution shuts" him out from enjoying mystical states "almost entirely," and that he "can speak of them only at second hand" (379), the experiences on nitrous oxide seem to be an exception. A few paragraphs later, he ascribes to them a "metaphysical significance" (388).

133 **often for our entire lives:** Doblin, "Pahnke's 'Good Friday Experiment.' "

133 **According to psychologist David Yaden:** David B. Yaden, Jonathan Haidt, Ralph W. Hood, David R. Vago, and Andrew B. Newberg (under review), "The Varieties of Self-Transcendent Experience."

133 **which they refer to as awe:** Dacher Keltner and Jonathan Haidt, "Approaching Awe, a Moral, Spiritual, and Aesthetic Emotion," *Cognition and Emotion* 17, no. 2 (2003): 297–314.

134 **Adam Smith wrote, awe occurs:** Quoted in Jesse Prinz, "How Wonder Works," *Aeon,* June 21, 2013.

134 **how awe affects our sense:** Michelle N. Shiota, Dacher Keltner, and Amanda Mossman, "The Nature of Awe: Elicitors, Appraisals, and Effects on Self-Concept," *Cognition and Emotion* 21, no. 5 (2007): 944–63.

135 **"a sense of timelessness and infinity":** Quoted in Andrew Newberg and Eugene d'Aquili, *Why God Won't Go Away: Brain Science and the Biology of Belief* (New York: Ballantine Books, 2002), 2.

135 **"I possessed God so fully":** Quoted in Newberg and d'Aquili, *Why God Won't Go Away*, 7.

135 **Cory Muscara has been there, too:** Author interview on September 2, 2015.

137 **Jon Kabat-Zinn, has put it:** Jon Kabat-Zinn, *Wherever You Go, There You Are* (New York: Hyperion, 1994), 4.

140 **practitioners of Tibetan Buddhist meditation:** Andrew Newberg, Abass Alavi, Michael Baime, Michael Pourdehnad, Jill Santanna, and Eugene d'Aquili, "The Measurement of Regional Cerebral Blood Flow during the Complex Cognitive Task of Meditation: A Preliminary SPECT Study," *Psychiatry Research: Neuroimaging* 106, no. 2 (2001): 113–22. See also Andrew Newberg, Michael Pourdehnad, Abass Alavi, and Eugene d'Aquili, "Cerebral Blood Flow during Meditative Prayer: Preliminary Findings and Methodological Issues," *Perceptual and Motor Skills* 97, no. 2 (2003): 625–30. Material from this section also comes from an author interview with Newberg on April 25, 2013.

141 **minds of meditating Sufi mystics:** Andrew Newberg and Mark Robert Waldman, *How Enlightenment Changes Your Brain: The New Science of Transformation* (New York: Avery, 2016).

141 **former astronaut Jeff Ashby:** Author interview on July 17, 2014.

141 **Within a decade of Shepard's flight:** Information about the early history of space exploration came via NASA's website and my conversation with Ashby.

142 **Archibald MacLeish wrote:** James H. Billington (preface), *Respectfully Quoted: A Dictionary of Quotations: Compiled by the Library of Congress* (New York: Dover Publications, 2010), 328.

143 **Their values, according to one:** Peter Suedfeld, Katya Legkaia, and Jelena Brcic, "Changes in the Hierarchy of Value References Associated with Flying in Space," *Journal of Personality* 78, no. 5 (2010): 1411–36. See also David B. Yaden, Jonathan Iwry, Kelley J. Slack, Johannes C. Eiechstaedt, Yukun Zhao, George E. Vaillant, and Andrew Newberg, "The Overview Effect: Awe and Self-Transcendent Experience in Space Flight," *Psychology of Consciousness* (in press).

144 **"You develop . . . 'son of a bitch'":** "Edgar Mitchell's Strange Voyage," *People*, vol. 1, no. 6, April 8, 1974.

144 **Ron Garan, for example:** Ron Garan, *The Orbital Perspective: Lessons in Seeing the Big Picture from a Journey of 71 Million Miles* (Oakland, California: Berrett-Koehler, 2015).

144 **Edgar Mitchell:** "Edgar Mitchell's Strange Voyage."

144 **"You cannot view . . . preservation":** This quote appears in his biography on the website for Mosaic Renewables.

145 **John Muir, the nineteenth-century naturalist:** Muir's biographical information comes from Donald Worster, *A Passion for Nature: The Life of John Muir* (New York: Oxford University Press, 2008); and John Muir, *The Story of My Boyhood and Youth* (Boston: Houghton Mifflin, 1913), retrieved from Google Books.

146 **was influenced by Transcendentalism:** James Brannon, "Radical Transcendentalism: Emerson, Muir and the Experience of Nature," *John Muir Newsletter,* vol. 16, no. 1 (Winter 2006), retrieved online at the Sierra Club website.

146 **Ralph Waldo Emerson's 1836 essay "Nature":** David Mikics (editor), *The Annotated Emerson* (Cambridge, Massachusetts: Belknap Press, 2012).

146 **"all nature is leaden . . . light":** Ralph Waldo Emerson and Waldo Emerson Forbes (editors), *Journals of Ralph Waldo Emerson with Annotations: 1824–1832* (Boston: Houghton Mifflin, 1909), 381.

147 **"If this is mysticism," as Emerson's:** Robert D. Richardson, *Emerson: The Mind on Fire* (Berkeley: University of California Press, 1995), 228.

147 **an awe-inspiring encounter:** Paul Piff, Pia Dietze, Matthew Feinberg, Daniel M. Stancato, and Dacher Keltner, "Awe, the Small Self, and Prosocial Behavior," *Journal of Personality and Social Psychology* 108, no. 6 (2015): 883–99, study 5.

148 **writes the psychologist Mark Leary:** Mark Leary, *The Curse of the Self: Self-Awareness, Egotism, and the Quality of Human Life* (New York: Oxford University Press, 2004), 86.

148 **Take the case of Janeen Delaney:** Author interview, June 18, 2014.

149 **Since ancient times:** Peter T. Furst, *Flesh of the Gods: The Ritual Use of Hallucinogens* (Prospect Heights, Illinois: Waveland Press, 1990).

150 **Roland Griffiths, the principal investigator:** Much of the information in the paragraphs that follow came from an author interview with Griffiths on February 28, 2013. See also Roland R. Griffiths and Charles S. Grob, "Hallucinogens as Medicine," *Scientific American* 303, no. 6 (2010): 76–79.

150 **"bad trip":** Hallucinogenic trips are not the only transcendent ex-

periences that can go wrong. Meditation can plunge people into terror, too. See Tomas Rocha, "The Dark Knight of the Soul," *The Atlantic,* June 25, 2014.

150 **Leary, an academic psychologist at Harvard:** Information about Leary from Timothy Leary, *Flashbacks: A Personal and Cultural History of an Era* (New York: G. P. Putnam's Sons, 1990); and Robert Greenfield, *Timothy Leary: A Biography* (Orlando, Florida: Harcourt, 2006).

151 **Nixon called Leary:** Quoted in Laura Mansnerus, "Timothy Leary, Pied Piper of Psychedelic 60's, Dies at 75," *New York Times,* June 1, 1996.

151 **studies have looked at the effects:** The research on religious leaders has yet to be published, but for findings on the other three groups, see Griffiths et al., "Psilocybin Can Occasion Mystical-Type Experiences Having Substantial and Sustained Personal Meaning and Spiritual Significance"; Charles S. Grob, Alicia L. Danforth, Gurpreet S. Chopra, Marycie Hagerty, Charles R. McKay, Adam L. Halberstadt, and George R. Greer, "Pilot Study of Psilocybin Treatment for Anxiety in Patients with Advanced-Stage Cancer," *Archives of General Psychiatry* 68, no. 1 (2011): 71–78; and Matthew W. Johnson, Albert Garcia-Romeu, Mary P. Cosimano, and Roland R. Griffiths, "Pilot Study of the 5-HT2AR Agonist Psilocybin in the Treatment of Tobacco Addiction," *Journal of Psychopharmacology* 28, no. 11 (2014): 983–92.

152 **cancer patients Griffiths has studied:** At the time of this writing, Griffiths and his colleagues were preparing to submit the study in which Janeen participated to journals to be published. They have already published one study on the effects of a psilocybin-induced mystical experience on terminal cancer patients, showing that it reduces anxiety: Grob et al., "Pilot Study of Psilocybin Treatment for Anxiety in Patients with Advanced-Stage Cancer."

153 **"Sooner or later," writes the Buddhist:** Thich Nhat Hanh, *No Death, No Fear: Comforting Wisdom for Life* (New York: Riverhead Books, 2002), 25.

6: Growth

156 **Welcome to The Dinner Party:** I attended a Dinner Party with Sarah, Raúl, Christine, and Sandy on October 19, 2014. The attendants asked that I maintain anonymity by giving them different names and, in some cases, changing identifying details of their

lives. Information about The Dinner Party as a movement and organization, and its founding, from an interview with Lennon Flowers and Dara Kosberg on May 7, 2014.

156 **For most of us, there is:** "Researchers estimate that about 75 percent of people will experience a traumatic event in their lifetime," writes Jim Rendon in *Upside: The New Science of Post-Traumatic Growth* (New York: Touchstone, 2015), 27.

157 **shatter our fundamental assumptions:** Ronnie Janoff-Bulman, *Shattered Assumptions: Towards a New Psychology of Trauma* (New York: Free Press, 1992).

157 **can also push us to grow:** Good overviews of this research are Rendon, *Upside;* and Stephen Joseph, *What Doesn't Kill Us: The New Psychology of Posttraumatic Growth* (New York: Basic Books, 2011).

162 **new idea in mainstream psychology:** Joseph, *What Doesn't Kill Us.* Joseph mentions some exceptions that prove the rule in his book, like the work of Viktor Frankl (whom I cover in the conclusion). See also chapter 1 of Richard G. Tedeschi, Crystal L. Park, and Lawrence G. Calhoun (editors), *Posttraumatic Growth: Positive Changes in the Aftermath of Crisis* (Mahwah, New Jersey: Routledge, 1998).

163 **added post-traumatic stress disorder:** Matthew J. Friedman, "PTSD History and Overview" at the Veterans Administration website, ptsd.va.gov/professional/PTSD-overview/ptsd-overview.asp.

163 **The story of Bob Curry:** Author interviews on May 30, 2014, and January 27, 2015.

167 **Robert Jay Lifton:** Robert Jay Lifton, "Americans as Survivors," *New England Journal of Medicine* 352, no. 22 (2005): 2263–65.

167 **others don't have to go through:** This tendency has also been called "altruism born of suffering," as Kelly McGonigal points out in *The Upside of Stress: Why Stress Is Good for You, and How to Get Good at It* (New York: Avery, 2015).

167 **Survivors of sexual assault:** Examples of survivor mission from Lifton, "Americans as Survivors," and Lauren Eskreis-Winkler, Elizabeth P. Shulman, and Angela L. Duckworth, "Survivor Mission: Do Those Who Survive Have a Drive to Thrive at Work?" *The Journal of Positive Psychology* 9, no. 3 (2014): 209–18.

167 **less depression . . . and meaning in life:** McGonigal reviews this body of research in chapter 5 of *The Upside of Stress.*

168 **most people will experience some:** Rendon, *Upside.*

168 **half to two-thirds of trauma survivors:** Based on his research and

knowledge of the field, psychologist Richard Tedeschi provided this figure in an email to me on January 27, 2015.

168 **small percentage suffer:** According to the American Psychological Association, "almost 8% of adult Americans will experience PTSD at some point in their lives": apa.org/research/action/ptsd.aspx.

168 **Richard Tedeschi and Lawrence Calhoun:** The information about post-traumatic growth came chiefly from an author interview with Richard Tedeschi on January 28, 2015. See also Richard G. Tedeschi and Lawrence G. Calhoun, "Posttraumatic Growth: Conceptual Foundations and Empirical Evidence," *Psychological Inquiry* 15, no. 1 (2004): 1–18.

168 **"We'd been working":** Quoted in Shelley Levitt, "The Science of Post-Traumatic Growth," *Live Happy,* February 24, 2014.

169 **"are the most important things":** Shelley E. Taylor, "Adjustment to Threatening Events: A Theory of Cognitive Adaptation," *American Psychologist* 38, no. 11 (1983): 1161–73.

169 **"I've become more empathetic":** Tedeschi and Calhoun, "Posttraumatic Growth: Conceptual Foundations and Empirical Evidence," 6.

169 **oncology nurse:** Lawrence G. Calhoun and Richard G. Tedeschi, *The Handbook of Posttraumatic Growth: Research and Practice* (New York: Psychology Press, 2006).

169 **"vulnerable yet stronger":** Ibid., 5.

170 **rape survivor who admitted:** Janoff-Bulman, *Shattered Assumptions.*

170 **survivor of an airplane crash:** Ibid.

170 **Trauma shatters those assumptions:** Ibid.

171 **"It is not the actual trauma":** Suzanne Danhauer of Wake Forest School of Medicine, quoted in Rendon, *Upside,* 77.

171 **James Pennebaker:** Information about expressive writing and Pennebaker's work from author interview, December 22, 2014; Anna Graybeal, Janel D. Sexton, and James W. Pennebaker, "The Role of Story-Making in Disclosure Writing: The Psychometrics of Narrative," *Psychology and Health* 17, no. 5 (2002): 571–81; James W. Pennebaker and Janel D. Seagal, "Forming a Story: The Health Benefits of Narrative," *Journal of Clinical Psychology* 55, no. 10 (1999): 1243–54; and James W. Pennebaker, *Writing to Heal: A Guided Journal for Recovering from Trauma and Emotional Upheaval* (Oakland, California: New Harbinger Publisher, 2004).

174 **less depressed and report higher well-being:** Vicki S. Helgeson, Kerry A. Reynolds, and Patricia L. Tomich, "A Meta-analytic Re-

view of Benefit Finding and Growth," *Journal of Consulting and Clinical Psychology* 74, no. 5 (2006): 797.

174 **Viktor Frankl tells about consoling:** Viktor Frankl, *Man's Search for Meaning* (Boston: Beacon Press, 2006), 113.

175 **through dance didn't benefit:** Anne M. Krantz and James W. Pennebaker, "Expressive Dance, Writing, Trauma, and Health: When Words Have a Body," in Ilene Serlin (editor), *Whole Person Healthcare, Volume 3* (Westport, Connecticut: Praeger, 2007), 201–29.

175 **One of those people is Shibvon:** Shibvon's story, and all of the quotes from it, appear in chapter 2 of Gina O'Connell Higgins, *Resilient Adults: Overcoming a Cruel Past* (San Francisco: Jossey-Bass, 1994), 25–43. To protect her privacy, Higgins used a pseudonym, "Shibvon," and changed the identifying details of individuals in the story. The other aspects of the story, Higgins explains, are rendered factually.

176 **psychological and physical scars:** For a good review of the research on the psychological and physical effects of childhood adversity, see Donna Jackson Nakazawa, *Childhood Disrupted: How Your Biography Becomes Your Biology, and How You Can Heal* (New York: Atria Books, 2015).

176 **Childhood adversity has been linked:** These research-based findings are summarized at "Child Maltreatment: Consequences" on the CDC's website, cdc.gov/violenceprevention/childmaltreatment/consequences.html.

177 **research on resilience began:** Information from this paragraph from Ann S. Masten, "Ordinary Magic: Resilience Processes in Development," *American Psychologist* 56, no. 3 (2001): 227–38; and email exchanges with Masten in March 2016.

177 **Steven Southwick . . . Dennis Charney:** For the following paragraphs on the factors that explain resilience, as well as the quotes from the POWs, see Steven M. Southwick and Dennis S. Charney, *Resilience: The Science of Mastering Life's Greatest Challenges* (Cambridge: Cambridge University Press, 2012).

178 **For children, especially:** "Toxic Stress," Harvard University's Center for the Developing Child, developingchild.harvard.edu/science/key-concepts/toxic-stress/.

179 **religious and patriotic services:** There, a young John McCain delivered sermons. See Jill Zuckman, "John McCain and the POW Church Riot," *Chicago Tribune,* August 15, 2008; and Karl Rove, "Getting to Know John McCain," *Wall Street Journal,* April 30, 2008.

179 **by our genetic makeup:** McGonigal, *The Upside of Stress.*

179 **early-life experiences:** The influence of early-life experiences on our stress response is touched upon by McGonigal, ibid. See also Linda L. Carpenter, Cyrena E. Gawuga, Audrey R. Tyrka, Janet K. Lee, George M. Anderson, and Lawrence H. Price, "Association Between Plasma IL-6 Response to Acute Stress and Early-Life Adversity in Healthy Adults," *Neuropsychopharmacology* 35, no. 13 (2010): 2617–23; and Pilyoung Kim, Gary W. Evans, Michael Angstadt, S. Shaun Ho, Chandra S. Sripada, James E. Swain, Israel Liberzon, and K. Luan Phan, "Effects of Childhood Poverty and Chronic Stress on Emotion Regulatory Brain Function in Adulthood," *Proceedings of the National Academy of Sciences* 110, no. 46 (2013): 18442–47.

179 **Charney has said:** "The Science of Resilience and How It Can Be Learned," *The Diane Rehm Show,* National Public Radio, August 24, 2015.

179 **resilience can be taught:** Michele M. Tugade and Barbara L. Fredrickson, "Resilient Individuals Use Positive Emotions to Bounce Back from Negative Emotional Experiences," *Journal of Personality and Social Psychology* 86, no. 2 (2004): 320–33.

181 **Gregory Walton and Geoffrey Cohen:** Description of this study from Gregory M. Walton and Geoffrey L. Cohen, "A Brief Social-Belonging Intervention Improves Academic and Health Outcomes of Minority Students," *Science* 331, no. 6023 (2011): 1447–51; and email exchanges with Walton in March of 2016.

183 **Abelson at the University of Michigan:** James L. Abelson, Thane M. Erickson, Stefanie E. Mayer, Jennifer Crocker, Hedieh Briggs, Nestor L. Lopez-Duran, and Israel Liberzon, "Brief Cognitive Intervention Can Modulate Neuroendocrine Stress Responses to the Trier Social Stress Test: Buffering Effects of a Compassionate Goal Orientation," *Psychoneuroendocrinology* 44 (2014): 60–70. I also exchanged emails with Abelson on March 16–18, 2016, about this study.

184 **Research led by David Yeager:** Yeager et al., "Boring but Important: A Self-Transcendent Purpose for Learning Fosters Academic Self-Regulation."

184 **As Stanford's Kelly McGonigal writes:** McGonigal, *The Upside of Stress*, 219.

184 **In his classic work on grief:** Harold Kushner, *When Bad Things Happen to Good People* (New York: Anchor Books, 2004), 147.

185 **suffer well:** The late University of Michigan psychologist Christo-

pher Peterson used to say, I'm told, that resilience is the ability to "suffer well."

7: Cultures of Meaning

187 **St. Mark's Cathedral in Seattle:** I visited St. Mark's for mass and Compline on October 4, 2015. Further information about the church and Compline from author interview with Jason Anderson on October 5, 2015; and Kenneth V. Peterson, *Prayer as Night Falls: Experiencing Compline* (Brewster, Massachusetts: Paraclete Press, 2013). Anderson is the director of the Compline Choir of St. Mark's, and Peterson is a member of it. If you'd like to hear the service, check out the choir's website, complinechoir.org.

188 **handful of other churches:** For example, Compline is offered at St. Andrew's Episcopal Church in Ann Arbor, Michigan; Christ Church in New Haven, Connecticut; St. David's Episcopal Church in Austin, Texas; and Trinity Church in New York City.

188 **"unmediated experience of the Divine Presence":** Peterson, *Prayer as Night Falls,* 9.

190 **"Adults spend":** Paul Piff and Dacher Keltner, "Why Do We Experience Awe?" *New York Times,* May 22, 2015.

191 **Joshua Bell stood in a Washington:** Gene Weingarten, "Pearls Before Breakfast: Can One of the Nation's Great Musicians Cut through the Fog of a D.C. Rush Hour? Let's Find Out," *Washington Post Magazine,* April 8, 2007.

191 **"work-and-spend" mentality:** Gregg Easterbrook, *The Progress Paradox: How Life Gets Better While People Feel Worse*, 250.

191 **social connections are becoming less:** See Putnam, *Bowling Alone: The Collapse and Revival of American Community*; and Stefano Bartolini, Ennio Bilancini, and Maurizio Pugno, "Did the Decline in Social Connections Depress Americans' Happiness?" *Social Indicators Research* 110, no. 3 (2013): 1033–59.

192 **"A transition from material want":** Easterbrook, *The Progress Paradox,* 211.

192 **In his research, Inglehart discovered:** Ronald Inglehart, *Culture Shift in Advanced Industrial Society* (Princeton: Princeton University Press, 1990).

192 **"fourth great awakening":** Robert William Fogel, *The Fourth Great Awakening and the Future of Egalitarianism* (Chicago: University of Chicago Press, 2000).

193 **Many teenagers are unsure:** Damon, *The Path to Purpose: How Young People Find Their Calling in Life.*

194 **DreamCon:** I attended DreamCon, and interviewed Kanya Balakrishna as well as a number of high school students there, on December 13, 2014. Information about The Future Project came from those interviews, as well as subsequent emails with Balakrishna and others at the organization. See also The Future Project for research findings about the program: thefutureproject.org.

196 **society's interest in purpose:** Gabriel Bauchat Grant, "Exploring the Possibility of an Age of Purpose," papers.ssrn.com/sol3/papers.cfm?abstract_id=2618863.

196 **As Bert and John tell it:** Author interview with John Jacobs on June 12, 2014; and Bert and John Jacobs, *Life Is Good: How to Live with Purpose and Enjoy the Ride* (Washington, DC: National Geographic Society, 2015).

199 **the foundation has trained over:** According to Charles Veysey, Chief Business Optimist at the Life Is Good Kids Foundation, on March 2, 2016.

200 **Ian Mitchell . . . Craig Marcantonio . . . Allison Shablin:** Three separate author interviews on November 3, 2015.

200 **Aaron Hurst has called:** Aaron Hurst, *The Purpose Economy: How Your Desire for Impact, Personal Growth and Community Is Changing the World* (Boise, Idaho: Elevate, 2014), 28–29. I also interviewed Hurst on June 3, 2014.

201 **John Mackey . . . Raj Sisodia:** John Mackey and Raj Sisodia, *Conscious Capitalism: Liberating the Heroic Spirit of Business* (Boston: Harvard Business Review Press, 2014); see appendix A for the "business case for conscious capitalism," 275–89.

201 **"People are increasingly":** Rajendra S. Sisodia, David B. Wolfe, and Jagdish N. Sheth, *Firms of Endearment: How World-Class Companies Profit from Passion and Purpose* (Upper Saddle River, New Jersey: Wharton School Publishing, 2007), 4.

201 **"not engaged" . . . "actively disengaged":** Amy Adkins, "Majority of U.S. Employees Not Engaged Despite Gains in 2014," Gallup, January 28, 2015.

201 **feel satisfied with their jobs:** Julianne Pepitone, "U.S. Job Satisfaction Hits 22-Year Low," CNNMoney, January 5, 2010.

201 **more engaged . . . far likelier to stay:** For engaged and likelier to stay, see Tony Schwartz and Christine Porath, "Why You Hate Work," *New York Times,* May 30, 2014. For more productive, see the research by Adam Grant covered in chapter 3; and Adam M.

Grant, "Does Intrinsic Motivation Fuel the Prosocial Fire? Motivational Synergy in Predicting Persistence, Performance, and Productivity," *Journal of Applied Psychology* 93, no. 1 (2008): 48–58.

201 **a very potent motivating force:** Adam M. Grant, "The Significance of Task Significance: Job Performance Effects, Relational Mechanisms, and Boundary Conditions," *Journal of Applied Psychology* 93, no. 1 (2008): 108–24.

201 **Teresa Amabile of Harvard:** Teresa Amabile and Steven Kramer, "How Leaders Kill Meaning at Work," *McKinsey Quarterly,* January 2012.

202 **serious problems, especially at long-term-care:** See Catherine Hawes, "Elder Abuse in Residential Long-Term Care Settings: What Is Known and What Information Is Needed?" in Richard J. Bonnie and Robert B. Wallace (editors), *Elder Mistreatment: Abuse, Neglect, and Exploitation in an Aging America* (Washington, DC: National Academies Press, 2003); Claudia Cooper, Amber Selwood, and Gill Livingston, "The Prevalence of Elder Abuse and Neglect: A Systematic Review," *Age and Ageing* 37, no. 2 (2008): 151–60; and the National Center on Elder Abuse, which compiles the research on elder abuse and neglect on its website, ncea.aoa.gov/.

202 **In one study:** The studies cited in this paragraph are summarized in a review of the research on elder abuse in long-term-care centers: Hawes, "Elder Abuse in Residential Long-Term Care Settings."

202 **a classic psychology experiment:** Ellen Langer and Judith Rodin, "The Effects of Choice and Enhanced Personal Responsibility for the Aged: A Field Experiment in an Institutional Setting," *Journal of Personality and Social Psychology* 34 (1976): 191–98. For the follow-up study, see Judith Rodin and Ellen J. Langer, "Long-Term Effects of a Control-Relevant Intervention with the Institutionalized Aged," *Journal of Personality and Social Psychology* 35, no. 12 (1977): 897–902. Also, this study is described in Ellen Langer, *Counterclockwise: Mindful Health and the Power of Possibility* (New York: Ballantine Books, 2009). Beyond the plant manipulation, people in the experimental group were told that they were responsible for their own schedules and well-being, while those in the control group were told that the nursing home staff was responsible for them.

203 **more purpose in life live longer:** Patricia A. Boyle, Lisa L. Barnes, Aron S. Buchman, and David A. Bennett, "Purpose in Life Is Associated with Mortality among Community-Dwelling Older Persons," *Psychosomatic Medicine* 71, no. 5 (2009): 574–79.

203 **longevity:** Neal Krause, "Meaning in Life and Mortality," *The*

Journals of Gerontology Series B: Psychological Sciences and Social Sciences 64, no. 4 (2009): 517–27.

203 **better immune functioning:** Michael Steger, "Is It Time to Consider Meaning in Life as a Public Policy Priority?" *Ewha Journal of Social Sciences* 30, no. 2 (2014): 53–78.

203 **more gray matter in the brain:** Gary J. Lewis, Ryota Kanai, Geraint Rees, and Timothy C. Bates, "Neural Correlates of the 'Good Life': Eudaimonic Well-Being Is Associated with Insular Cortex Volume," *Social Cognitive and Affective Neuroscience* 9, no. 5 (2014): 615–18.

203 **cognitive impairments, Alzheimer's:** Patricia A. Boyle, Aron S. Buchman, Lisa L. Barnes, and David A. Bennett, "Effect of a Purpose in Life on Risk of Incident Alzheimer Disease and Mild Cognitive Impairment in Community-Dwelling Older Persons," *Archives of General Psychiatry* 67, no. 3 (2010): 304–10.

203 **strokes:** Eric S. Kim, Jennifer K. Sun, Nansook Park, and Christopher Peterson, "Purpose in Life and Reduced Incidence of Stroke in Older Adults: 'The Health and Retirement Study,'" *Journal of Psychosomatic Research* 74, no. 5 (2013): 427–32.

204 **chances of having a heart attack:** Eric S. Kim, Jennifer K. Sun, Nansook Park, Laura D. Kubzansky, and Christopher Peterson, "Purpose in Life and Reduced Risk of Myocardial Infarction Among Older US Adults with Coronary Heart Disease: A Two-Year Follow-Up," *Journal of Behavioral Medicine* 36, no. 2 (2013): 124–33.

204 **for cardiovascular disease:** Toshimasa Sone, Naoki Nakaya, Kaori Ohmori, Taichi Shimazu, Mizuka Higashiguchi, Masako Kakizaki, Nobutaka Kikuchi, Shinichi Kuriyama, and Ichiro Tsuji, "Sense of Life Worth Living (Ikigai) and Mortality in Japan: Ohsaki Study," *Psychosomatic Medicine* 70, no. 6 (2008): 709–15.

204 **psychologists speculate that people:** Michael Steger suggested this in a lecture he delivered at a conference in Vancouver in July 2014.

204 **take better care:** For research on the connection between meaning and healthy habits, see Kristin J. Homan and Chris J. Boyatzis, "Religiosity, Sense of Meaning, and Health Behavior in Older Adults," *The International Journal for the Psychology of Religion* 20, no. 3 (2010): 173–86; László Brassai, Bettina F. Piko, and Michael F. Steger, "Meaning in Life: Is It a Protective Factor for Adolescents' Psychological Health?" *International Journal of Behavioral Medicine* 18, no. 1 (2011): 44–51; and Carole K. Holahan and Rie Suzuki, "Motivational Factors in Health Promoting Behavior in Later Aging," *Activities, Adaptation & Aging* 30, no. 1 (2006): 47–60.

204 **use preventive health services:** Eric S. Kim, Victor J. Strecher, and

Carol D. Ryff, "Purpose in Life and Use of Preventive Health Care Services," *Proceedings of the National Academy of Sciences* 111, no. 46 (2014): 16331–36.

204 **Michael Steger has put it:** From a class I took with Steger in May 2015.

204 **According to the World Health Organization:** "Ageing and Health," World Health Organization, who.int/mediacentre/factsheets/fs404/en/.

204 **in the United States, one fifth:** "Rising Demand for Long-Term Services and Supports for Elderly People," Congressional Budget Office, June 26, 2013.

204 **their sense of purpose declines:** Maclen Stanley, "The Pernicious Decline in Purpose in Life with Old Age," *Psychology Today,* April 15, 2014.

204 **Marc Freedman:** Author interview on December 10, 2014.

205 **"Nothing is so insufferable":** Blaise Pascal, *Pensées,* retrieved online via Project Gutenberg.

205 **Pam Mulhall . . . Tom Hendershot:** These examples are from the Encore website.

206 **Global Age-Friendly Cities project:** "Global Age-Friendly Cities: A Guide," a report of the World Health Organization, 2007, who.int/ageing/publications/Global_age_friendly_cities_Guide_English.pdf.

206 **New York:** The information about the New York Age-Friendly initiative came from an author interview with Lindsay Goldman; the website agefriendlynyc.com, which contains a number of reports about the initiative, including "Toward an Age-Friendly New York City: A Findings Report" (New York Academy of Medicine, 2008), and "Age Friendly NYC: Enhancing Our City's Livability for Older New Yorkers" (City of New York, 2009); and Hari Sreenivasan, "Age Friendly New York City Helps Seniors Stay Active in the Big Apple," *PBS NewsHour,* September 4, 2013.

207 **As a result of such programs:** There are "Experience Corps" programs in a number of cities, and researchers have studied their impact on the students and the adults involved. See "Research Studies," AARP Foundation, Experience Corps, aarp.org/experience-corps/our-impact/experience-corps-research-studies.html.

208 **Isay got hooked:** For information about Isay and StoryCorps, I relied on author interview with Dave Isay on October 6, 2015; and Dave Isay (editor), *Listening Is an Act of Love: A Celebration of American Life from the StoryCorps Project* (New York: Penguin Books, 2007).

210 **Research confirms this:** See Greg J. Stephens, Lauren J. Silbert, and Uri Hasson, "Speaker-Listener Neural Coupling Underlies Successful Communication," *Proceedings of the National Academy of Sciences* 107, no. 32 (2010): 14425–30; and Harvey Max Chochinov, Thomas Hack, Thomas Hassard, Linda J. Kristjanson, Susan McClement, and Mike Harlos, "Dignity Therapy: A Novel Psychotherapeutic Intervention for Patients Near the End of Life," *Journal of Clinical Oncology* 23, no. 24 (2005): 5520–25.

211 **more self-oriented . . . less meaning:** See Kathleen D. Vohs, Nicole L. Mead, and Miranda R. Goode, "Merely Activating the Concept of Money Changes Personal and Interpersonal Behavior," *Current Directions in Psychological Science* 17, no. 3 (2008): 208–12; and Todd B. Kashdan and William E. Breen, "Materialism and Diminished Well-Being: Experiential Avoidance as a Mediating Mechanism," *Journal of Social and Clinical Psychology* 26, no. 5 (2007): 521–39.

212 **Mary Anna Elsey:** Author interview, both inside and outside the booth, on October 24, 2015.

Conclusion

217 **William Breitbart:** Author interview on May 30, 2014; and William Breitbart, "It's Beautiful," *Palliative and Supportive Care* 9, no. 3 (2011): 331–33.

218 **"Everybody said how important":** Quoted in Melinda Beck, "A New View, After Diagnosis," *Wall Street Journal,* July 15, 2009. This and several other quotes come from Beck's article.

219 **Jack Kevorkian:** Dennis McLellan, "Dr. Jack Kevorkian Dies at 83; 'Dr. Death' Was Advocate, Practitioner of Physician-Assisted Suicide," *Los Angeles Times,* June 4, 2011.

219 **the Northern Territory . . . the Netherlands:** Marlise Simons, "Dutch Becoming First Nation to Legalize Assisted Suicide," *New York Times,* November 29, 2000.

219 **legal in California . . . Oregon:** Ian Lovett, "California Legislature Approves Assisted Suicide," *New York Times,* September 11, 2015.

219 **the *Journal of Medical Ethics* released:** Saskia Gauthier, Julian Mausbach, Thomas Reisch, and Christine Bartsch, "Suicide Tourism: A Pilot Study on the Swiss Phenomenon," *Journal of Medical Ethics* 41, no. 8 (2015): 611–17.

220 **an "existential vacuum":** Colleen S. McClain, Barry Rosenfeld,

and William Breitbart, "Effect of Spiritual Well-Being on End-of-Life Despair in Terminally-Ill Cancer Patients," *The Lancet* 361, no. 9369 (2003): 1603–7; and William Breitbart, Barry Rosenfeld, Hayley Pessin, Monique Kaim, Julie Funesti-Esch, Michele Galietta, Christian J. Nelson, and Robert Brescia, "Depression, Hopelessness, and Desire for Hastened Death in Terminally Ill Patients with Cancer," *JAMA* 284, no. 22 (2000): 2907–11.

220 **eight-session group therapy:** For a description of each stage, see William Breitbart and Allison Applebaum, "Meaning-Centered Group Psychotherapy," in Maggie Watson and David W. Kissane (editors), *Handbook of Psychotherapy in Cancer Care* (Chichester, United Kingdom: John Wiley & Sons, 2011).

221 **"BC and AD":** Quoted in Beck, "A New View, after Diagnosis."

222 **"This is what I will teach":** Ibid.

222 **three randomized controlled experiments:** William Breitbart, Barry Rosenfeld, Christopher Gibson, Hayley Pessin, Shannon Poppito, Christian Nelson, Alexis Tomarken, et al., "Meaning-Centered Group Psychotherapy for Patients with Advanced Cancer: A Pilot Randomized Controlled Trial," *Psycho-Oncology* 19, no. 1 (2010): 21–28; William Breitbart, Shannon Poppito, Barry Rosenfeld, Andrew J. Vickers, Yuelin Li, Jennifer Abbey, Megan Olden, et al., "Pilot Randomized Controlled Trial of Individual Meaning-Centered Psychotherapy for Patients with Advanced Cancer," *Journal of Clinical Oncology* 30, no. 12 (2012): 1304–9; and William Breitbart, Barry Rosenfeld, Hayley Pessin, Allison Applebaum, Julia Kulikowski, and Wendy G. Lichtenthal, "Meaning-Centered Group Psychotherapy: An Effective Intervention for Improving Psychological Well-Being in Patients with Advanced Cancer," *Journal of Clinical Oncology* 33, no. 7 (2015): 749–54.

223 **"extraordinary growth":** Quoted in Beck, "A New View, after Diagnosis."

223 **"I didn't have to":** Ibid.

223 **"the deathbed test":** A version of the deathbed test appears in Peterson and Seligman, *Character Strengths and Virtues: A Handbook and Classification.*

224 **Their principal regrets:** Bronnie Ware, *The Top Five Regrets of the Dying: A Life Transformed by the Dearly Departing* (London: Hay House, 2012).

224 **In September 1942, Frankl:** I drew on the following sources for Frankl's story: Viktor Frankl, *Man's Search for Meaning*; Frankl,

Recollections: An Autobiography (Cambridge, Massachusetts: Basic Books, 2000); Anna Redsand, *Viktor Frankl: A Life Worth Living* (New York: Clarion Books, 2006); and Haddon Klingberg Jr., *When Love Calls Out to Us: The Love and Lifework of Viktor and Elly Frankl* (New York: Doubleday, 2002).

Index

About the Author

EMILY ESFAHANI SMITH writes about culture, psychology, and relationships. Her work has appeared in the *Wall Street Journal*, the *New York Times*, *The Atlantic*, and elsewhere. She is also a columnist for *The New Criterion* and an editor at Stanford University's Hoover Institution, where she manages the Ben Franklin Circles project, a collaboration with the 92nd Street Y and Citizen University to build community and purpose across the country. She studied philosophy at Dartmouth College and has a master's in positive psychology from the University of Pennsylvania. She lives with her husband in Washington, DC.

EmilyEsfahaniSmith.com